Moodle 1.9 for Design and Technology

Support and enhance Food Technology,
Product Design, Resistant Materials, Construction,
and the Built Environment using the Moodle VLE

Paul Taylor

[PACKT] PUBLISHING open source community experience distilled

BIRMINGHAM - MUMBAI

Moodle 1.9 for Design and Technology

First published: May 2010

Production Reference: 1240510

Published by Packt Publishing Ltd.
32 Lincoln Road
Olton
Birmingham, B27 6PA, UK.

ISBN 978-1-849511-00-1

www.packtpub.com

Cover Image by Duraid Fatouhi (duraidfatouhi@yahoo.com)

Credits

Author
Paul Taylor

Reviewers
Kent Villard
Mark Bailye
Mary Cooch

Acquisition Editor
Sarah Cullington

Development Editor
Reshma Sundaresan

Technical Editors
Aditya Belpathak
Ajay Chamkeri
Vishal Wadkar

Copy Editor
Leonard D'Silva

Editorial Team Leader
Aanchal Kumar

Project Team Leader
Priya Mukherji

Project Coordinator
Ashwin Shetty

Proofreaders
Aaron Nash
Lynda Silwoski

Indexer
Monica Ajmera Mehta

Production Coordinator
Shantanu Zagade

Cover Work
Shantanu Zagade

About the Author

Paul Taylor has been working at the cutting edge of IT since the early 1990s after completing a Masters in Political Philosophy in the US, following an Undergraduate degree at Durham University. In those pioneering days he was working for a company that made digital video recorders for a then unknown company called Pixar. At the time, the BBC told him, "this digital video stuff will not catch on old boy".

The early introduction to the Unix OS as part of this manufacturing experience led Paul ultimately into Linux and open source in the latter part of the decade. Paul returned to the UK and trained as an IT teacher and spent ten years evangelizing the use of open source in UK schools. It was during the latter part of this experience that Paul first came across Moodle and began using this software and promoting it in schools.

In 2006 Paul became self-employed and now works exclusively on open source projects, particularly Moodle, as well as supporting a UK awarding body. He is slowly learning Japanese to try to keep up with his two young daughters, though his wife correctly asserts that he should be fluent by now.

The majority of Paul's time is spent working for a UK Moodle partner, `Pteppic.net`, owned by Sean Keogh, but he also works for a Moodle Partner in Japan, Manabu3. In addition to Moodle work, Paul works for an awarding body, The Learning Machine, which developed INGOTs, an open source friendly IT and Business qualification certificated by the QCA. Paul also supports a number of schools in the UK, and has his own website: `www.osict.net`.

I would like to thank Sean Keogh of `Pteppic.net` and Ian Lynch of The Learning Machine for believing in my open source credentials from an early stage. I would also like to thank Martin Dougiamas and all the Moodle team for developing such a fantastic product for the educational community and their constant support and inspiration. I would also like to thank the team at Packt for giving me this opportunity and for the professionalism and quality support they have so tirelessly given. Thanks also extend to the team who provided feedback on the early drafts, especially Anthony Borrow, who has always been an inspiration to me in terms of time and energy devoted to the Moodle community.

Most of all I would like to thank my wife Miyako, and my daughters Koyuki and Kiyono for putting up with my time worshipping the phosphor face.

About the Reviewers

Kent Villard is the E-Learning Coordinator for the University of Prince Edward Island and has been administrating Moodle for four years. Kent particularly enjoys the process of converting traditional curriculum to work in an online form.

When he's not administering Moodle or evangelizing the Mac platform, Kent likes to spend quality time with his wife Denise and children, Maxwell and Samantha.

Kent lives in Cornwall, Prince Edward Island in Atlantic Canada. He can be reached at `kent.villard@gmail.com`.

Mark Bailye describes himself as a developer, teacher, and learner, who discovered Moodle about four years ago. He is passionate about medical education and training, and has introduced Moodle as the platform to support the needs of a flexible workforce, to cater for different learning styles and to develop and provide access to a variety of e-learning opportunities. Mark is currently working with Medical Education Units and junior doctors across South Australia to tailor and develop Moodle to enhance, enrich, and engage learners in medical education.

I would like to thank Packt Publishing, and in particular, Ashwin, for giving me the opportunity to review another book.

Mary Cooch is the author of *Moodle 1.9 for Teaching 7-14 Year Olds*. She has taught languages and geography in the UK for 25 years, and now spends part of her working week travelling the country as a VLE trainer specializing in Moodle. She regularly promotes its benefits in schools and has a deep understanding of what works best for younger children. Known online as the *moodlefairy*, Mary is a Moodle Certified Teacher and moderator on the help forums of `moodle.org`. She runs her own blog on `www.moodleblog.org` and can be contacted for training or consultation on `mco@olchs.lancs.sch.uk`.

Mary is based at Our Lady's Catholic High School Preston, Lancashire, UK.

I would like to thank my family for their patience and Our Lady's Assistant Head Mark Greenwood for his support.

Table of Contents

Preface

This book is written to show readers how best to use the tools and elements of Moodle to improve their Design Technology courses and to make their courses more dynamic and challenging. The various modules have been chosen for their suitability and flexibility and will hopefully act as comprehensive enhancements. The book is written using real world examples and situations in order to better show the reader how and why the modules are used, as well as give some possible teaching methods based on course specifications. It is hoped that this book will help the reader to design their courses in order to maximize their students' learning and use the built-in tools of Moodle to fully assess their progress and development. The chapters can be read in a linear fashion for people new to Moodle, or in a more random way for experienced users. There should be something for everyone.

What this book covers

Chapter 1 – Setting Up a Basic Moodle Site for Design Technology (DT), provides you with an overview of how Moodle can be used as a system to help teaching and learning of Design Technology subject matter. You will learn how to construct and the basic categories in order to organize your courses, as well as the design and set-up of the courses themselves. You will then learn how to create resources for your students learning and add interactive activities to challenge and excite your students. Finally, you will be shown how to track and assess your students' learning through the Gradebook incorporated into Moodle.

Chapter 2 – Organizing Information using Moodle Modules, introduces you to the interactive tools in Moodle called Modules. Two of these modules, the Database and Questionnaire, are used to illustrate how students can be encouraged to enhance their understanding and knowledge. You will learn how to create and structure a database for students to gather and analyze the materials and components they will use for their design and construction. You will then work through a basic example of how to use the Questionnaire module to allow students to gather a wide variety of opinions from potential customers in order to make their final products more suited to their target audience. Since this chapter introduces third party add-on modules, such as the Questionnaire module, you will be guided through the process of adding extra modules to your Moodle site.

Chapter 3 – Encouraging Reflective Practices using Forums and Blogs, tells you, through worked examples, how best to encourage and support reflective practices in your students with the use of Blogs, Forums, Galleries and Personal Learning Plans. You will learn how to enable and configure Blogs for your courses and how to use these tools to guide students in their development of ideas and practices. You will then be guided through the creation and usage of Forums in order to test students in their ability to role play and deal with simulations of working in their chosen discipline of Design Technology. You will be shown how to set up a Gallery to allow students to post their on-going work details, such as images taken during the construction of their projects. Finally, you will be introduced to a Personal Learning module which allows you and your students to set and evaluate targets and personal goals. All of these tools collectively will help your students reflect on their work and allow you to better guide them in their ideas and practices.

Chapter 4 – Exploring Design Portfolios, introduces Electronic Portfolios (e-portfolios) and shows you how best to use the variety of available e-portfolios to support your student's learning. You will be shown how to set up the Exabis e-portfolio to allow students to store and organize their own work and be able to share it with their peers or external examiners. You will then be shown how to configure and use the Open University e-portfolio MyStuff, which allows students more flexibility in building up digital resources in order to show their complete understanding of Design Technology with their own digital artifacts. Finally, you will be guided in the process of using Mahara to allow students to build up digital views of their material for assignments and assessment.

Chapter 5 – Testing Students' Knowledge using Moodle Modules, explains how best to support and reinforce your students' understanding of some of the disparate knowledge they need to engage in their courses. You will be shown how to set up the Glossary module to allow students to construct and maintain their own dictionary of key terms used in their courses. You will also be shown through a worked example how the linking capability of the Glossary module can be used to reinforce key ideas throughout your course. You will be shown how to incorporate the Mind Mapping module into your course to allow students to brainstorm some of their project ideas. Finally, you will be shown how to use the Quiz module to construct various formal and informal tests to better gauge your students' level of understanding of the courses.

Chapter 6 – Helping your Students Gather Data about their Potential Markets, explores in more detail the Questionnaire module introduced briefly in Chapter 2 and shows how it can be used effectively to support detailed market analysis for students. You will be shown how the data can be gathered and analyzed in order for students to make more informed choices about their projects and how markets might react to their designs. You will then be guided through the implementation of the Feedback module to allow students to get an impression for their potential customers about the suitability of their design ideas. Finally, you will be shown how to use interactive on-line meeting tools like DimDim to allow students to discuss their ideas with a wider audience, such as representatives from local manufacturing companies.

Chapter 7 – Adding Multimedia Resources to your Moodle Site, provides you with an introduction to e-learning materials and resources such as the Lesson module and SCORM (Shareable Content Object Reference Module) packages, as well as on-line materials provided by governments. You will be shown how to set-up and use the Lesson module to create a self-contained lesson for assessing and supporting your students' learning. You will be shown how to enable on-line repositories of SCORM material to provide your students with more media rich materials and examples. Finally, you will be shown how to create your own multi-media rich SCORM material with free web-based tools such as MyUdutu.

Chapter 8 – Assessing Student Progress, shows you how to assess your students' progress through creating assignments to monitor their development. You will be shown how to create a variety of different assignments for different purposes such as multiple file uploads for complex projects involving documents, images and video files. You will be shown how to grade and scale these assignments and how to add quality feedback to make sure the students reach their full potential in your courses. You will also be shown how to add enhancements to the course such as progress indicators and blocks to show you how much marking you have left to complete.

Chapter 9 – Tracking Progress with the Gradebook, explains in detail how to use the Gradebook in Moodle to fully assess your students' progress and achievement. You will be shown how to configure and use the Gradebook to assess learning in an informal way through homework assignments and a formal way through examinations. You will also be shown how to use the Gradebook to set and mark outcomes such as competence in literacy and numeracy. You will be shown how to organize the Gradebook to display different categories of grades such as coursework and examination work, and how to tally these for a final mark. Finally, you will be shown how the Gradebook can be customized to display the reports of grades required for your specific courses.

What you need for this book

For Moodle, you must have the following components up and running on your server:

- Database: MySQL (version 4.1.6 or later), PostgreSQL (version 7.4 or later), Microsoft SQL Server (version 2005 or later), Oracle (version 8 or later).
- Web server: Apache is the preferred web server though IIS 6 is also fine.
- PHP: PHP 4.30 is required to run Moodle, but it might be advisable to use PHP 5.24 or higher as this will be necessary in the forthcoming 2.0 version of Moodle.
- PHP extensions: Moodle makes use of a number of PHP extensions, most of which are compiled into PHP by default.

Depending on your specific setup, additional software or hardware might be required.

Who this book is for

The primary focus of this book is on the support of teaching Design Technology subjects and would therefore be useful for teachers and instructors in this field. However, the modules covered here, such as e-portfolios, are more generally used in teaching and therefore this book would be useful to all educational staff teaching secondary level students and above.

Conventions

In this book, you will find a number of styles of text that distinguish between different kinds of information. Here are some examples of these styles, and an explanation of their meaning.

Code words in text are shown as follows: "Depending on the type of system your Moodle site is running on, you now need to unzip this file into the `mod` folder of your server."

New terms and **important words** are shown in bold. Words that you see on the screen, in menus or dialog boxes for example, appear in our text like this: "Setting outcomes to **Yes**—the default is **No**."

> Warnings or important notes appear in a box like this.

> Tips and tricks appear like this.

Reader feedback

Feedback from our readers is always welcome. Let us know what you think about this book—what you liked or may have disliked. Reader feedback is important for us to develop titles that you really get the most out of.

To send us general feedback, simply drop an email to `feedback@packtpub.com`, and mention the book title in the subject of your message.

If there is a book that you need and would like to see us publish, please send us a note in the **SUGGEST A TITLE** form on `www.packtpub.com` or email `suggest@packtpub.com`.

If there is a topic that you have expertise in and you are interested in either writing or contributing to a book, see our author guide on `www.packtpub.com/authors`.

Customer support

Now that you are the proud owner of a Packt book, we have a number of things to help you to get the most from your purchase.

> **Downloading the example code for the book**
>
> Visit `https://www.packtpub.com//sites/default/files/downloads/1001_Code.zip` to directly download the example code.
>
> The downloadable files contain instructions on how to use them.

Errata

Although we have taken every care to ensure the accuracy of our contents, mistakes do happen. If you find a mistake in one of our books—maybe a mistake in text or code—we would be grateful if you would report this to us. By doing so, you can save other readers from frustration, and help us to improve subsequent versions of this book. If you find any errata, please report them by visiting `http://www.packtpub.com/support`, selecting your book, clicking on the **let us know** link, and entering the details of your errata. Once your errata are verified, your submission will be accepted and the errata added to any list of existing errata. Any existing errata can be viewed by selecting your title from `http://www.packtpub.com/support`.

Piracy

Piracy of copyright material on the Internet is an ongoing problem across all media. At Packt, we take the protection of our copyright and licenses very seriously. If you come across any illegal copies of our works in any form on the Internet, please provide us with the location address or website name immediately so that we can pursue a remedy.

Please contact us at `copyright@packtpub.com` with a link to the suspected pirated material.

We appreciate your help in protecting our authors, and our ability to bring you valuable content.

Questions

You can contact us at `questions@packtpub.com` if you are having a problem with any aspect of the book, and we will do our best to address it.

1
Setting Up a Basic Moodle Site for Design Technology (DT)

Most readers, by now, will be familiar with Moodle through the excellent publications from Packt, but a quick overview is useful to remind ourselves of why it has been chosen for this subject guide. In addition, the methods and practices in this book will be supported through a Moodle site set up to support **Design Technology** (**DT**).

Support can be found at `www.dtmoodle.org.uk`. Please feel free to register and join in with the discussions and help each other out. The more material we can amass together, the easier it will be for all of us.

In this chapter, we will take a look at setting up a very basic Moodle course in order to begin building our more DT specific elements. We will briefly look at setting up some basic resources and then add some interactive materials. These on their own would build a useful course, but we will then extend the facilities and features in order to maximize student participation and curriculum support. We will also look at the basic reporting and assessment tools available and how to enhance the look of your course. These will build the foundations from which we can build more sophisticated and comprehensive sites to support DT.

Setting up Moodle Virtual Learning Environment

Moodle is a **Virtual Learning Environment** (VLE) that is based on open source principles and the educational philosophy called **social constructivism**.

> You can find out more about the philosophical underpinnings through a search on the Internet or through Moodle's own document page at `http://docs.moodle.org/en/Philosophy`.

This methodology holds that the best and most effective way for people to learn is by a collaborative sharing of knowledge and practice. Moodle is therefore designed from the ground up to support collaborative learning practices and methods. In addition, Moodle is part of the open source movement, which is a large community of people who support each other and work towards some shared goals. At the time of writing, this number is close to 850,000. If you join in with the Moodle community through forums and conferences, you will find a wealth of information and help available from people throughout the world. This large pool of people is really what makes Moodle work so well. There is a good chance that any problem that you may have had with an aspect of using Moodle has already been solved by someone else or a group of people. This will save you a great deal of valuable time and energy.

Assigning access rights to roles

Once you have logged in to a Moodle site, you will have been granted some sort of role. In most instances, as we are dealing with supporting students, this is likely to be a teacher role. This role will allow you to customize your own courses and add material to them, as well as support and assess the progress of the students who are also enrolled in the course.

The three key roles you are likely to deal with will be your own as teacher, the non-editing teacher role for class-based assistants, and the student role. The basic overview of roles can be found on the Administration panel under **Users**. The overview of the roles is displayed there, as shown in the following screenshot:

Teacher	Teachers can do anything within a course, including changing the activities and grading students.
Non-editing teacher	Non-editing teachers can teach in courses and grade students, but may not alter activities.
Student	Students generally have fewer privileges within a course.

When you log on to your own course, you will see the various roles that users have been granted. Once you log in to Moodle, you will see which courses you have access to. If you are watching a particular course, you will see the role that you are assigned, as shown in the following screenshot:

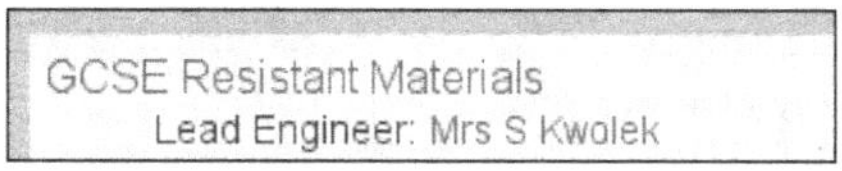

Creating a new course

In the example site, there is a course for each of the key areas of the DT subjects, and these are broken down into the levels that correspond with qualifications in the UK:

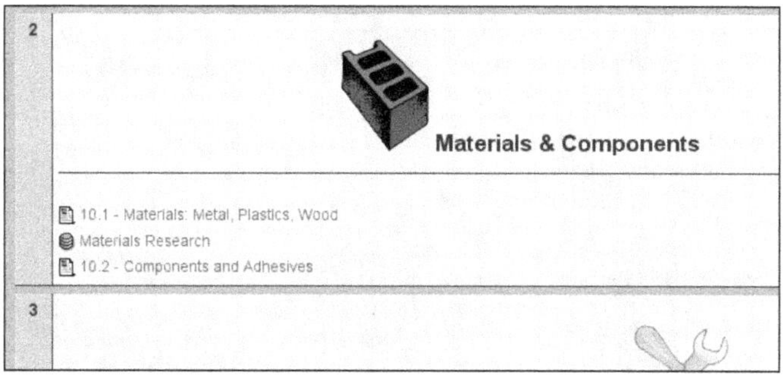

There will obviously be some overlap as many of the subjects will cover all of these levels. However, for now this is a useful way to organize the subject matter. The courses themselves can then be created in one or all of these categories. The way that they are organized will depend on how the institution manages all teaching on a VLE. As you can see in the previous screenshot, you have the **Add new category** and **Add a new course** buttons to add new categories and courses respectively. The following example shows a possible approach to structuring the courses within a level. It shows all **Level 2** courses:

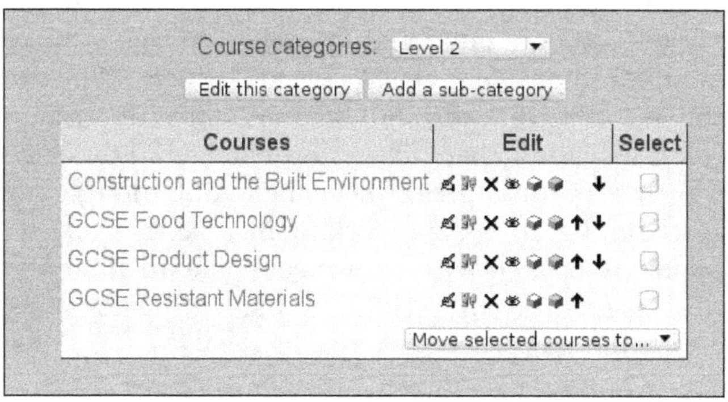

As stated earlier, these are the UK subject areas, but they are the subject areas that are general to the field of DT and therefore useful as vehicles for understanding the processes of this book.

The courses themselves are then organized in relation to the exam board specifications. For example, the main areas of resistant materials then become the labels that make up a course structure.

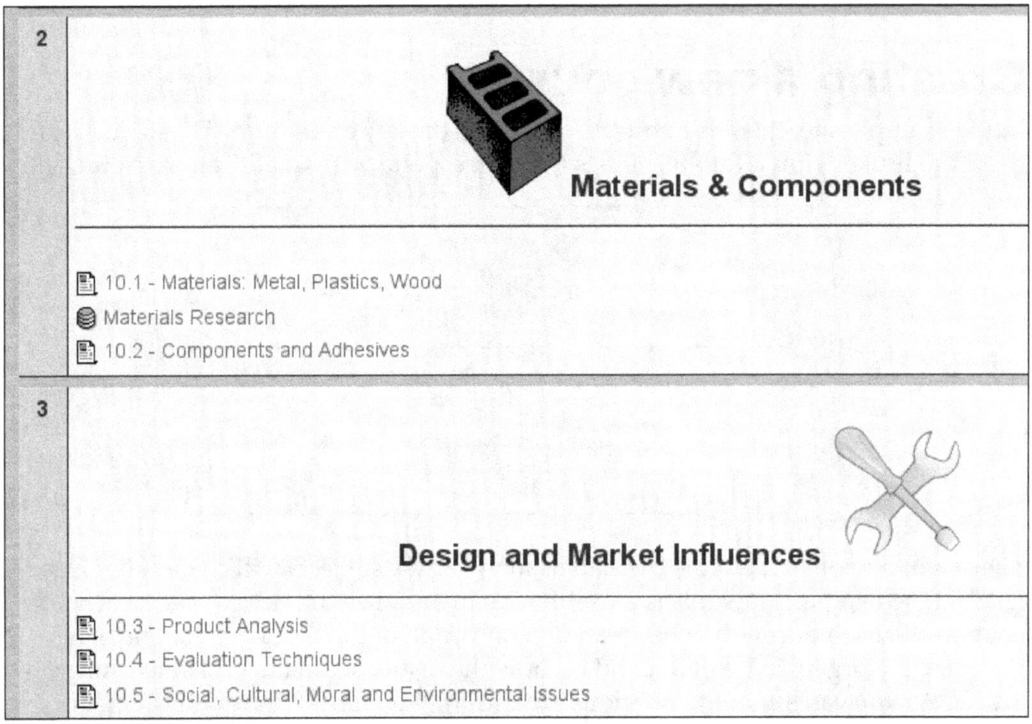

The type of layout shown in the previous screenshot has been organized by the topic's course format. When setting up a course, there are currently several styles that can be used, such as topics or weekly. The style chosen would depend on how you wish to deliver your learning material. It could also be organized on a monthly basis, which is useful for intensive revision periods before public examinations. In many cases, students will work through the material at different times, so a topic-based approach will allow them to access the material they need, while still seeing the overall picture of the course. A weekly layout, though more detailed, may be somewhat overwhelming. If you are working in a blended environment, where there are specific dates associated with your meetings with students, you may choose the weekly format. This format will track the course with dates so that students know very specifically the stage they have reached.

Adding resource materials to your basic Moodle site

Once you have set up the basic working course layout, it is time to start adding the resources and materials, as well as interactive elements that will bring the course to life for your students.

Adding static resources to your Moodle site

The most basic building blocks of Moodle, or indeed any VLE, are static resources. Chances are that you have already created a wealth of worksheets and supporting documents for your subject area and these may already exist on an Intranet. An **Intranet** is an internal network, as opposed to the Internet, which is the network of computers outside of your organization. The Intranet resources can easily be added to Moodle, but in a more structured way than just allowing students access to a named folder on an Intranet. In addition, they can be organized with a more meaningful context and linked in to other more interactive resources to build a detailed learning resource.

In order to add material to the site, it first needs to be placed on the server itself. Moodle is a web-based system that links material stored in an area designated for the course being used to an easy-to-use web interface. Therefore, you need to upload your material to the site in order to make the resource available.

In order to do this, you first need to enable the edit functions on the course itself. You can achieve this by clicking the following button, which appears at the top-right corner of all your courses:

To add a file to the site, choose the **Add a resource** drop-down bar, as shown in the following screenshot, and select the option to **Link to a file or web site**. The resource menu that opens will be common to most elements you add to Moodle, so is worth looking at in some detail. Once you have understood this process, it is easy to modify and replicate it for all other aspects of Moodle; again, this is a very useful design feature in and of itself.

The process of adding material to Moodle courses involves the following steps:

1. Naming the element.
2. Summarizing the element.
3. Linking to the resource (such as a file or website).
4. Presentation of the information.
5. Assigning permissions to user groups.

Naming the element

As you can see in the following screenshot, the name is required (designated by the *) as this will appear as the link in the course itself:

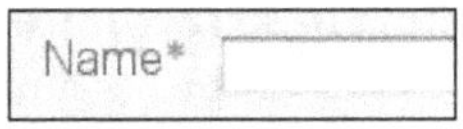

Summarizing the element

Giving some detail to the element may help students understand its purpose better if it is not immediately obvious. The field itself is labeled as **Description** and will be displayed to students in the main window when they first access the resource. You could use this to add some more detail if the resource or website link itself is not obvious. For example, you might note that the website link you have provided will help them with a specific aspect of their coursework.

Linking to the resource (such as a file or website)

As you can see, you can either type in a web address as the link to the resource, or you upload a file to the system and then click on **Choose** to make it available. If you choose an uploaded file, the system will present you with a file manager window and ask you to select a file to upload. This can be done from anywhere, which gives a great deal of flexibility. If the file is already there, then simply click on the **Choose or upload a file** button, as shown in the following screenshot:

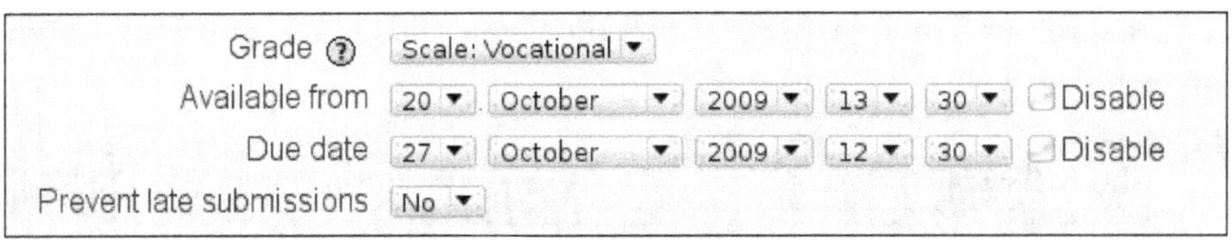

Moodle is an online system, and as such, it is based on open standards and practices. Many students may not have access to proprietary office software at home and may therefore be disadvantaged by being asked to use that software for their homework, though Microsoft does provide free readers for Word and PowerPoint. If you use something such as OpenOffice, you can give your students a copy to take home on a CD, thus guaranteeing they have the same software and are not using something that was illegally obtained. OpenOffice also outputs files as `.docs` and `.pdfs`. A PDF reader is also freely available on the Internet.

Presentation of the information

Once you have chosen the material, such as a health and safety guideline for working with metals or corrosive construction materials such as lime, you need to decide if it is easier to display in the same window or a new one. I find it less distracting if the resource opens into another window, but this is a personal choice.

Grouping

The grouping feature needs to be explained briefly, though it will be covered in a later chapter as it is very useful. It also needs to be enabled by the site administrator in order to be available (for details, please see *Chapter 9, Tracking Progress with the Gradebook*). Its main use here is for the purpose of differentiation. If grouping has been enabled at the site level, and assuming you have set your class up into groups such as Intermediate and Advanced, you can specify a grouping for this particular element resource. The students who make that group will see and use the resource, but all other students will not. This makes it useful for either advanced material for gifted and talented students, or more remedial material for students who have not yet grasped the concepts fully and need extra support. For example, a sub-group of your Product Design group may be working on some extra credit work relating to the electronic elements used in circuit design. These students can work on this material without the remainder of the group being distracted by material that they do not understand yet.

Adding instructions with the web page resource

The other key (resource) feature of Moodle, which can be used to build up the structure of the course, is the web page (element) resource. This is accessed by choosing the **Compose a web page** in the drop-down resource list, which is part of resources, as shown in the following screenshot:

The nature of this should be quite self-explanatory as it presents a basic HTML editor for composing instructions or extra research material. However, the other great advantage is that once it has been composed, it becomes part of the system's database, and as such, can then be searched as with any other data. This is not possible with pre-formatted files, such as word-processed documents, though obviously they are convenient as they can be downloaded.

Since it is a web-based resource, it means that pictures and links can be embedded and the HTML features such as color coding can be used as well. In addition, if the auto-linking feature of Moodle has been enabled, any word that appears in this web page, that is, also in a glossary, will be linked. This is obviously an advantage in a jargon-rich subject such as design technology; it helps reinforce the student's grasp of the key terms. This will be shown in more detail in *Chapter 5, Assessing Student Progress*.

Adding interactivity to the basic Moodle site

Once you have created some static resources and web-based instructional pages, you should have enough initial material to start carrying out some assessment. Moodle has a detailed and sophisticated gradebook and all aspects of the site that have some method of grading can be used to build up a picture of your student's learning progress. The most basic type of assessment, however, will probably be the assignment.

Increasing user interactivity by adding assignments

There are various ways to assess your students, and even though this is an online learning system, you can still have assignments that are not necessarily uploaded and stored. Many elements in Design Technology will be such that they may not lend themselves to an online system. For example, you may have students create some basic recipe for homework to test their ability to follow instructions or to make base sauces. You can obviously take a picture of the result and include this as part of the assessment, but the assessment itself is an aesthetic one based on taste and smell. In this instance, you can set up an assignment that does not require an accompanying file upload called **Offline activity**, but still allows a mark to be recorded. The following screenshot shows this type of assignment choice:

For another assignment, there may be a requirement for multiple file uploads, such as in a product design, and some of these may require several drafts. Both of these instances (as well as many others), are well catered for in Moodle and we will go into these in some depth in *Chapter 8, Assessing Student Progress*, but for now, we need to add an assignment.

By choosing the **Add an activity** drop-down menu, seen in the following screenshot, you can see that there are four types of assignment that can be added:

- Advanced uploading of files
- Online text
- Upload a single file
- Offline activity

The interface for all assignments is broadly similar and requires, as a minimum, the naming of the assignment and the type of grading associated. If it is an informal piece of work, you can leave it so that no grade is required. You can also use some of the features in this setup interface to determine whether or not it is based on a deadline or even if they are allowed to re-submit based on any feedback improvements you suggested.

In this screenshot, there is a customized scale based on the vocational specifications of some exam boards in the UK, which is marked from pass to distinction. Scales will be discussed in more detail in *Chapter 9*. Once you add this type of custom scale to your course, students will be notified of its presence the next time they log in. Also, if the calendar is enabled, they will see any due dates. Once they submit some work (even by handing it to you) and you assign a grade, the grade will appear in the gradebook.

Increasing user interactivity by adding forum discussions

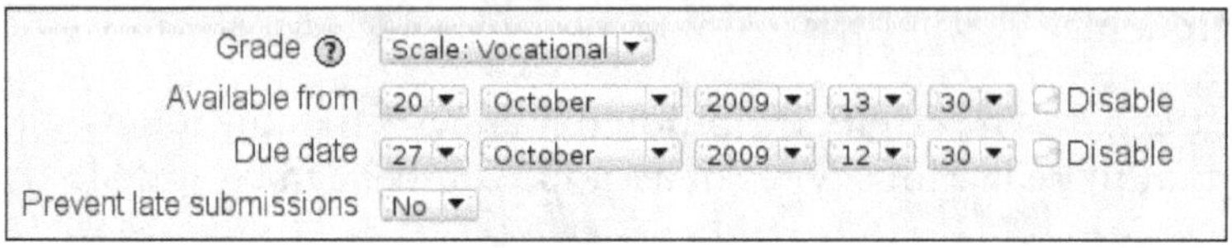

Much that is created in the world of design is often brought about through discussion and an interchange of ideas. With this in mind, it is useful to be able to create some areas for student discussion. These can be quite formal discussions where you present design ideas and get some feedback from students in order to assess their grasp of the principles, or they could be more informal discussions to let them test out some of their more esoteric ideas. The module to use for this type of activity is the forum, which we look at in detail in *Chapter 3, Encouraging Reflective Practices Using Forums and Blogs* as part of reflective practice.

As with the assignments explained before, forums are added from the **Add an activity** drop-down menu once editing has been enabled. The interface is similar to assignments we looked at previously and the basic requirements here are the name of the forum, a description of what it is for, and the basic layout. The layout, as listed, refers to the organization of the forum, such as how comments are displayed to the users. As with the assignment module, there are a few basic options to choose from:

- A single simple discussion
- Each person posts one discussion
- Q and A forum
- Standard forum for general use (the default)

In the forum description box, you can set the scene for what this discussion is about and possibly pose a question that will prompt the student's responses. The rest of the settings determine whether or not students are forced to subscribe and if they can use the "read tracking" feature to monitor their own participation. You may, for example, want to force all students to be subscribed in a discussion relating to health and safety, as it is so fundamental to all aspects of Design Technology because students are working with dangerous equipment such as lathes or making food for the public in Food Technology. In the following screenshot, we have chosen the option to not force everyone to be subscribed:

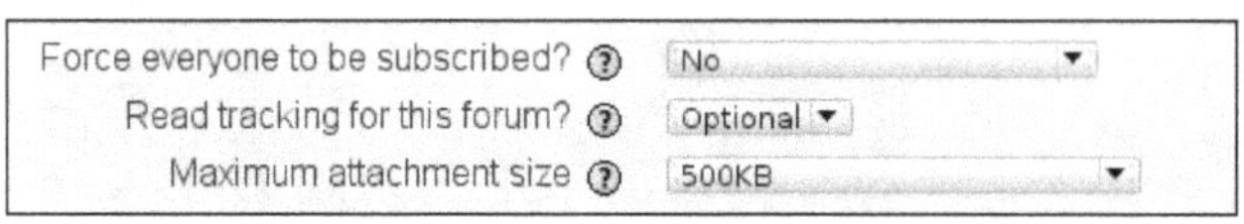

If the forum is something that you would like to use for formative assessment, by this we mean part of the student's publicly recognized qualification such as a GCSE in the UK, you can assign grading, which may be another way to assess how well students understand design principles. Much of what is created in Design Technology is peer assessed, so this acts as a good model for what they will encounter in the real world and may set some good habits. In the following screenshot, this marking is based on a **Vocational** scale, which in the UK would be: Pass, Merit, or Distinction.

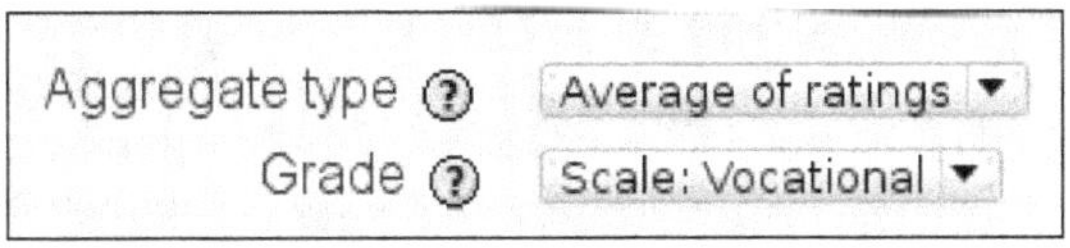

This type of marking makes a useful starting point for other discussions. It may be that you attach a picture of an iconic chair design. You may then prompt a discussion to ask if students agree that it is well designed. If the bulk of them disagree and rate it as only so-so, perhaps it could be a generation thing. What is it about this design that makes it so unattractive to the group? How would they change it? The discussion can be limited to a number of posts to make sure it does not go too far off topic. Grading is discussed in depth in *Chapter 9*.

Increasing user interactivity by adding quizzes

Once you have added some static resources and hopefully promoted some lively discussions, it might be useful to give some short tests to the students for you to gauge their current knowledge. For example, after a lesson on hydraulics, you may design a short quiz of the key words and functions in a model of a hydraulic pump. If all students miss a certain key term, you can then address this in more detail in a follow-up lesson. It also acts as a useful signpost for students to know where they are in terms of understanding key concepts. As with all activities on Moodle, quizzes can be somewhat informal and not use a rigid number scale. Alternatively, they may be limited to a time and a specific computer for more formal assessment that forms part of a recognized qualification. All of their attempts will be placed into their gradebook and can be set to measure a highest grade or an average, depending on what you are measuring. Quizzes will be dealt with in depth in *Chapter 5*.

The quiz interface is the same as other modules in Moodle in terms of naming the activity, describing what it is about, and then creating the content of it—the quiz questions in this case. Once you select **Quiz** from the activities drop-down menu, you will see the basic naming and description fields. The following table lists a series of presentational options available:

Option name	Sub-options	Description
Timing	Open the quiz Close the quiz	A range of options here allow you to make the quiz appear to students in a set date range.
	Time limit	You can also assign a time so that students can get practice of a 30 minute public exam.
	Time between attempts	You can also make sure that they don't take the quiz quickly after the first attempt as they have memorized a few answers.
Display	Questions per page	How many questions should students see? Maybe one per page so that they can focus.
	Shuffle	You can make questions shuffle each time they retake so they don't learn the answer patterns only.
Number of Attempts	Attempts allowed	Maybe use one attempt for exam practice, but many attempts for practice drills.
	Adaptive	Students can see their mistakes and try again so that they learn from their errors.
Grades	Method	Use the highest or average grade.
	Penalties	Students' grade is marked down after each unsuccessful answer.
Security	Browser security	The quiz will take over the desktop so they can't copy and paste.
	Password	The quiz will require a password
	Require network address	The quiz will only be available on a specific computer or set of computers.

These options described briefly are hopefully self-explanatory and the help buttons associated with them are quite detailed if you are unsure. The main issue is what type of quiz you are creating: is it formal or informal? For example, are you asking a small number of yes/no questions to students in order to make sure that they followed today's lesson or will this form part of their certificated course? The security option allows you to specify a range of computer IP addresses, so that you could specify 10 computers in one part of your school. This would allow manual supervision at least.

> For a more detailed overview of some of the security issues discussed here, you might look at the corresponding Moodle docs at: `http://docs.moodle.org/en/Adding/updating_a_quiz#Security_section`.

Once you have chosen your options for the quiz such as the time and display as previously discussed, you can save it. You then need to return to the course and click on the newly-created link to the quiz in order to add the questions. The resulting window shows that you can create questions for this specific course, albeit they can be used on other courses if required or add them to a more general category to form a question bank. The **edit** tab displayed will open some sub-menus, one of which will be **Questions** where you can add your questions. The quiz module is dealt with in greater detail in *Chapter 5*. There are several question types to choose from:

- Multiple Choice
- Short Answer
- Numerical
- True/False
- Matching
- Embedded Answers
- Random Short-Answer Matching
- Random
- Description
- Calculated
- Essay

The type of question chosen will be determined by what it is you are testing. In most cases, the multiple-choice type will be most commonly used due to familiarity. However, you may use the short answer type when you are testing for something very specific such as the properties of plastics are: `x`, `y`, `z`, or even to test for spelling skills. Short answer quiz questions can be used when students are expected to know and be able to write very specific pieces of information and where you are testing this recall ability. You may also use an essay type question like those that exist in a more formal exam situation such as showing a picture and asking students to write what the picture tells them about a certain recipe, or type of material, for example. Do bear in mind, however, that the essay type of a question will still need to be graded manually.

The most basic type of question, as indicated, is likely to be the multiple-choice style of question. Once you have chosen this from the drop-down option for a question, you will be presented with the usual box to enter a name for the question and a box for the actual question text. As this is an HTML box, it is easy enough to upload and embed an image here. The advantages to this in design are quite clear. You may also insert a table with multiple pictures if the question is trying to determine the differences or similarities between a certain number of items such as wood working joints or metal joins. If there is more than one possible answer, this can be specified in the interface, as long as you remember to add up the possible answers to make the requisite 100 percent for the total.

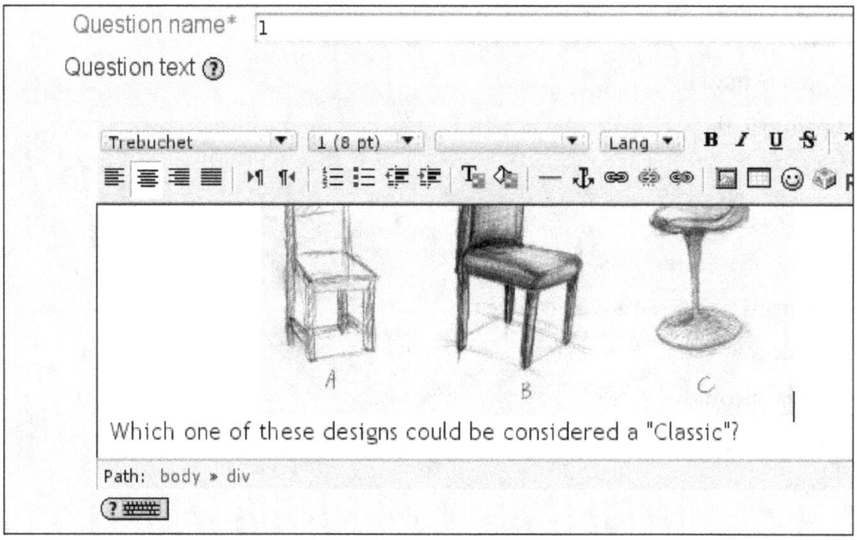

In the previous screenshot, you can see that a sketch has been scanned and uploaded to the quiz to create the question. This could be work carried out by you or some other image (always bear in mind the copyright issues). It might be likely in this case that all of the chairs are "Classics", in which case you would need to enable multiple answers and assign the appropriate marks to each correct choice, such as 25 percent each or 33.333 percent each, as shown in the following screenshot:

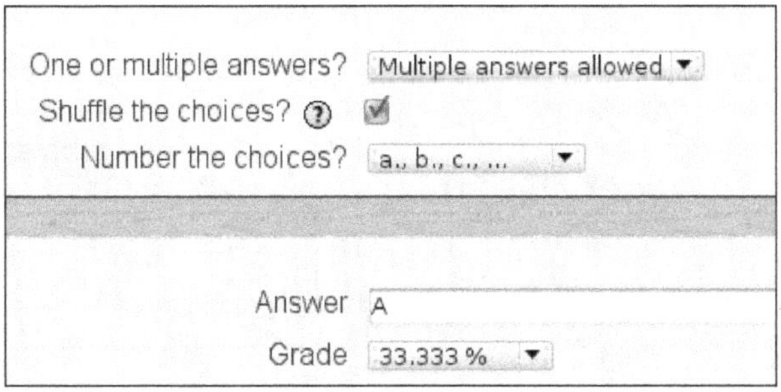

The previous screenshot shows that the quiz will allow three correct answers for this question and that each correct answer will carry a mark of **33.333** %. Students will need to get all three answers correct to get a full mark. Each wrong answer will reduce their score for the question.

Students taking the quiz, or any other assessed module, would then gain grades in their gradebook, which could then be used to assess their progress or achievement.

> Further guidance and suggestions on the use and creation of quizzes can be found at: `http://docs.moodle.org/en/Effective_quiz_practices`.

Assessing student progress

As students interact with your course materials, join in with discussions, and take various quizzes, they build up some marks in the gradebook that we will look at in detail in *Chapter 9*. Some of these marks will be automatically assigned, as with quizzes and peer assessed forums, but others will require a mark from staff and some feedback.

> Please note that an over reliance on automated grading may not be as effective as a teaching method, so it needs to be used in conjunction with more hands-on methods of feedback and encouragement.

Depending on how the gradebook is set up, the students will be able to see their grades when they log in and staff or teachers enrolled on that course will be able to see all their students' grades.

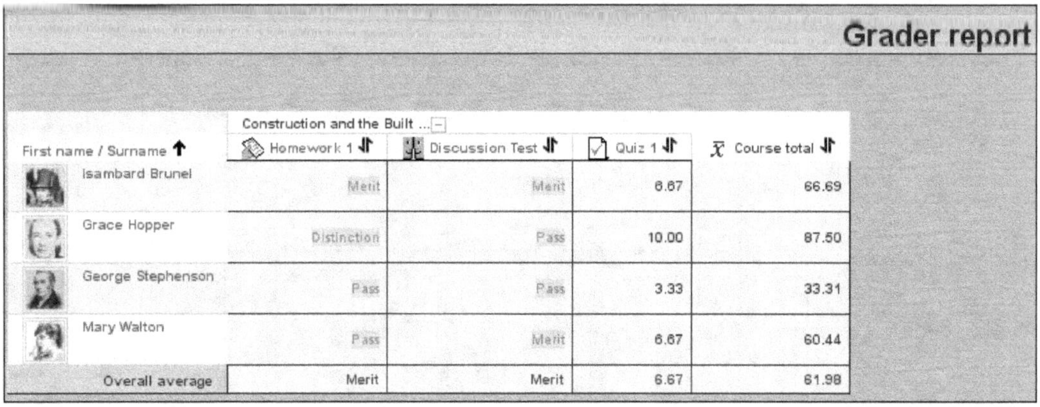

Gradually, as you can see in the previous screenshot, you can build up a clear picture of how your students are doing and can spot problems to intervene as quickly as possible. You can also give detailed feedback on assignments and posts to forums in order to guide your students and create an effective framework for their learning in the subject. The gradebook itself, as we shall see in *Chapter 9*, can also be divided into categories of marks such as coursework or extra credit; so, it could be a useful guide for students' ability in all areas of their learning. It can be used to track homework assignments that might be a fast and effective way of gauging areas where students are having difficulties with your material. Information here would therefore allow you to modify your resources or discuss with the students other strategies that they could employ.

Managing student participation with Moodle generated reports

The report features of Moodle allow you to get an idea of when and how students are accessing and participating in your courses. The level of participation and quality of participation might be useful for **Continuing Professional Development** (**CPD**) as a gauge as to the effectiveness of your teaching strategies and material. If a student is not meeting their targets, but claims that they are spending the requisite number of hours on the online material, it is easy enough to create a report about this to see if they are indeed logging on at home and what they are looking at. For example, you could choose the **Participation report** under the **reports** menu on the course, as shown in the following screenshot:

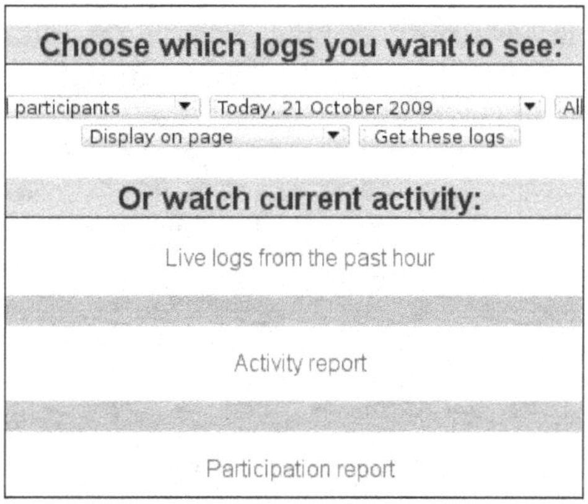

You can select the homework assignment activity or activities, and quickly see who has accessed them. The following screenshot shows a report of student's activity (or lack thereof) on the assignments associated with a Food Technology course. In this case, three students have not read the material set for homework so they are not allowed to undertake a practical assignment in class as they are underprepared.

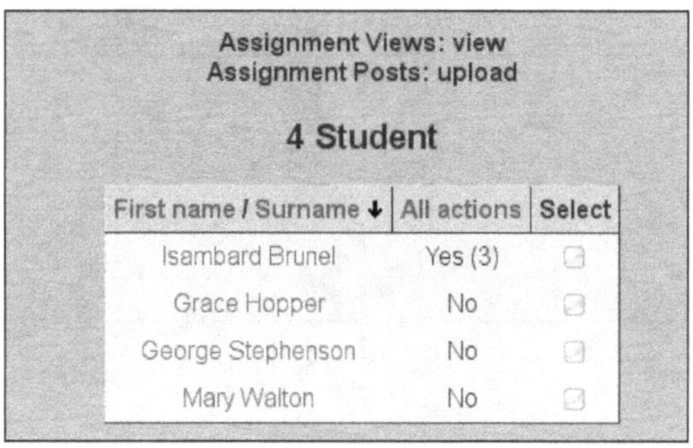

Setting up your Moodle environment

The final element of setting up your working course on Moodle is the course format. Various blocks can be added to the course in order to support and enhance learning and communication among course participants and these can be positioned in a way that makes your course more interactive and perhaps conducive to learning. You can add a calendar, which will tell students about upcoming events such as guest speakers, assignments that are pending, construction demonstrations held at local colleges, or quizzes that have been added. You can also enable a blogging facility so that students can post their own personal reflections on the course for others to read and comment upon their recent work placements. Blogs will be addressed in more detail in *Chapter 3*. You can add RSS blocks that will pull in information from other websites and keep students up-to-date in developments from companies and government departments. All of these can be arranged in the course format to encourage and stimulate learning and the exchange of information as much as possible. The more interactive these elements, hopefully the more engaged and interactive the students will become.

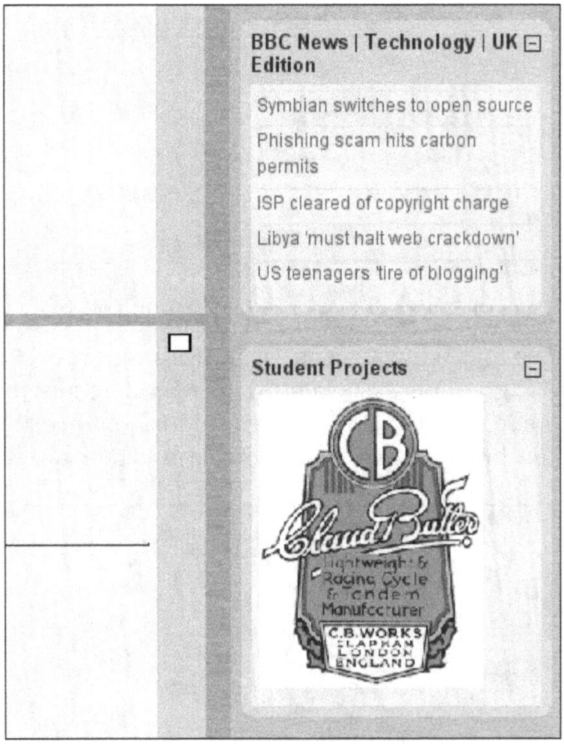

The previous screenshot shows that this course has a rolling news feed from the BBC technology website and also an add-on block called **slideshowgallery**, which rotates some of the student's work in a small block. These are only some of the multitude of blocks that can be added to a course, though it is always good not to overdo it. The amount of modules and blocks that can be added to your site is growing daily. Some of these are heavily developed by members of the Moodle core team, while others are personal projects that have been uploaded by users to share. It is best to try these on a test site before placing them on your main site.

Summary

Now that we have a basic grasp of the key aspects of creating a Moodle course and using some of the available tools, we will now delve deeper and introduce some other tools and functions to extend this repertoire. We also introduce some third-party tools, which bring even more functionality and features to the way in which we can teach DT in Moodle. Some of these are not part of the downloadable Moodle, but have been tested by the wider community. In the next chapter, we will begin to compile our course by introducing methods to assist students in data gathering by using the Database and Questionnaire modules.

2

Organizing Information using Moodle Modules

In Design Technology, perhaps more than any other subject in educational settings, students need to be very aware of their market. Whether they are designing a product, or trialing a new recipe in Food Technology, the clear purpose for this activity is the possibility of some future sales. In light of this, we will take a detailed look at using specific modules in Moodle to support students research into finding out exactly what the public wants, in relation to their product, and how best to determine how successful it might be. This will then inform their overall design brief in a better way.

Coupled with this understanding of the market, one of the key areas of technology that is central to all of the design-based subjects addressed in this book is the clear understanding of materials. Students are required to build up a detailed and organized set of knowledge and evidence to show that they know what materials are used in their subject area and can justify their possible choice at a later date for practical work. They also need to show a level of competence in how they work with materials. We will look in detail at how to use modules in Moodle to organize and display the research that students gather so that they can justify their usage of materials and forms in their projects.

Preparing for market research

All students, whether young or old, tend to have a great deal of difficulty with the concepts and ideas surrounding a market. Most people feel that when they have created something that they think is particularly good, all other people will feel the same way. In their obvious pride with their creations, they tend to become insensitive to slight nuances that would probably put other people off. Likewise, students will conduct a straw poll with their friends, who already share their values, and conclude from this that their design is suitable for all. Some of this is a difficulty of availability; it is not easy to gather the opinion of thousands of diverse people. However, some of this market reach is possible with the right sort of tools in Moodle and there are techniques that can be deployed to extend the reach beyond a student's best friends.

Worked examples in this chapter

For this chapter, we will look at two useful modules: the Database module and the Questionnaire module. We will briefly look at how to install the Questionnaire module at the end of this chapter, as it is not part of the "out of the box" Moodle, and then look at worked examples about how to use the two modules.

For the Database module, we will look at how a student can create a database to track their research and organize their findings and evaluations of the types of materials they encounter in Design Technology. This could be food items and utensils used in Food Technology or the properties and design uses of materials used in construction.

For the Questionnaire module, we will look at how a student might design a questionnaire to find out the suitability of a certain type of fast food in their local area. This will involve finding out what people prefer and testing whether or not they are open to change, such as a new type of food that they would not normally encounter locally in the UK, such as Mexican.

Organization of research using the Database module

As students work through their design brief and other aspects of their design technology courses, they will be introduced to a range of materials and design concepts in order to give them the breadth of understanding to make the best possible designs themselves. These ideas and concepts need to be well organized so that they are easily accessible for the students. Many of the students' reports will be collections of paper-based resources and possibly even hard artifacts such as plastics or metals for reference, but all of the artifacts can be organized through the use of a database facility. Fortunately, a database activity module comes as standard with Moodle.

Students will need some help in setting up their own database, if that is part of the teaching methodology, but they can also use a shared system so that they can pool each other's knowledge. This approach can also be useful for a homework or extra research activity, by assigning different data gathering tasks to different students in the group in order to build up a resource for everyone. The shared knowledge implicit in a group-based approach to data gathering ties in well with the ideas of social constructivism.

Enabling the Database module for your course

As with all modules in Moodle, the database is accessible from turning on the edit function. The following image shows the **Turn editing on** button:

Once the editing has been activated, an activity drop-down menu will appear and **Database** will be one of the possible choices, as shown in the following image:

This action will result in the database configuration window being displayed, and you can then set up your database properties.

Naming your database

As with all modules in Moodle, the database requires a name and a brief description. The name and introduction fields are the first two options that appear in the general options section. For this demonstration, we are going to name it Materials Research. This would apply to most Design Technology subjects, though you could have a specific database for Food Technology where the focus is on food and equipment. The two fields are **Name** and **Introduction**, which you can use to give a small amount of detail about the database such as the purpose or who will be accessing it.

Setting the general options on your database

The second part of the general options section relates to how the database is going to be used. The options include how and when the database will be available for students. For example, will it always be viewable so that students can enter data throughout the year? Alternatively, will it only be open for a short period as a revision exercise to allow students to gather specific data about materials in preparation for a public exam?

Controlling the availability of the database

If you are using the database as part of your teaching, you may want to make it viewable only when it is complete, or if you are using a specific set of materials in a database for examination preparation, you may have a viewable time for students to revise and then switch it off. The options relating to the availability and view ability of the database are shown in the following image, such as **Available from** and **Available to**, or **Viewable from** and **Viewable to**, though here they have all been disabled in this example. For our purposes here we want it to always be available and viewable, as students will use it as a reference and add to it themselves through homework and research assignments throughout their course.

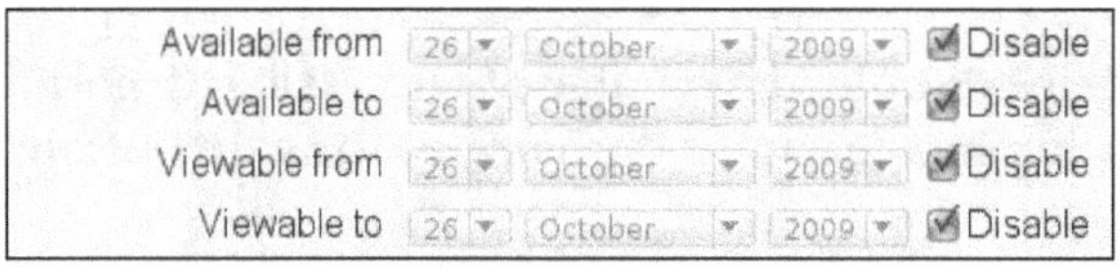

Prompting students to complete their tasks

If you have a fixed group of students and are assigning them specific tasks, you may want to choose the option of required entries so that the students will be encouraged to meet their task deadlines and be reminded that they are still due to add some entries. The same applies to the settings for number before viewable and maximum number. These can be used as a prompt for students to get them more engaged. The following image shows these settings and options. How they are used will depend on how you are using this database to teach.

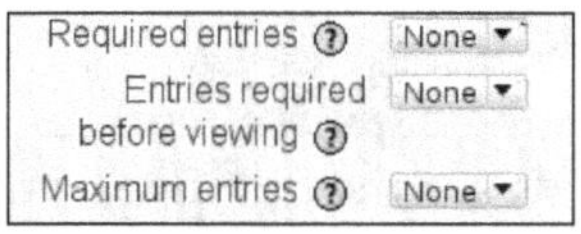

Allowing comments and ratings

Allowing comments and ratings will help students take ownership of the data they put into this module and hopefully motivate them to do their best under peer review. If you allow comments as well, they can interact with each other. This again refers back to the social constructivist pedagogy at the heart of Moodle where knowledge is built up by collaboration and review.
The following image highlights the options available:

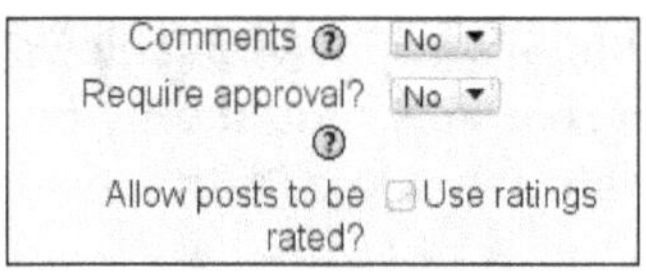

Applying grades to the student entries

The final option available when setting up the database for the students is whether or not to apply a grade. This will be discussed in more detail in *Chapter 9, Tracking Progress with the Gradebook*, when we look at the gradebook, but we could use a competence based system to give the students some formal feedback on the quality of the information they are storing in the database. If you select the **Allow posts to be rated?** option, shown in the previous image, the **Grade** option will appear. This will have a drop-down menu, and you could choose to apply some competencies to the database entries, as shown in the following screenshot:

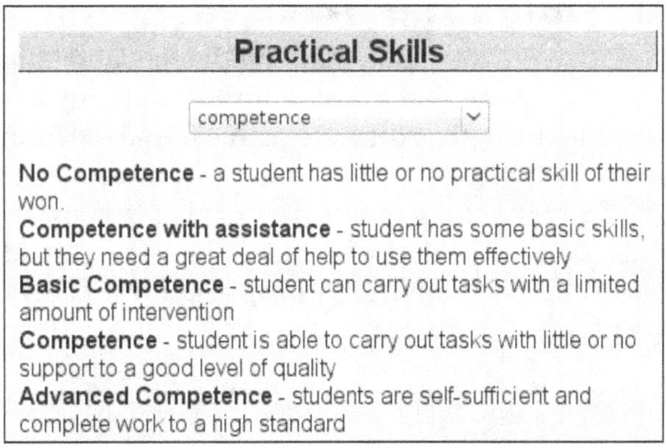

In the example shown in the previous screenshot, a scale has been created for **Practical Skills** and competence. When staff or students look at the entries of other students, they can use this drop-down list and apply the level they feel is appropriate to the entry, as shown in the following screenshot. In this instance, a more traditional grading scale has been applied and a comment left by the teacher:

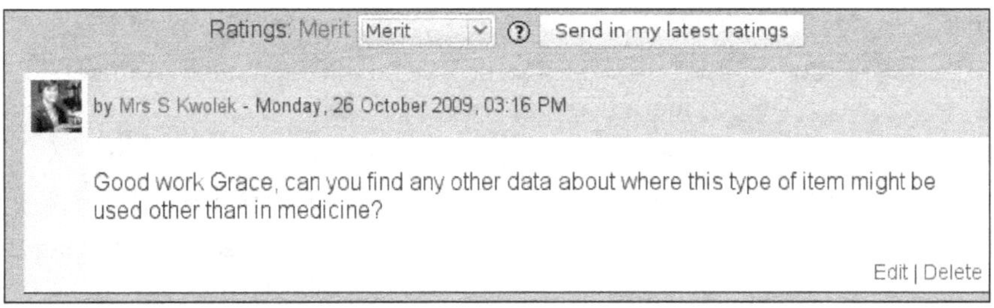

Creating the database

Once you set the options for the database, you can then save it and begin designing its structure for data entry and use. The following screenshot shows all the options available when designing the database, as well as options to export the data:

Designing the database fields

The first thing to do is to make the fields that will display and store the information. As with all things, this may be a good exercise for the students to work on through a forum or via an assignment so that they are active in the creation of the resource. Discuss with them what details they might need to know and ask them to come up with a list of data to store. This can then be discussed as you make the database itself so that they understand how and why data is stored. It could also be a wiki activity so that they can edit each other's findings and ideas. This will be useful for their IT requirements.

The following table shows the fields available on the database module:

Fields	Example
Checkbox	Is this food item vegetarian? Yes/No
Date	Date on which the item was first manufactured
File	Upload a document or PDF of specifications on an item
latitude/longitude	What country the item is located in, such as tropical hardwood
menu	A list of properties: vegetable, animal, or mineral
menu (multi-select)	A list of properties: vegetable, animal, or mineral but more than one choice possible
number	The tensile strength of an item or atomic number
picture	Upload of an image file to show the object
radio buttons	A number of options that can be selected by ticking the radio buttons such as possible uses for an item
text	A short text field to name a manufacturer
text area	A longer text area where you can put in some description of how you might use the material
url	A weblink to a manufacturer's site

Adding a text field

The first task we need to do is get some basic textual information about the data we are storing. Therefore, the first field we will be using will be a text field. All fields in the database are added from the **Fields** tab. As shown in the following image, there is a button to **Create a new field** and a drop-down menu from all of the choices in the previous table:

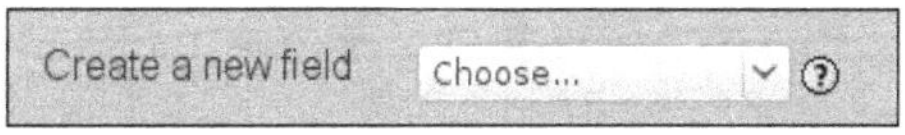

From the resulting drop-down box, you will need to choose the **Text field**. The following option box will then appear:

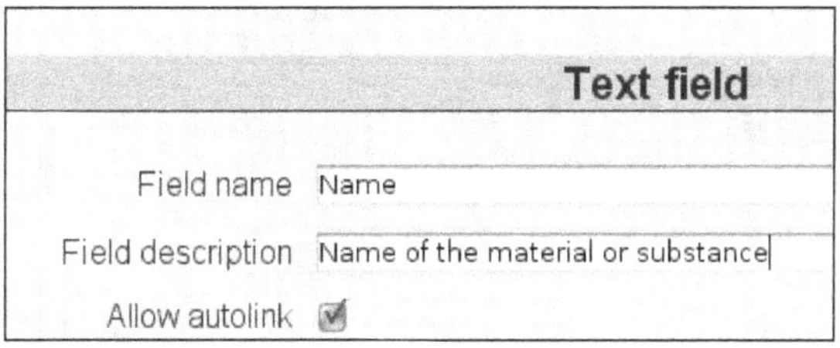

If you enable the **Allow autolink** option, as shown in the previous screenshot, the data you enter into this text field can be linked to other resources.

Adding a picture field

It would be useful here to have a picture of the item that students can upload to show what it actually looks like, so a picture field is a useful addition. The following screenshot shows the options available when setting up the picture field option, such as the name and description of the image and how big it will appear in the database when previewed:

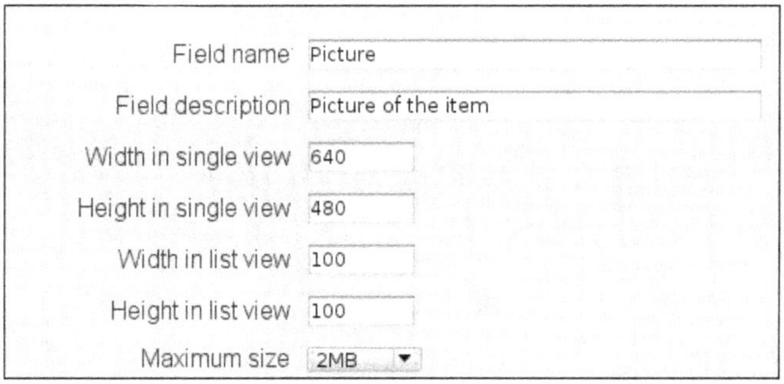

Adding a menu field

We now need a field to look at the type of material or item. For this, we could use another text field, but the danger is that students will not enter the name consistently and make searches quite hard. As this is probably quite important for their overall research work, it is worth making it slightly more foolproof. By using a menu field, we can pre-specify most of the possible items and therefore minimize mistakes (as much as possible). Also, as some items may cross over a number of properties, a multi-select menu would be better suited. The menu can always be added too if it is not complete or if some other material presents itself to your students.

The following screenshot shows the format for entries in the menu field:

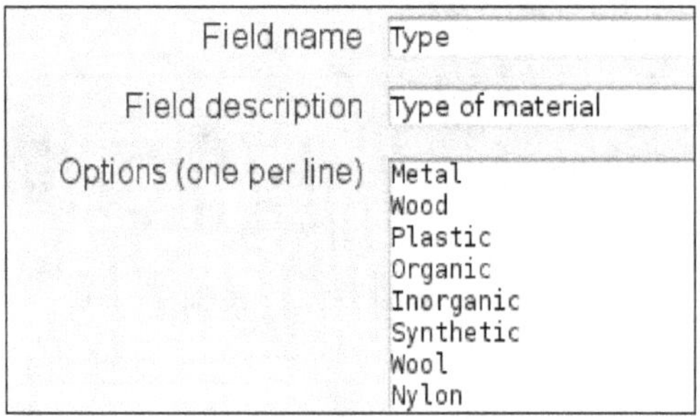

When students enter the data, they can use the *Ctrl* + click combination of keys to choose multiple entries.

Menu fields can then be entered for more factual details such as:

- Use of material
- Characteristics
- Advantage
- Disadvantage

This will then give a number of fields for students to enter some of their observations about the material in question.

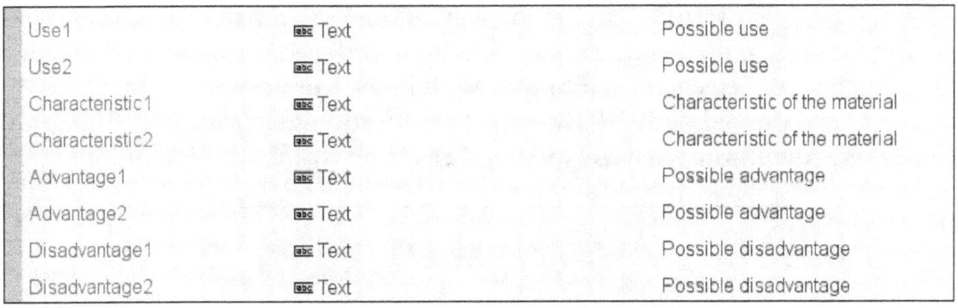

If these fields have been chosen through consultation with the students, they will be more meaningful and keep them focused. The previous screenshot shows some possible fields for a materials database, such as characteristics of the material and some of the advantages and disadvantages.

Adding a number field

The students might then be encouraged to incorporate some more technical details into the database, such as measurable data (for example weight or tensile strength). This may not apply to all items that they research, but would need to be included for the ones that do warrant it, such as metal items.

For this, you could use a number field and compare it to something like steel so all other items are measured against its strength, again, as long as students understand this aspect of the activity or have decided this measure among themselves or in consultation with staff.

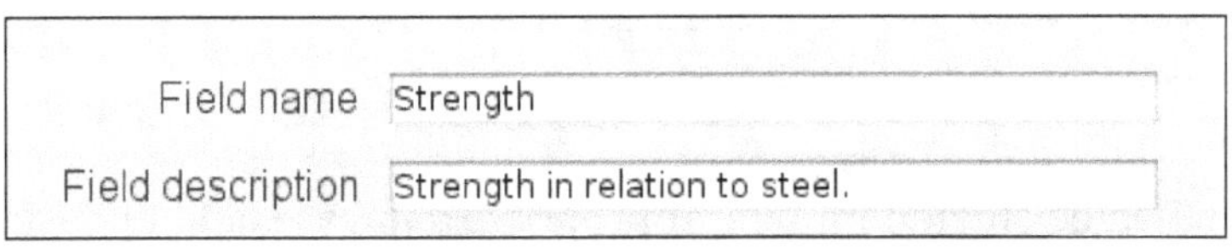

Using a menu field for the type of industry

The next set of fields to store data needs to relate the item to its intended use and where it can be found and sourced. It is also useful to keep a record of what type of industry it might be used in. Here again, a menu list with some selection options would be useful, as an item such as steel would be used in many different types of industry.

Adding a latitude / longitude field

If the students need to gather data relating to something such as the carbon footprint of an item, it may be useful to have some way of tracking the item's location. This may help to reinforce the need to source locally in order to bring down costs, or at least reinforce where cost comes into play with items from other nations to their own. This can be carried out with the use of the location field (latitude / longitude), which can use something such as **Google Maps** to show the location of items:

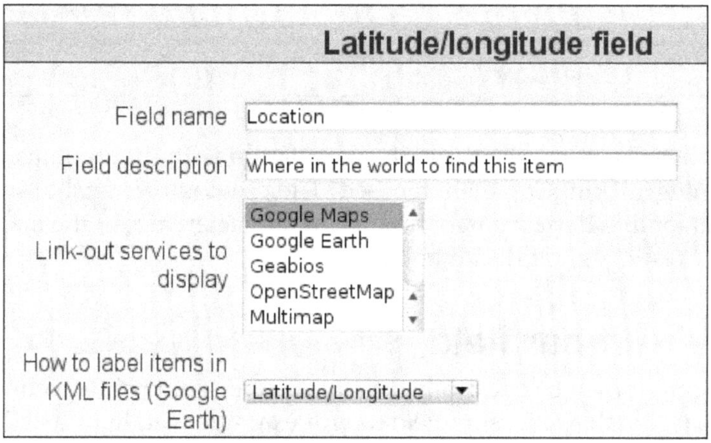

Students will need to be shown how to find the data they need on Google Maps for this to work. For example, if the material is a tropical hardwood that is found in Brazil, they will need to find it and look for the nearest latitude/longitude data.

Once you select search in Google Maps, you should see the coordinates that you need:

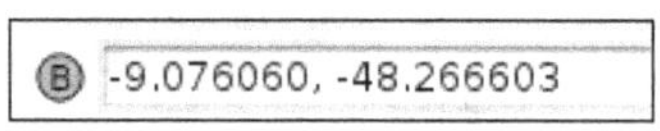

This data can then be entered into the appropriate database field once set up, as shown in the following screenshot:

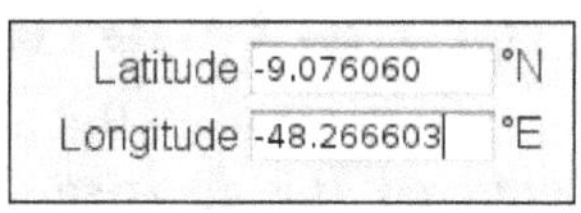

Once a user clicks on this option in the database, they will be taken to this location on Google Maps and can therefore see slightly more detail about the item in terms of where it comes from.

Adding a Textarea field

The next piece of data would be some more details of what the student knows about the item; about where it might be used, and possible examples that they have found. For this, they will need a fairly big field such as a text area, which will give them the usual HTML edit window to fill in:

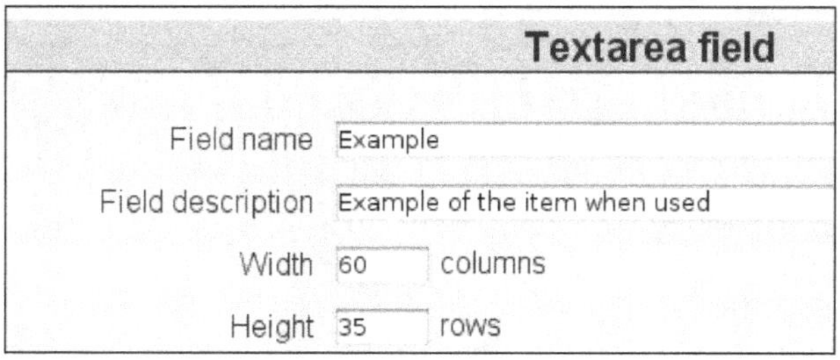

Adding a URL field

In addition to their own research details, they can add some details from existing sites such as Wikipedia or maybe a manufacturer's site via a website link. This is through the URL field:

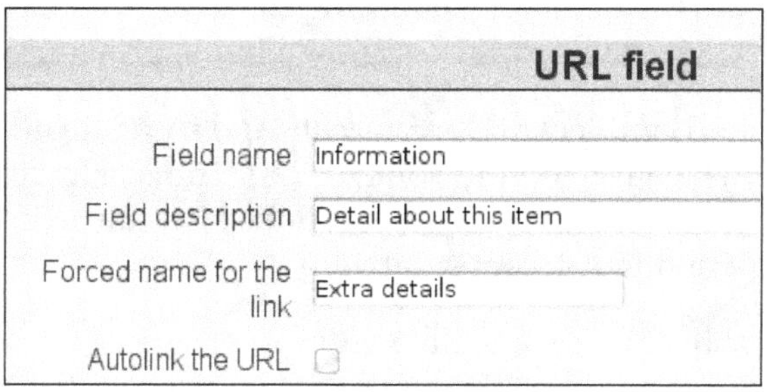

You can choose to link the URL if you feel it would help tie all the data together, but it will perhaps be enough to just open the source from the database itself.

The last real requirement may be to enter a text field so that you can record the name of the person who has carried out the data entry.

Adding database entries

Once this has been done and the structure saved, the database is ready for some data entry from the students.

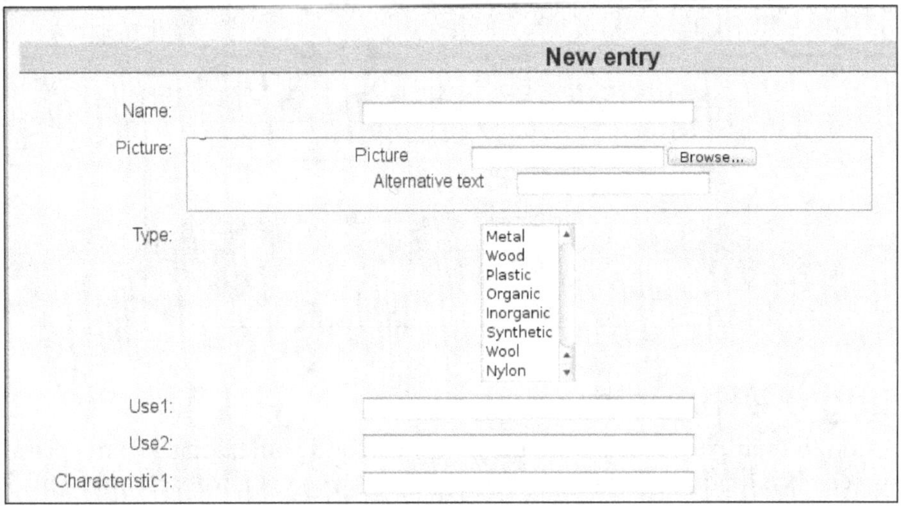

The layout table we have designed by choosing the fields in the preceding sequence will result in an entry window display, as shown in the previous screenshot.

You can change the look and feel of the template and move around some of the fields within the template, as well as modify some color settings. However, for now, this will be enough to gather some useful data. Students can start entering their research work when they click on the **Add entry** tab.

The previous screenshot shows some data entry in progress. If you are using the database as part of the assessment element of the course and have enabled this option, the staff can comment on the quality of the data and also add marks for feedback purposes, as shown in the following screenshot:

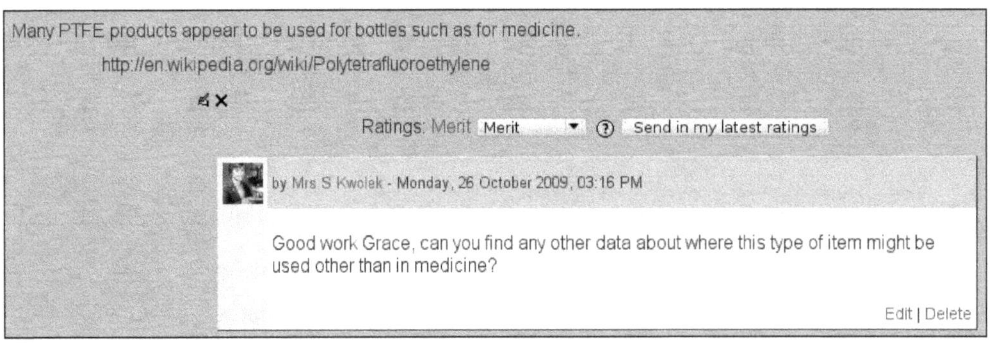

As with the information gathered through the questionnaire module, this data can also be further analyzed by the use of a spreadsheet application such as Open Office Calc. The following screenshot shows that you can choose the application you wish to export to, as well as which particular fields to include with the data:

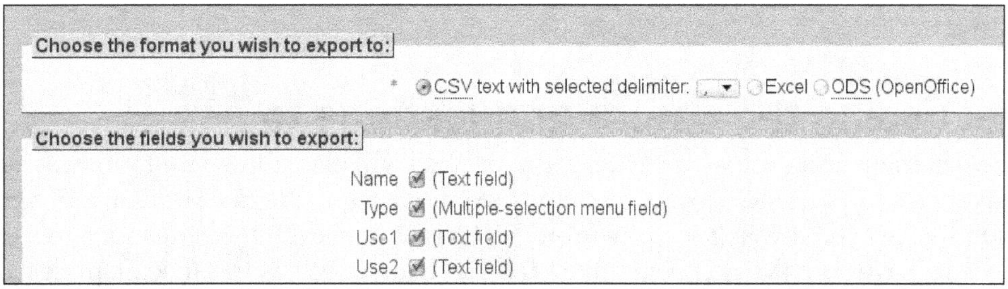

This would also be a useful practice for students and cross references nicely with other subject areas, showing that design technology does not happen in isolation of all other disciplines in the real world.

Designing a good questionnaire to gather opinions on your designs

The main purpose for this module, in terms of your design technology students, is to gather potential client opinions to help the students make the best possible product and to make sure that they have properly identified the market and their client's needs.

This is not as easy as it sounds. The design of a good questionnaire with the use of questions that gather the sort of data they need is crucial. In light of this, it is probably worth spending some time with your students to find out what they consider to be good questions and discussing with them best practices.

A good starting point for a discussion on the best practice could be by looking at the Wikipedia definition here:

`http://en.wikipedia.org/wiki/Questionnaire_construction`

One possible way to address this might be to create a forum discussion with a good and bad questionnaire attached to find out what they think and to guide them in their own designs. If you are familiar with wikis, which are a default module of Moodle, you might use these so that students can help construct the best possible questions together through editing each other's work. More detail on wikis can be found here:

`http://docs.moodle.org/en/wiki`

For example, you might create a wiki page about work experience in a local company. As each student finishes their work experience they can add their thoughts about the placement and details of what they carried out at the company. Other students can then use this material to decide whether or not they would like a work placement at this company and discuss some of the merits of the placement with staff.

Discussing the nature of questions to use

The discussion and exchange of ideas as a process will also allow you to introduce ideas such as 'open' and 'closed' questions, assuming they are not familiar with these from other subject areas. It is quite important to get a mix of these questions to make sure they have some very specific or quantitative data such as the specific price people will pay, as well as more open questions, which will gather qualitative data such as how often you might buy this item or what type of shape they like in a chair and so on.

Once you have a set of questions, you can begin designing the actual questionnaire. One consideration that needs to be made is how to maximize the gathering of data. It would be useful to make a publicly accessible course that contains all of the students' questionnaires so that they can advertise the site and allow as many people as possible to participate. It might also be useful, if you have a relationship with local firms, to get them to participate. This should ensure that the students get a broad range of opinions from lots of backgrounds and ages.

A worked example

In this example, we will be designing a questionnaire for a Food Technology class where students are identifying possible gaps in the fast food market in their local area. They need to find out what is currently available and offer some alternatives to respondents to see if they will have any success with their ideas.

For this example, the student here has recently been on holiday in Mexico and they feel that there is a definite gap in the market and a subsequent need for Mexican based snacks. The added dimension to these foods is that they can be relatively healthy so they can be marketed as such and hopefully appeal to a wide audience. However, how do they know this is the case?

Enabling the questionnaire module

To start making the questionnaire, switch editing on by choosing the **Turn editing on** button:

Then, choose the **Questionnaire** option on the activities drop-down menu:

Naming and describing the questionnaire

The screen that will be displayed, once editing of the questionnaire is enabled, will be familiar and consistent with other modules with name and description fields. However, there will be some questionnaire-specific options to be considered. Under the **General** tab, you need to define the questionnaire link, which will appear on the course itself. In this example, we are designing a questionnaire using questions designed by a specific student. The purpose here is so that the student can use the data gathered for their own design project. The following screenshot shows how the name will appear on the course:

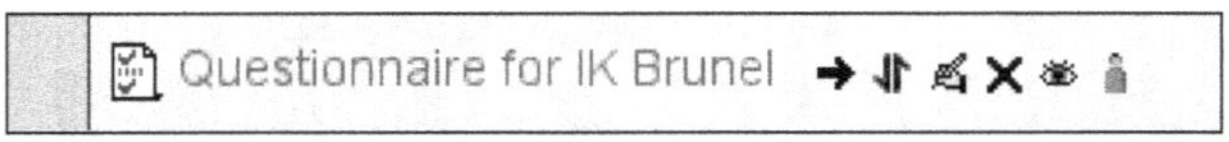

Deciding on the Timing options

The **Timing** tab will allow the questionnaire to be limited to a certain date range. You can specify here when the questionnaire is open and ready to use and when it is closed for further comments. This could be useful in order to encourage students to work, to set deadlines, and to show students the importance of meeting these deadlines. The following screenshot shows the timing options:

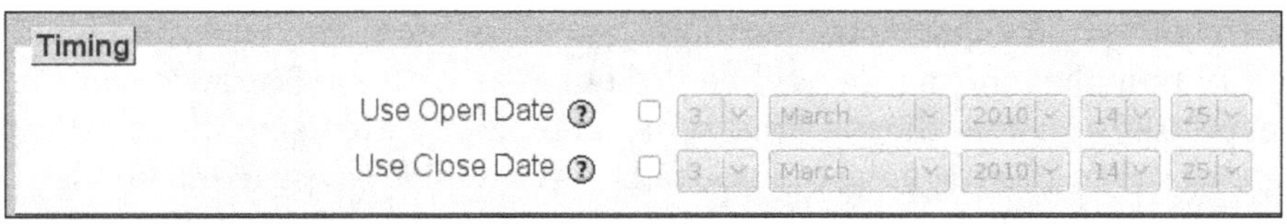

Displaying Respondents' Responses

The **Response options** allow you or your students to determine how information is saved and how the information is subsequently presented. For example, you can determine how many times each respondent can fill in the form. For some questionnaires, it may be useful to allow people to complete the form as many times as they like. In other instances, you may want to restrict this to just one response. You can also determine whether or not to find out who filled out the form by selecting to display the full name in the responses. Likewise, you can gather data anonymously by selecting the anonymous option under respondent type. It might be worth discussing these options with the students in terms of the type of data they require and the implications in terms of privacy. You can allow students to see the responses immediately or at a later date, that is, when the questionnaire is closed. It can also be assigned a grade in terms of its actual completion and if you use outcomes such as spelling (discussed in *Chapter 9*) you can mark the data to these competence criteria.

The following screenshot shows the **Response options** available on each questionnaire you design:

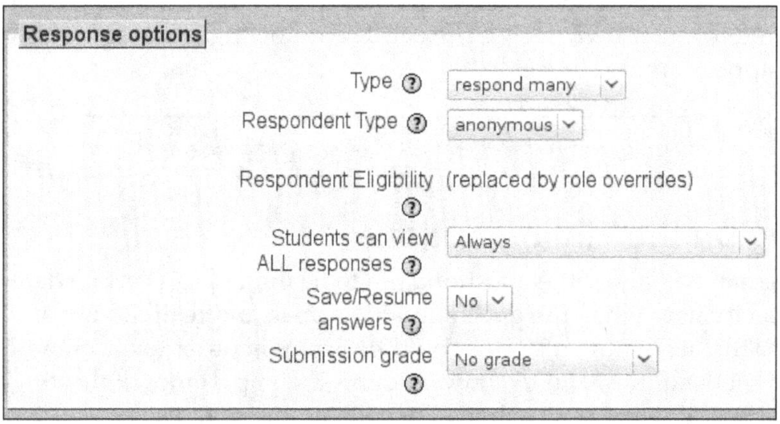

For the majority of the questionnaire module settings, your consideration will be in terms of how the information will be presented as with the **Students can view ALL responses** option in the previous screenshot. If you are using the questionnaire throughout the course to gauge opinions, then you will allow students to view responses at all time. If, however, you have a limit on the gathering of responses as part of a deadline, you might change this to **After the questionnaire is closed**.

Controlling student participation

The type of response you allow relates to how many times each participant can respond to the questionnaire. The five choices available are: many, once, daily, weekly, and monthly. Each response type will suit a different style of data gathering questionnaire and will need to be decided in each separate instance. In this example of our new local fast food restaurant, we want to get a volume of responses so we have chosen **Respond many**, as shown in the following image:

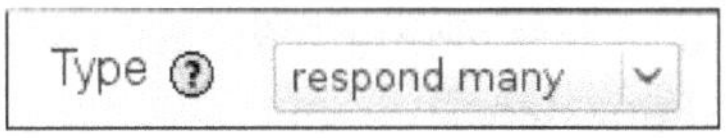

Each participant can choose many times and the overall responses can show a trend towards a favorite choice for each question.

Controlling the display of user identity

The two choices for this option are whether you want each respondent's full name, or whether the responses will be marked as anonymous. If you are using the questionnaire as part of a teaching process so that you can discuss each student's response with them individually or others in the group, you might allow a full name for reference. In most cases, due to privacy, you will likely choose to make response types anonymous.

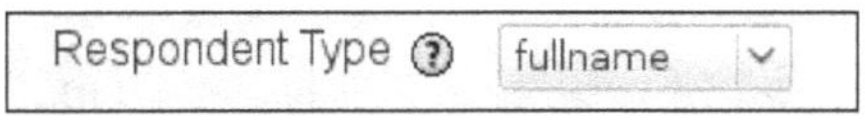

Allowing students to view their responses

The four choices for this option relate to whether or not students can see how they responded, and if so, how quickly.

Therefore, the choices are:

- **Never**
- **After answering the questionnaire**
- **After the questionnaire is closed**
- **Always**

You may wish to allow students to always see their responses, or you may wish the responses to only be available once everyone has answered and the questionnaire has been closed. This last method may be used in conjunction with an assignment deadline so that students have a controlled timescale to complete their research into the responses and to write up their findings.

Allowing students to save their work

If the questionnaire is particularly detailed or contains a huge number of responses, you may wish to give the students the option to save the point they reached to return and finish the questions at a later date:

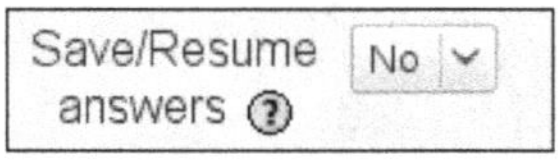

It might also be the case that some of the questions require some additional research or self-reflection to answer effectively so a save and resume option would be useful.

Assigning a grade to the questionnaire response

The submission grade option allows you to assign a grade to the questionnaire response:

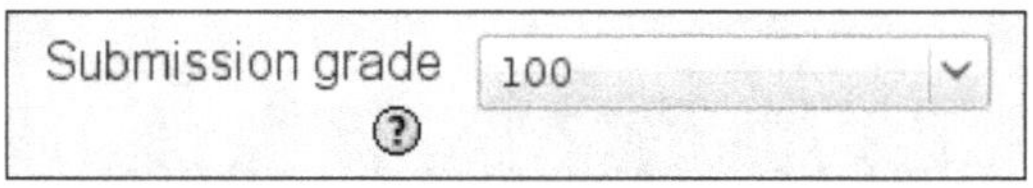

However, as it will merely place the corresponding grade into the user's grade book, it is only really useful as a guide to actual participation. If you assign a grade of 100, then 100 will be added to the student's gradebook which would not relate to the quality of their submissions. The best option would be to choose **No grade**.

In addition, if you have enabled groupings at the site level (discussed in *Chapter 9*), it will be possible to assign the questionnaire to a certain group only, as shown in the following screenshot:

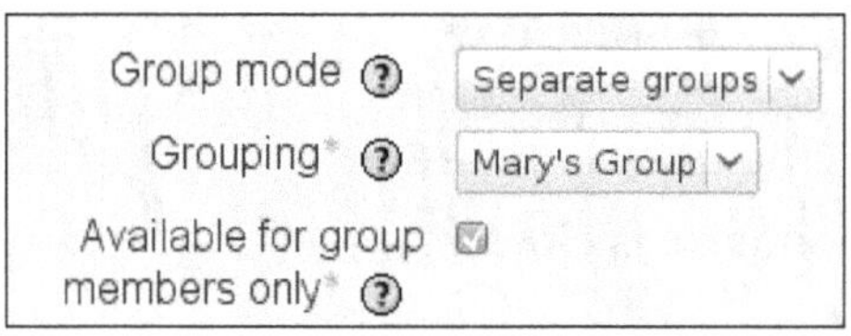

If you are working with a specific group of students within an entire year group, this may be a useful way of concentrating your time and effort on their work without changing the work of the year group. We have also chosen the option to make it available only for Mary's grouping so other students in the course will not be distracted by seeing it and believing they need to participate. For example, there may be a group working with a local company as part of their work placement, but no other students in the year.

Adding the questions to your questionnaire

Once you have chosen the settings on the questionnaire that match the working example, in this case for our fast food restaurant idea, and the type of responses you would prefer to see, you can then add the questions themselves. You do this by clicking on the questionnaire on the course with the edit function enabled. This will present you with four tabs to view the questionnaire and fill in the questions, namely, modify the **Advanced settings**, add the **Questions**, and **Preview** to see what the finished questionnaire will look like to respondents. The following screenshot shows these four tabs:

Customizing your questionnaire

The first tab is the **Advanced settings**. The options under the Advanced Settings tab allow you to customize some aspects of the questionnaire, such as allowing an e-mail of any responses to go to specific students. The advanced options menu is further divided into **Content** options and **Submission** options.

Setting the type of questionnaire

The first option is for the type of questionnaire and the choices are **Private** or **Public**. There is also the option to use this questionnaire to create a template, which can be used on subsequent occasions. The **Public** option allows you to make the questionnaire shareable between courses to gather more data; however, the course would still need to be accessible by other students and you would need to advertise that fact.

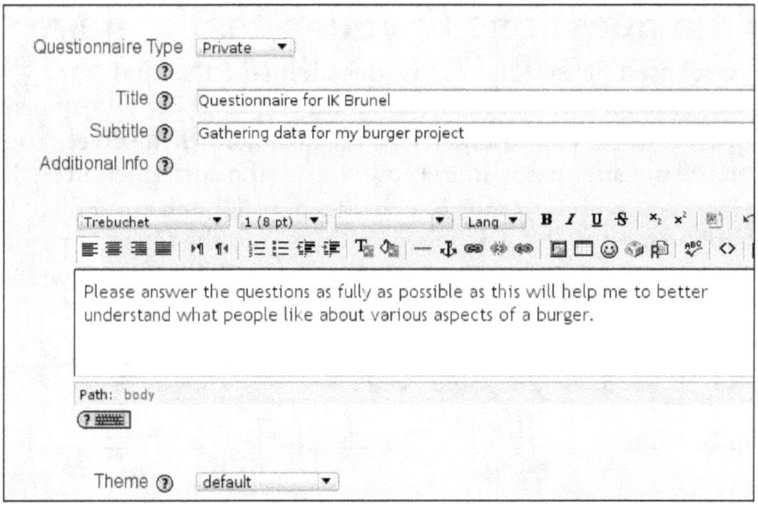

Adding further details to your questionnaire

The three fields below the option of questionnaire type allow you to add detail to the questionnaire so that respondents have a better idea of the purpose of the questionnaire, assuming it is not apparent elsewhere in the design.

Choosing a display theme for your questionnaire

The **Theme** option allows you to choose the colors and fonts that are used in the questionnaire when it is presented to the respondents.

There is currently a choice of four different themes, plus the default theme, which will reflect which overall theme you have chosen for Moodle. In this instance, it will use the Wood theme.

Redirecting students after response submission

The following screenshot shows the initial options available for submission of the questionnaire. By default, on submission of the questionnaire, the respondent will be taken to a page that thanks them for their submission and allows them to return to their course. However, there is the option to send them to another website where you can add a custom heading and message in the body of the web page.

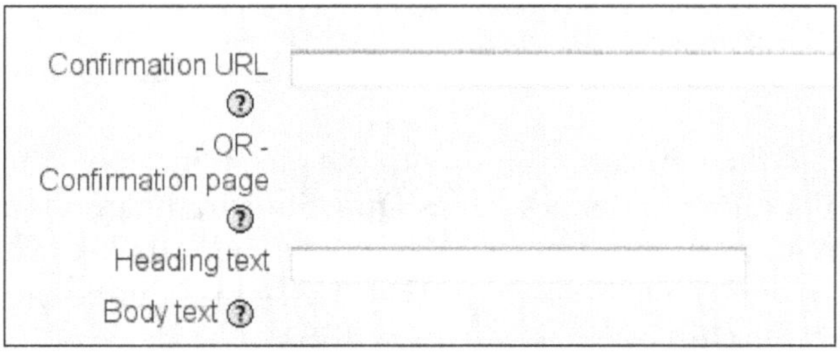

Sending e-mail to respondents on their completion of the questionnaire

The final option is for sending an e-mail to specified respondents. Each respondent's e-mail can be separated by an apostrophe for more than one.

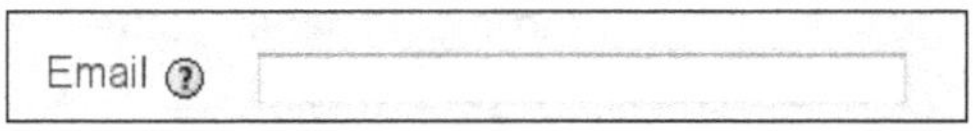

Once all the appropriate options have been chosen, it is time for the questions themselves to be formulated. For this example, as already mentioned, we will be devising a questionnaire in order to gather data relating to a student creating a new fast food menu or item to be sold in the local area. The scenario will be similar for all aspects of design technology, but this acts as a useful focus to discuss possible question formats and structure. Other examples might be a questionnaire to find out if there is a need in your institution for new furniture for certain areas such as the main hall, or you might devise a questionnaire to ask local businesses if they intend to purchase new items for their company and what these items might consist of. Part of the questionnaire might consider if they would allow these to be designed and made by a local school or college so that students have a clear idea of local community support before they begin.

Adding the questions

The **Questions** design page initially shows two buttons: one for the choice of question and the other button to add the choice to your design. The buttons are as shown in the following screenshot:

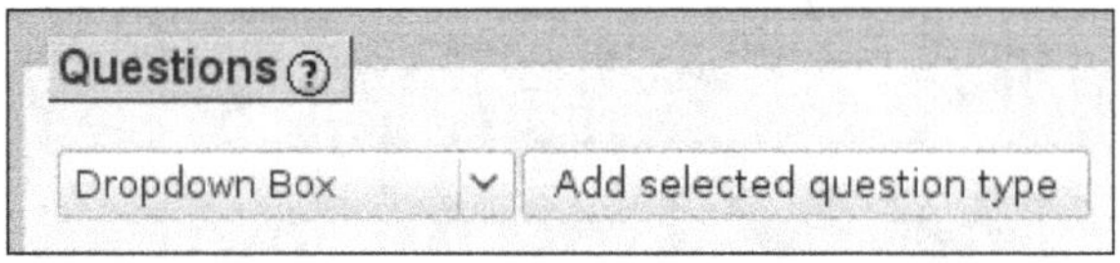

As you can see from the help associated with the question types (the yellow circle with a question mark next to items such as **Questions** in the previous screenshot), there are currently nine different types of questions that can be created as well as two presentational elements: page break and label. These presentational elements can be used to break up larger forms (page break) or reintroduce a set of instructions for specific sections (label). The other nine questions are a mixture of open and closed forms, as we mentioned earlier in this chapter. The following table shows some of the possible uses for the question types:

Question Name	Type	Possible Use
Check Box	Closed	Finding out if someone has followed a health and safety course
Date	Closed	Finding out when someone would like something achieved by
Drop-down box	Closed	Giving respondents a choice of options, for example, Chinese Food, Italian Food
Essay box	Open	Asking for an opinion, that is, do you agree this is a good idea?
Numeric	Open	Asking for a number, that is, how much would you pay?
Radio buttons	Open	Giveing the respondents some choices to choose from
Rate (scale 1..5)	Closed	Giveing respondents a scaled choice, that is, which is your most important choice for food prices?
Yes/No	Closed	Asking for a basic yes/no response

The purpose of this questionnaire

In this example questionnaire, we are trying to find out how popular a type of fast food might be if it were introduced into a local community. This could be for the institution itself, such as a school, or it could be for a local community. For schools that are specialist schools, such as business and enterprise schools, this could be setting up a sandwich bar to sell at a local business park.

Creating our questions

The first set of questions will determine something about the potential market's habits as they currently exist.

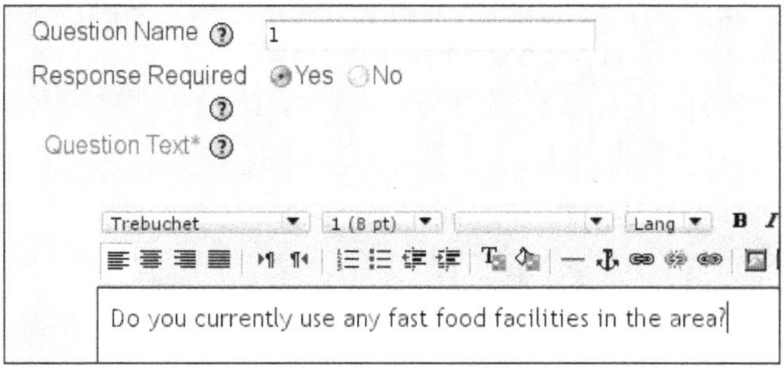

The first question can be a basic closed question to find out their preferences. This could be a yes/no type of question, which is selected from the drop-down list, or it could be some radio buttons. In either case, this would be a closed question, as there is a limited set of choices and no option to be 'open'.

It might be useful to make every question 'required', as shown in the previous screenshot, so that all data is gathered. This will really depend on the nature of the question asked, as some people may not be comfortable being forced to answer something that could be construed as very personal, especially if you are using real names in the responses.

Enabling the option "require a response" means that people will be notified that the response is a required one. Also, they will be reminded that they can not submit the questionnaire until the required questions have been answered.

The next question could be used to get a clearer idea of possible tastes and could therefore be a list of options. We can achieve this with the checkbox type of question. As with the previous question, there is the option to make the response a required one or not and also to force a certain number of responses. If you want a top five for this example, you would make a maximum of five responses allowed and respondents would be notified when this is reached. It may also be referenced in the question itself.

The final **Possible answers** box allows you to enter the possible choices that the respondent will be asked to choose from:

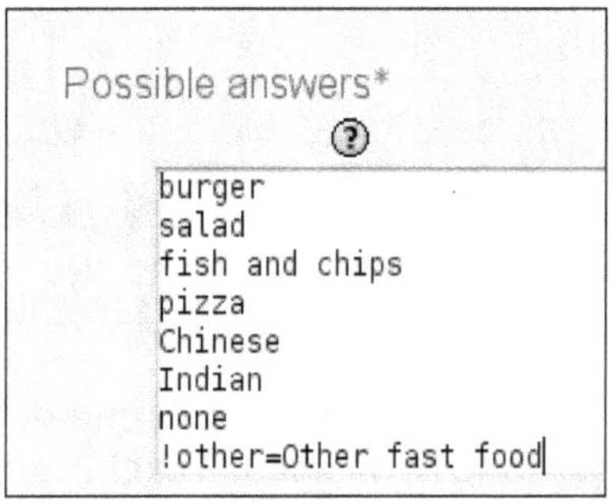

If you require a response such as 'Other fast food' as a catch-all statement, you can add a line **!other=Other fast food**, as shown in the previous screenshot. This will allow respondents to enter something not in the list.

The output for the respondent is as shown in the following screenshot:

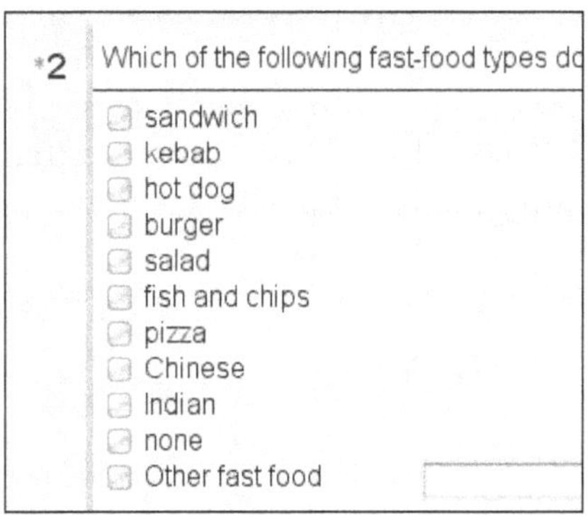

Using this form of question type, and using the same lists, it might be useful to ask such questions as:

- Which type of fast foods would you prefer to eat?
- Which type of food not currently in the area would you like to see?

These will gather quite a lot of useful data on people's preferences. As the student is hoping to introduce Mexican food, it would be useful to include this as an option and possibly ask if people are happy to have slightly more spicy food. These can be handled with yes/no type responses.

Similarly, checkbox questions can be used to gather more detailed data, as shown in the following screenshot:

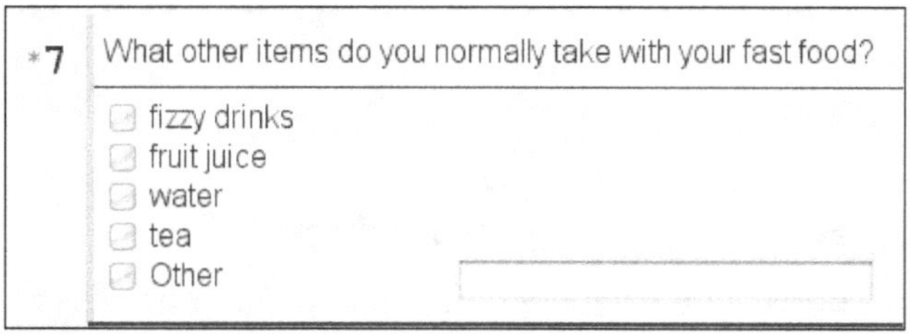

All of these questions should build up a detailed picture of the student's potential market, as well as some other items that could be used to supplement the food that they are likely to sell.

Useful information might also be gathered in relation to times when people might eat so that students can determine a strategy for when they might offer food for sale. This could be achieved with a checkbox format as used already or it could be achieved with the use of a rating question. This allows you to gather from respondents a range of possible times so that students can make a best choice based on the data. In the question, the range of responses needs to be told to the respondents, such as 1 means prefer strongly, and 5 means not at all. The output then becomes one of some differentiated choices shown in the following screenshot:

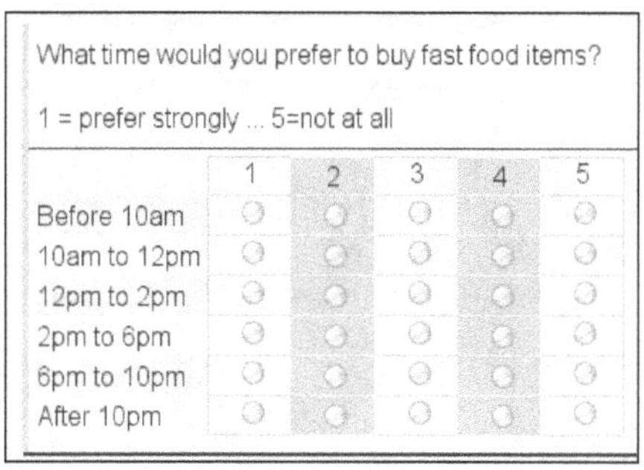

Some aspects of the questionnaire might need to be more open in their format. For this type of open response, you can incorporate an essay type of question. This is a very open format so it may be harder to quantify, but could gain some useful data for design consideration. The essay type of question allows an empty HTML box for the respondent to write in more detail and would be used for responses where you are perhaps gathering opinions on aesthetic choices such as whether you enjoy eating hot food and why. The following screenshot shows the essay type question format:

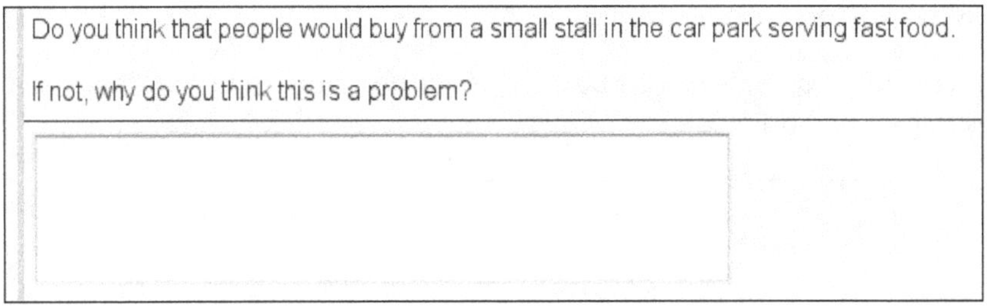

Checking the responses to questions

Once all of the questions have been designed, the questionnaire is ready to be published. As the respondents take the questionnaire, they can see their own responses. However, the overall responses are only available to the teacher on the course. If there is a deadline set for the questionnaire, it will then accept no more responses, and the data can be analyzed for trends and possible problems. All responses are collated and presented as bar charts or boxes if the essay type of response was used.

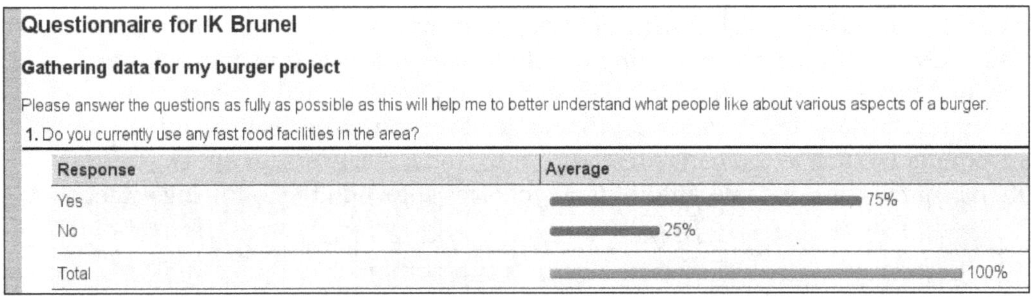

This type of output makes it easy to quickly see if any trends and decisions can then be made by students about particular aspects of their product design or placement in the market. For example, an important consideration would be the respondent's idea of cost:

10. How much would you pay for a fast food item?

Response	Average
Less than £1	25%
£1--£3	75%

Here, the majority of respondents are clearly happy to pay a higher price for food.

The questionnaire can be modified at any time, should the results not be gathering the required data, by using the module update feature. Access to this editing is via the button shown in the following screenshot:

This button allows you to update the questionnaire to some extent, such as changing the open and close dates if required.

Exporting the responses for detailed analysis

Once the questionnaire is complete, there is also the option to export the results as a Comma Separated Values file (`.csv`) for further analysis in a spreadsheet program. The option to export in a text format is shown in the following screenshot:

The option to export the results becomes visible as a menu item when viewing the overall results of the questionnaire. You are also given two further options to determine the format of the data output. The following screenshot shows the options with the checkboxes:

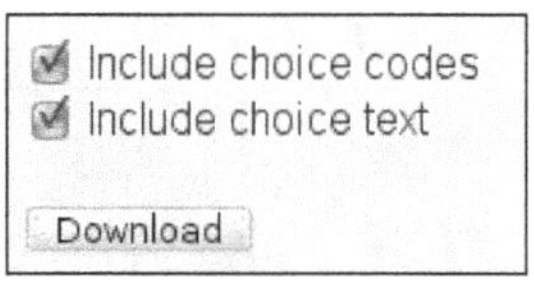

The two choices shown here refer to the way that data from questions constructed with radio buttons are handled when downloaded. Depending on how much data you require, your students can try these options to see which one works best. Once the download has completed, in most cases it can be analyzed with a spreadsheet and stored in the student's e-portfolio for additional evidence against any IT criteria they may need to meet (see outcomes in Chapter 9). They can customize the data output as needed.

	F	G	H	I	J	K	L	M	N
	Group	ID	Full name	Username	Q01_1	Q02_2->sandwich	Q02_2->kebab	Q02_2->hot dog	Q02_2->burger
nology		3	Isambard Brunel	ikbrunel	1	0	0	0	1
nology		5	George Stephenson	gstephenson	0	0	1	0	0
nology		6	Mary Walton	mwalton	1	1	0	0	0

If the students design the questionnaire carefully and ask the right sort of questions, it will gather invaluable data as to what product they should choose and what market to target for effective results.

In addition, with product design or resistant material, students can use the HTML features of the questionnaire module to incorporate images into the questions to make it clearer to respondents what it is they are trying to make and sell. Certain aspects of their proposed design can be shown as part of the response making it very clear what is being asked.

Downloading the questionnaire module

The current version of Moodle, 1.9, does not include a module for gathering specific opinions, although a Feedback module is currently being recommended for the 2.0 release of Moodle. The ability to gauge people's opinions to a series of specific questions, or even images, is something which is very important to a subject such as design and a great starting point for a project brief. A module which I have found very effective in meeting the demands of gathering opinions for the purpose of gauging people's views to a proposed project design is the Questionnaire module. The questionnaire activity module is freely available on the Moodle website `http://www.moodle.org` under the **Modules and plugins** section. The following screenshot illustrates the **Modules and plugins** link, which you use to find the activity module:

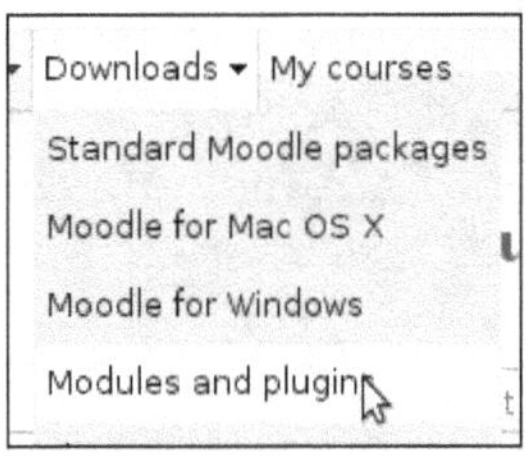

Once you are in the Modules and Plugins window, you can then search for the Questionnaire module since there are currently over 400 different modules and blocks available. The search box is as shown in the following screenshot:

The search will show a number of results, but Questionnaire will be highlighted. You can then click on the link to take you to the correct page.

`http://moodle.org/mod/data/view.php?d=13&rid=84&filter=1`

Here you will see some basic descriptions of the module and some links to other areas that may be of help such as forums to discuss the module and documentation. You will need to download the version that is appropriate to your particular version of Moodle. The version used for this book is version 1.9.

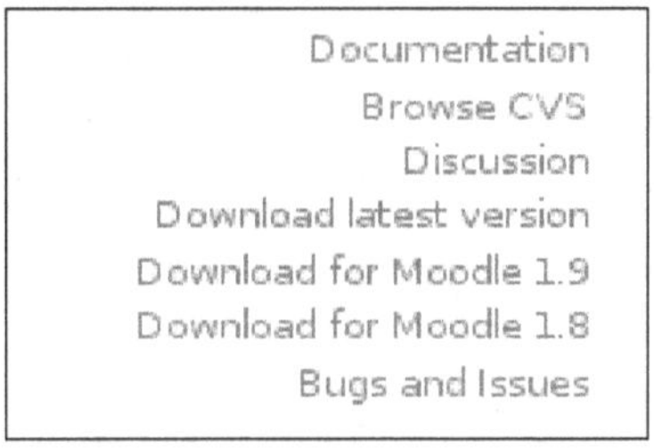

Clicking on the link, in this case, **Download for Moodle 1.9**, will begin downloading a ZIP file.

> Please bear in mind that modules and plugins in the database are referenced as part of the Moodle core (which means they are already in Moodle and supported by the developers) or they are called "third party". Third party modules and plugins are designed and maintained by people who may not be part of the core Moodle developer team and as such, they may work and be supported with upgrades, or they may have problems which you would not be able to fix and would be reliant on the good grace of developers to fix. Some modules and plugins require some form of financial support, and if you find the facility useful, you may consider supporting the developer with some financial aid.

Depending on how your Moodle site is set up, you will need to carry this out yourself or ask your service provider to do it for you. If you have a site hosted by a Moodle Partner, they will also tell you whether or not the module is well supported and advise you to the suitability of the module.

`http://moodle.com/partners/`

> I have access to a Linux-based web server where my sample site is hosted, and I am experienced in installing and supporting Moodle. This illustration is provided only to give some background to how modules are added to a Moodle site and are not intended as a comprehensive guide for readers to follow.

Installing the questionnaire module

We are assuming here that you have access to your site so that you can install these modules for yourself. The process, in most cases, is quite straightforward, but does require access to your Moodle files that form part of the root of your Moodle site. The following procedure is just a suggestion, as there are many different ways to carry this out and many different operating systems on which Moodle might be running. There are a number of excellent books on the subject available from PACKT or on the Moodle website:

`http://www.packtpub.com/moodle-books`

`http://docs.moodle.org/en/Installing_contributed_modules_or_plugins`

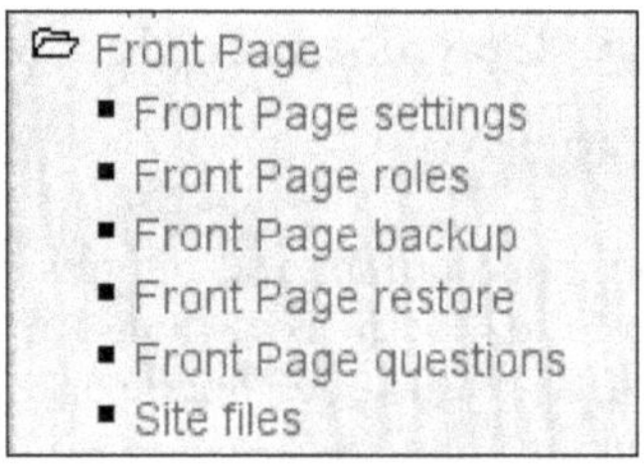

The ZIP file will be downloaded to your local machine and will then need to be transferred to your Moodle site, unless you are the administrator of the site running your Moodle website. The process will vary a great deal, but the following site gives the basic steps required:

`http://docs.moodle.org/en/Installing_contributed_modules_or_plugins`

In all instances, the ZIP file needs to be added to the server to be unzipped. One possible way to do this is via the Moodle site itself. On a Moodle installation, all of the courses and the front page itself have a corresponding folder in the `Moodledata` folder. In the previous screenshot, the folder is accessed with the link called **Site files**. This folder is readable and writeable by the web server that runs the Moodle site. If you upload the ZIP file to the **Front Page** files, it will then be available to unzip via a computer command line once you are logged on to your server. The following screenshot shows that it has been added to the `Site files` folder (`moodledata/1`):

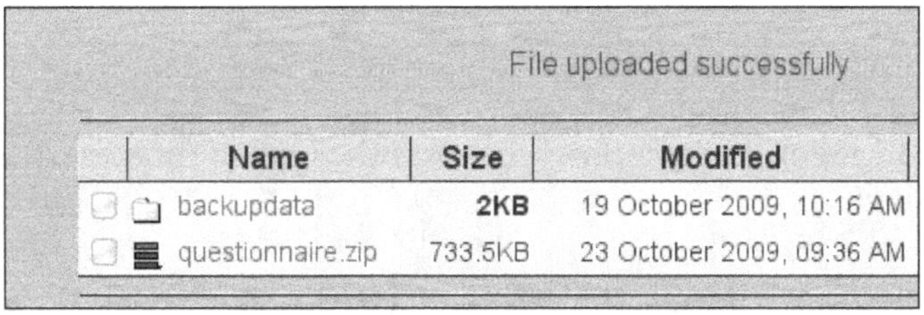

Depending on the type of system your Moodle site is running on, you now need to unzip this file into the `mod` folder of your server. With a Linux server, this can be accomplished easily by using the command line and a program such as Midnight Commander.

Using Midnight Commander to install a module

Midnight Commander (mc), in the following screenshot, shows two window panes. On the left, you can see the ZIP file that was uploaded to the front page folder (`moodledata/1`). The right pane shows the `mod` folder on Moodle where you need the questionnaire folder copied into (`your site/root folder/mod`). This folder, in the root of a Moodle installation, contains all of the directories and files that make the modules, such as forums, work.

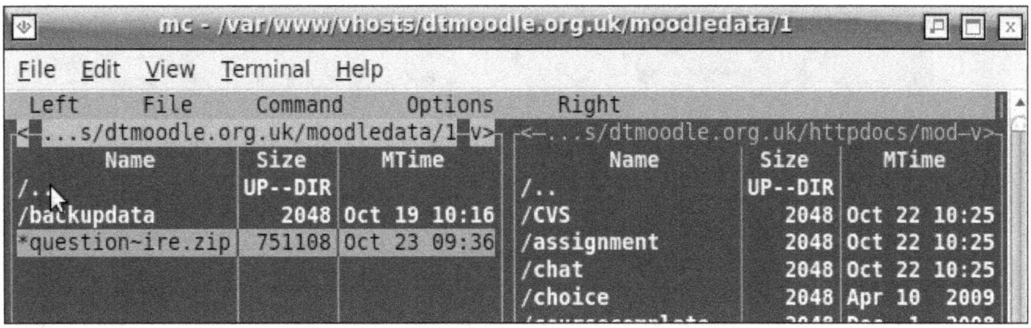

1. Pressing *Enter* on **mc** with the ZIP file highlighted will unzip the file as an entire folder.
2. You can then press *F5* and it will be copied across to the `mod` folder. You may need to check the permissions, but it should inherit the correct ones.
3. Once this has been done, you need to log in as the site administrator and click on the **Notifications** link on the **Site Administration** panel, as shown in the following screenshot:

4. This will trigger the install process and the Questionnaire module will be installed.

Installing the Questionnaire module on Windows servers

If you are using Windows, you would need to unzip the files and copy the folder in with the window manager, as illustrated below:

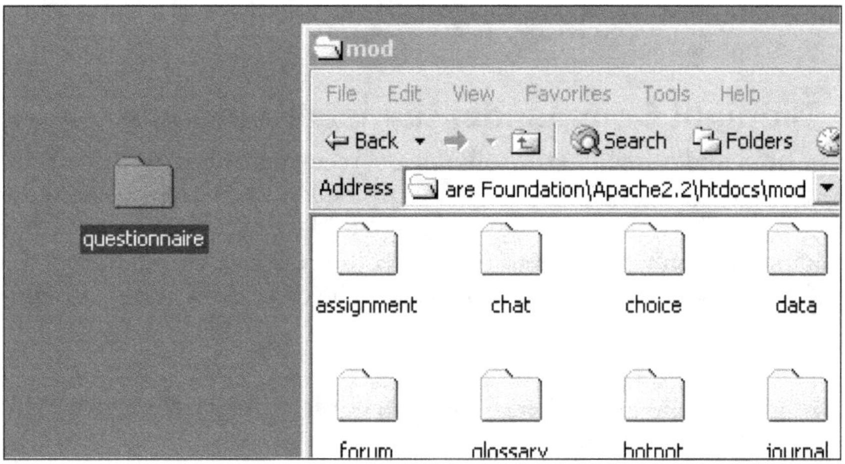

Either way, you will end up with a new module called **Questionnaire** in your modules interface of the **Administration** panel.

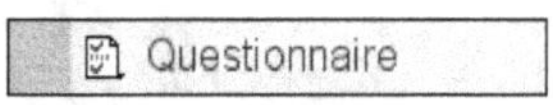

The module itself will now be available from the list of available activities when you enable editing on your course.

Summary

The two activity modules highlighted here, the Database module and the Questionnaire module, will allow students to gather and organize their research material in a great deal of detail and also allow them to better understand their target market through detailed questioning. Both of these sets of data combined will ensure that students are better equipped to build better quality products that meet some identified market needs and demographic populations. The experience they gain through designing and analyzing quality questionnaires, as well as a better understanding of database principles, will also go some way towards making them more effective users of Information Technology. In both cases, the use of these two activities will be underpinned with the interaction and communication facilities built into Moodle. The students can see how data is linked through embedded links to websites and use of geographical data through search websites.

In the next chapter, we will further enhance this data gathering by allowing students the opportunity to reflect on their work, or the gathering of their data, through forums and through the use of galleries.

3

Encouraging Reflective Practices using Forums and Blogs

In the previous chapter, we introduced students to modules that would allow them to organize and structure their research and information acquisition, such as *questionnaire* and *database*. Through the process of data gathering, the students will have begun to form some opinions and possibly some questions relating to the material they have gathered or have been introduced to. At this point, it would be very helpful for students to be able to reflect on the material and for staff to assist them in reaching a deeper understanding. Much of the work carried out in relation to design technology carries implicit social considerations and ethical/moral dilemmas. For Product Design students, is the product they are hoping to design really going to help people, or will it merely contribute to additional waste in landfills? Should they care? Or for Food Technology students, is it ethical to make food products that contribute to heart disease or other health issues? Should health concerns really be considered in the completed product? The most important element of design is surely the "bottom line"?

These sorts of issues are essentially socially constructed. It is therefore important for students to be able to discuss these ideas and issues openly with people and receive constructive feedback to enable them to make informed decisions and hence better quality products.

It is also important for students, as they work through their projects and designs, to show how their development is progressing. If they can gain some insights and constructive comments on the nature and direction of their designs at an early enough juncture, they may well save themselves some time and also have some dialog with their peers and tutors. This is invaluable input that would more closely mimic the real world.

In order to fulfill this need, there are several components within Moodle's core functionality, but also available from third party sources. The core modules to achieve a level of reflective practice will be forums and blogs. In addition to forums and blogs, there are a number of third party modules such as galleries and personal learning plans that offer a slightly different way for students to reflect on their work and help construct a clearer understanding of the subjects studied. Therefore, in this chapter, we will investigate:

- **Blogs**: Reflecting on possible jobs in Design Technology
- **Forums**: Reflecting on the impact of design decisions through role-play
- **Galleries**: Gathering feedback and comments on design processes on industrial placements
- **Targets**: Setting personal targets and reflecting on the outcome and process

Engaging in reflective practices using blogs

A good starting point for students to engage in reflective practices is by maintaining their own blogs. Blogs (an abbreviation for "web log") are increasingly available on the Internet and students will no doubt be familiar with their usage through social networking sites or online blogging or micro-blogging sites. However, the key here is to tie blogs into their more structured learning and make them part of the informal assessment methods you employ. If students use blogs effectively, they can build up a useful resource for revision and research notes, or in the example discussed here, use the blogs to discuss what they might expect from a career in design technology.

Enabling blogs for your course

By default, blogs will be enabled on your site and any user can access them as there will be a tab for blogs on the user's profile page. Users can click on the link to their name once they are logged in to Moodle and the blogs tab will be one of the choices. However, in this example, we are going to add the Blog block to a course so that it is visible to the course users to encourage increased reflection. Blogs are a block, as opposed to a module, so are initiated slightly differently. Once you turn course editing on, you will see the **Blocks** menu on the right column of your course view, as shown in the following screenshot:

From the resulting drop-down menu available on the **Blocks** menu, you need to select **Blog Menu**, which will place the **Blog Menu** block on your course, as shown in the following screenshot:

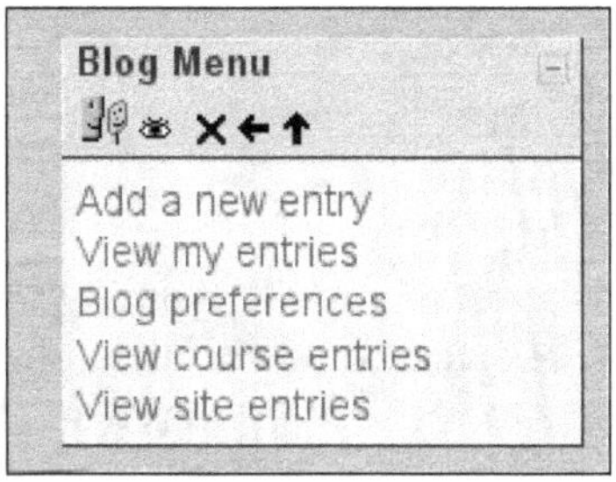

Blog menu options

There are different **Blog menu** options , which are explained as follows:

Blog preferences

The **Blog preferences** menu allows the user to choose how many entries they will see per page. The default for this is usually 8. You may want to adjust this or use some method as part of your teaching practice. It should be quite straightforward for students to grasp. As they add entries to their blog, they can choose to make them viewable by everyone on their site or keep them as private reflections.

Adding a new entry

By selecting **Add a new entry**, the student will be presented with a window to be able to create a new blog. The two options for this new blog entry are general and tags.

General options

The **General** options for a new blog entry are the name of the entry and the actual entry itself. Below these two fields, the student will further see a set of general options that allows them to add an attachment to their blog entry, as well as determine who will see the blog entry. The following screenshot shows the second set of options:

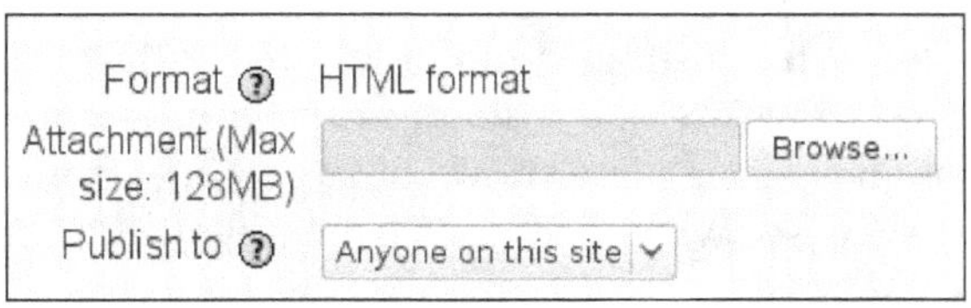

If the student clicks on the **Browse** button, as shown in the previous screenshot, they will be able to open their local computer files to add a picture or a document file, which may further illustrate the reflection they are making as part of this blog entry. In the previous screenshot, the **Publish to** option has been left as the default, so that it will be visible to anyone on the site. The other option students have is to publish the entry privately to themselves.

Tags options

The second of the two options available when creating a new blog entry are the tags that can be applied. A tag is a keyword or association that can be applied to an entry in order to make the item easier to retrieve in searches. The following screenshot shows the student view of these options:

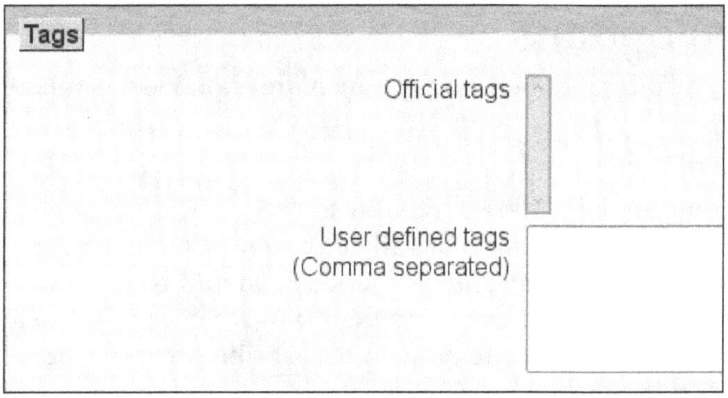

The **Official tags** are determined by the site administrator and are available under the administration block as part of the site **Appearance** options. A sub-menu under appearance is listed as **Manage tags** where the site administrator can add tags for the entire site and make them available to all bloggers. The use of official tags would be helpful for managing key search terms such as construction or hygiene for example. It might be worth creating a set of pre-determined tags and encouraging students to use these tags for consistency. In this example, there are no official tags, but the student has the option to determine their own set of tags for the entries they create.

Once these two options have been set, the blog entry can be saved.

Viewing entries

The remaining three links in the **Blog Menu** block are for the various views that are created. These three views are: the student's own entries, course-related entries, and site-wide entries. The course view shows blog postings from other people in the course. The site-wide view shows blog entries from anyone on the site.

Adding a Blog Tag block

In addition to the previous blog menu, you can also add a block to display the tags associated with the bog entries that students make. The block is entered in the same way as the **Blog Menu** block and will be available under the **Add block** drop-down menu as **Blog Tags**. The following screenshot shows the block once it has been added to a course:

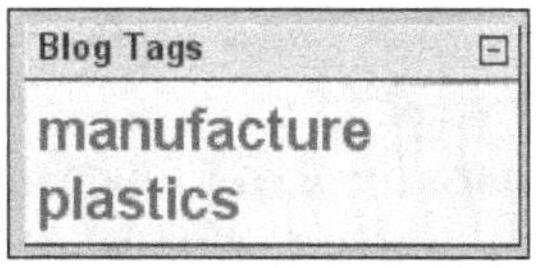

The entries that have the most tags associated with them will appear larger in the block, so that students have an instant visual clue as to which topics are most active.

The key point to emphasize to students in creating their blog entries is that they employ meaningful tags and this again may be something that should be part of the overall teaching plan. The more precise they are in defining the tags that identify their blog entries, the more useful they will be, in terms of revision, but also for others when they are searching for relevant data and posts.

In this example, the student has started writing a blog related to their interest in ship building. By creating a tag of "ships" for the post, it will then be useful for later reference.

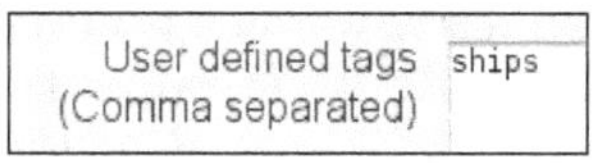

Blogs using this tag will then build up a display in terms of references—the more references, the bigger the font.

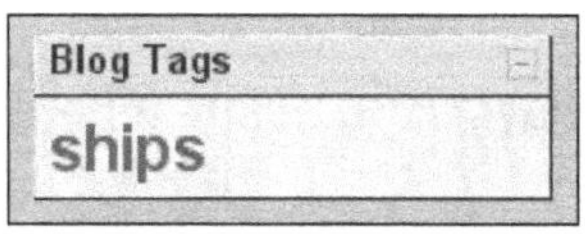

Worked example of reflective practice: Work Placement Blogs

In the UK, all Key Stage 4 students (Year 10) undertake a work placement organized by the school that normally lasts for two weeks. This placement is designed to allow students to explore possible careers. For Design Technology students, these placements would hopefully be in areas where they have a special interest or area of skill. The work placement is monitored by staff and they receive some official feedback from representatives of the company they are placed in, but a blog of the experience would be useful to share the experience and their thoughts with other students and staff. As places would be limited, especially in rural schools with limited access to manufacturing companies capable of absorbing large numbers, the experiences of student peers through their blogs would be invaluable. Equally, students who have secured a placement through a family firm could maintain a blog of the experience to show other students what such a career might entail. The personal nature of the blog would allow students to fully explore the work they undertake and reflect on whether or not they could sustain that for a number of years, and if it might lead to a promotion or branch to another profession.

Enabling and using blog syndication through RSS

Once the blogs begin to fill up with useful information, you might also encourage your students to syndicate some of the more popular ones. This will send them messages when new information is added if they do not have the opportunity to log in to check every day. You might also do this with blogs that you are using to send them vital and timely data. The syndication feed is accessed through the RSS icon on the blog itself.

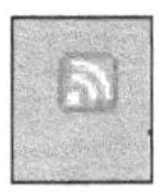

The link will take the user to a subscription site where they can choose which reader to use to follow the blog.

Engaging in reflective practices using forums

The forum activity module is one of the key elements of Moodle and central to Martin Dougiamas's driving ethos of social constructivism. To remind readers, the idea is that knowledge is best learned and remembered when it is collaboratively created. You can read more about the philosophy behind Moodle here: `http://docs.moodle.org/en/Pedagogy`.

With this in mind, students working within forums can discuss ideas and actions among themselves and with their tutors, or with the example here, use forums to reinforce their reflective practice through role-plays. This can be carried out in a number of ways from one-to-one meetings to group or even public exchanges.

Enabling and choosing a forum

The **Forum** module is enabled as with all modules by enabling editing within a course. This will display the **Add an activity** drop-down menu from which the option can be chosen to create a new forum activity for the course.

Once you choose to create a forum, you will have an initial choice of what type of forum it is going to be. The help file on this topic is very useful and lists four options:

Style of forum	Description and example of use
A single simple discussion	This type of forum would be useful when introducing a new topic or concept to students in order to see that they understand some key points you are trying to introduce. This type of short and focused forum can help both the staff and students identify possible areas of strength and weakness and therefore be able to adjust the course accordingly. It is also useful as an icebreaker in order to get students used to this type of activity.
Standard forum for general use	This forum is an open forum where anyone can start a new topic at any time. A standard forum might be used as an on-going discussion area that can be started by staff or students. The forum could be somewhere for students to introduce new ideas and concepts to each other and to be able to debate these ideas and even add files to more clearly understand the debate. If the forum becomes large and unwieldy or if it breaks away to a sub-topic, the forum can be moved to another more related forum.

Style of forum	Description and example of use
Each person posts one discussion	As the name suggests, this forum allows each person to post one topic for discussion. This might be a useful forum type to allow students to give feedback on each other's proposed projects. Each student can introduce their project and some of the outcomes they hope to achieve, or possibly some of the materials they might use. Other students in the group could then reply to the post with their own comments and suggestions.
Q And A forum	The Q & A forum requires students to post their perspectives before viewing other students' postings. After the initial posting, students can view and respond to others' postings. This feature allows equal initial posting opportunity among all students, thus encouraging original and independent thinking. For the aspects of design, which require student's views on social and moral issues, this forum would be useful to make sure that students were not being unduly influenced by other students in the group.

Each one of these forums has its own distinct attributes, as shown in the previous table, and these attributes will help us to determine how and why we will use a forum.

Creating a forum for role-playing

For this exercise, we have chosen the single simple discussion forum. The objective here is to create a role-play scenario for students to see how they might respond in character. The forum posts will be a useful guide for staff to see how fully students understand and can apply some of the key ideas and concepts in different situations. For example, you might pose as a health and safety officer visiting a company and the discussion would be about a violation that has been observed. Each student could then be assigned a role such as company owner, manager, safety officer, or shop floor worker, to see how they would respond to the post.

General options

The first task when creating a forum is the general options, as shown in the following screenshot:

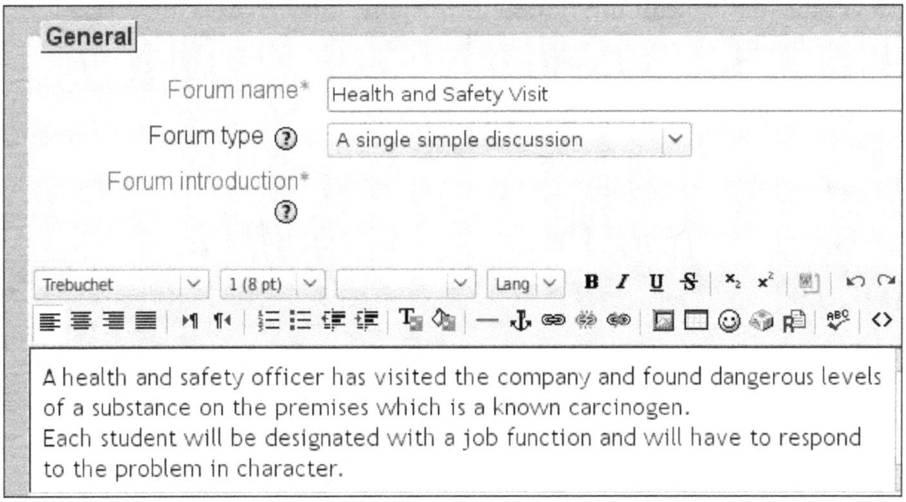

As we discussed, this example is for students to respond in character to a problem identified by a health and safety officer. The forum type chosen for this is **a single simple discussion** to allow each student to maintain their job position that has been designated.

The second group of options (once the type of forum has been decided and the introduction written) is to decide some of the ways the forum can be followed and also file attachment limits. The other key option here relates to the type of subscription allowed or preferred. In all courses, there is a default **News** forum, which every user on the course is subscribed to. This allows important notices to be posted to the course and an e-mail notification to be sent out to all users. However, in other forums, students may elect not to have constant updates from the forums, and in this case, you should not force them to be subscribed and they can choose to or not.

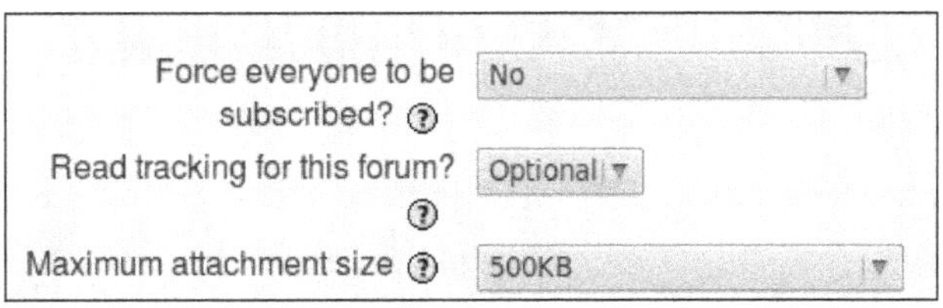

You may also choose the option to get students to subscribe initially, so they are at least aware of the first discussions, but they can unsubscribe themselves at a later date. If the forum has a great number of posts, the read tracking option will allow students to manage the posts they have viewed already and the posts they have not viewed. A good example of this would be from the busy forums on the `Moodle.org` site, as shown in the following screenshot:

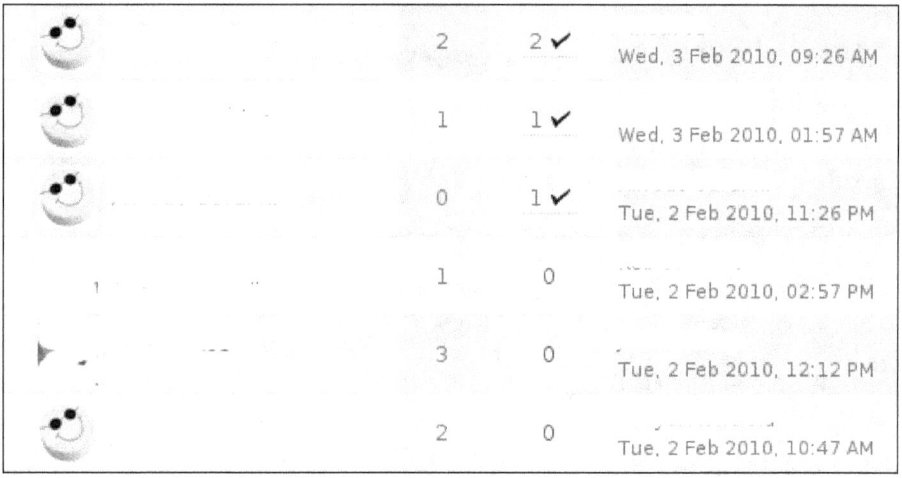

The tick marks indicate (or track) which replies to posts I have not yet read. This visual clue helps to manage large volumes of information on busy forums.

Grading forum posts

Many of the forum examples discussed here would be of a more formal nature. They would not necessarily be awarding grades to comments that students make, as in some cases these may be aspects of their character and therefore not really quantifiable. However, if the responses of students to key questions, such as with this health and safety example, are central to the way that students are assessed, then a forum can be used with a grading component. The grading itself forms a matrix. On one hand, you need to determine the aggregation of the forum posts that are awarded a mark. The options here are as shown in the following table:

Aggregation Type	Description
Average of ratings	The mean of all the ratings given to posts in that forum. This is especially useful with peer grading when there are a lot of ratings being made.
Count of ratings	The number of rated posts becomes the final grade. This is useful when the number of posts is important. Note that the total cannot exceed the maximum grade allowed for the forum.
Maximum rating	The highest rating is returned as the final grade. This method is useful for emphasizing the best work from participants, allowing them to post one high-quality post as well as a number of more casual responses to others.
Minimum rating	The smallest rating is returned as the final grade. This method promotes a culture of high quality for all posts
Sum of ratings	All the ratings for a particular user are added together. Note that the total is not allowed to exceed the maximum grade for the forum.

On the other hand, you need to establish the type of grade used for the rating of posts. You can used a standard scale such as 0 to 100, or use a custom scale such as **Excellent**, **Very Good**, **Good**, **Average**, **Poor**. The settings available are shown in the following screenshot:

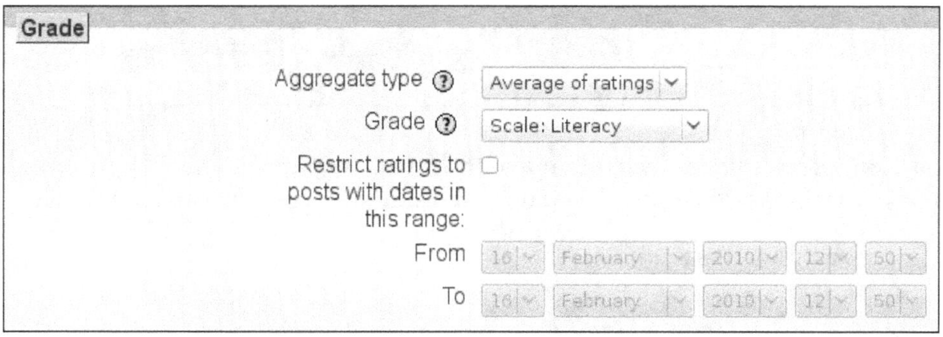

In the example shown here, we are using the forum as an assessment of basic literacy skills. We have discussed with the students in the group that they need to rate the posts of their peers in terms of quality of the writing. In this **Grade** option, there is also the possibility to assign a date range for postings. This option can be used in order to drive discussions forward against strict deadlines so that students do not go off topic.

Blocking posts on forums

The option to restrict posting numbers and in relation to time is useful as it reminds students that they are approaching a pre-determined threshold such as a number of posts within a week. This setting encourages students in the quality of their reflective practices.

Differentiating users on forums

The final set of options when creating a forum relates to the users that can participate. If you are using groups and groupings (discussed in other chapters, particularly *Chapter 9, Tracking Progress with the Gradebook*) then you can create forums only for selected users and also for the grades to be applied to a section of the grading (also discussed in greater detail in *Chapter 9*). The following screenshot shows some of these options for our forum:

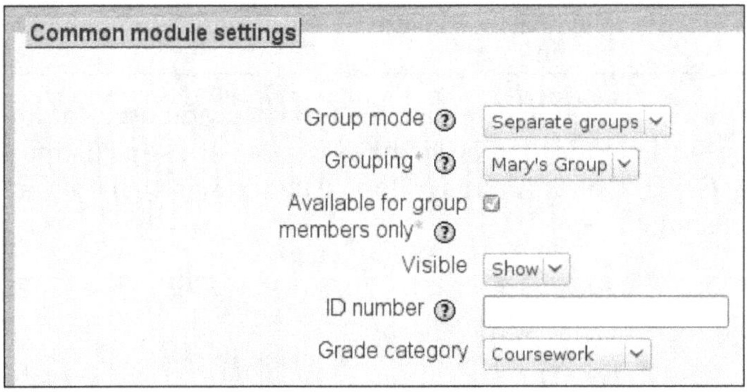

In this example, we have elected to make the forum available to Mary's grouping and so that any ratings will be saved as part of the student's coursework assessment.

The forum can now be saved.

User view preferences

The way forum posts are presented to the user can be controlled by the user and they can adjust how posts are displayed. If it is a really active forum, then it is perhaps best to show the most recent first or even to collapse the forum by displaying the threads. This type of forum could also be used to focus on a particular issue in order to make sure that students do not go too far off topic. The presentation of the posts available to the user is shown in the following screenshot. There is also the option to move the posts to another forum if they begin to veer off the initial topic too much.

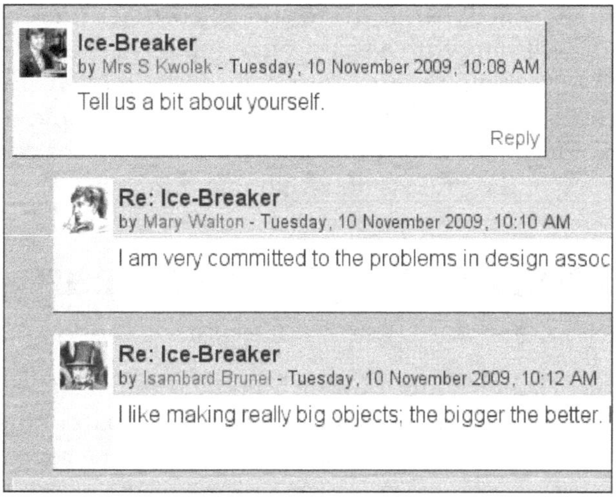

Additional forum suggestions

In order to encourage more independent thinking and reflective practice, you could create a forum and ask the students to post their thoughts on a specific project using the perspective of their assigned role. All of the other students in the group can then post messages on the forum to attack or defend that view. This role-playing aspect of forums makes them a powerful teaching tool and often students will feel more comfortable assuming a role alien to themselves when carried out through a forum. It also forces students to better understand the key players involved in any project undertaken in a design setting and hopefully reinforces the need to understand good working practices.

The question and answer forum can also be used in this way. The main difference is that students will not have time to reflect on the other student's views. They can post their thoughts on a particular issue and then see how closely this ties in with other people in the group. Again, if they have been briefed to research a role in a given situation, it will be interesting to see how they respond to other views on the fly.

Creating galleries to track student progress

The nature of design and technology is very much a visual one. In all of the sub-disciplines, there is a need for an aesthetically pleasing, though still functional, form. The most obvious example here would be with food technology, but also product design. In the area of construction, it would be the need to be visually correct and of the right proportion when building something like a wall for example.

In all cases, there is a visual dynamic that could be useful to track development. In most cases, students will start with a basic rough model of their finished product and take it through to the final production piece. This will likely involve many failed designs along the way. If they can track this process visually, and more importantly, receive some form of feedback and commentary, it would perhaps better help their overall understanding of the process of development in their subject design.

Using Lightbox gallery: A third party gallery resource

One possible means to achieve this through Moodle is the integration of a third party resource such as the Lightbox gallery. This module is not part of the Moodle core and would need to be installed by the site administrator. The code is available at the following URL:

`http://moodle.org/mod/data/view.php?d=13&rid=1021&filter=1`

In the previous chapter, we discovered how to use the database module to store and organize data. The Lightbox gallery allows students to manage their own image files whereby they can show their own product development.

Before you set up the gallery, you will need to decide how it will be used. In some instances, you may wish to control the gallery yourself, in terms of what gets added to it. By default, the only person that can add images to the gallery will be staff. If you use this approach, you can use it as a demo area to show all of the students how their work is progressing so that others can see it and make some comments. The comments could be directly on the images themselves or you could link in to another activity such as a feedback module or a forum. If you are using it as a staff controlled activity, then you will need this following procedure.

You could achieve a similar effect by creating a directory of images such as a directory view. However, students could not add comments to the gallery so you would need to use this in conjunction with a forum or encourage students through their blogs. You could also link to media sites that would store sequences of images such as `www.slide.com`.

Gallery general settings

When you set up a gallery, the default settings for viewing images will be the course file area, so any images that are in this file area will be displayed. It is more likely that you will want to set up a more specific area. To do this, you need to:

1. Create a new folder in the file area of the course. This is accessible via the **Files** folder icon on the administration panel:

   This will open the file manager area of your course.

2. Click on the **Make a folder** icon in order to make an area for the course images for your gallery.

3. As this will be used to highlight students' work, you may wish to make it a showcase area or you might create a gallery to highlight a specific aspect of their work. Here we have named it Exemplar Work:

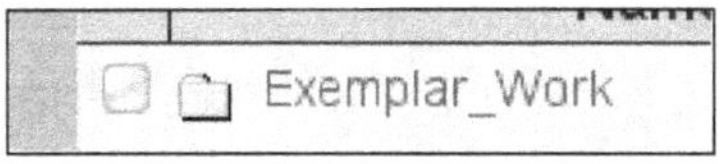

4. Once created, you can select the folder to add your images. To do this, choose the Lightbox gallery in the **Resource** drop-down menu. You will then see the setup menu, as shown in the following screenshot:

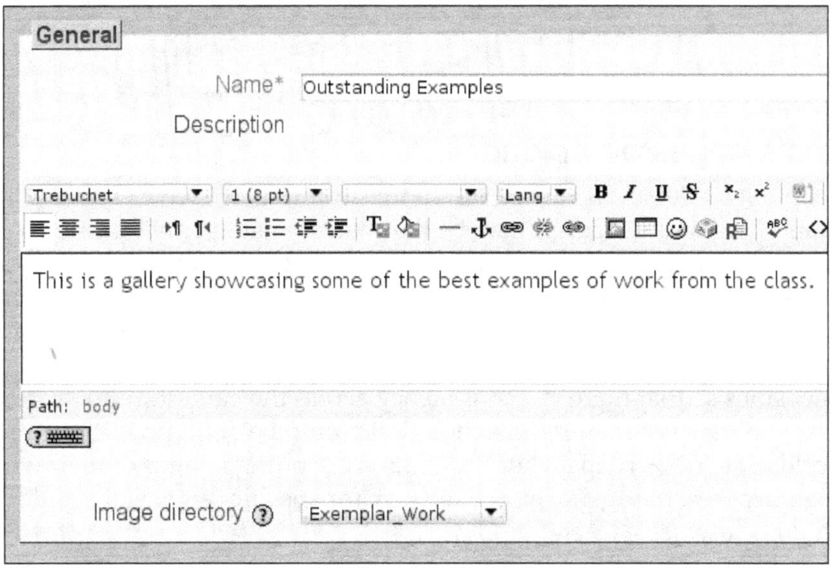

The key element to remember on this **General** section, as you can see in the previous screenshot, is to choose the appropriate **Image directory**. In this case, it is the **Exemplar_Work** gallery that we created earlier. The next set of options is accessed by clicking on the advanced options.

Gallery advanced settings

The advanced options allow you to control some aspects of how the images are handled as well as if you will allow any interactivity at all.

Images allowed

The number of images that will be viewable will likely depend on how many students you have and the nature of the gallery you are setting up. If the work is to show all stages in the development of a student's work, then you may wish to use the maximum number of images. In this case, we have decided to use 25.

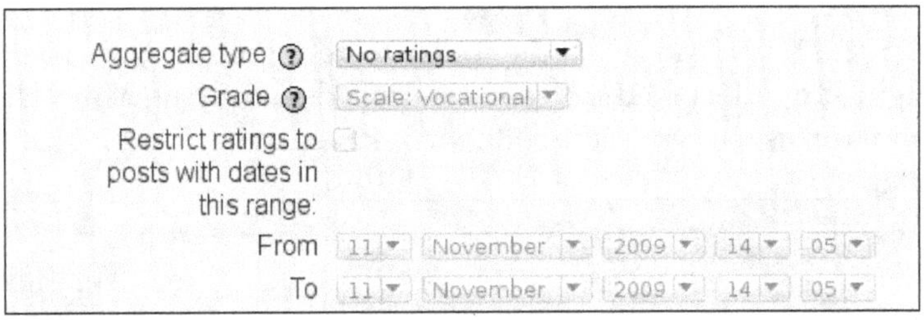

Resize of images on upload

The next option by default is turned off. In this example, we have enabled the ability to automatically resize images. It may be that you are using only one media capture device and therefore know the dimensions of every image that will be generated. In most cases, these images will come from a variety of sources. Many students these days use their mobile phones to capture images for Internet upload. Since there are a great variety of image capture devices, it is best to have some sort of de facto dimensions so that there is a consistency across the gallery. With students' own work, you may not require this, though it would be good practice to install. In the world of work, perhaps when students are sending images of their work for marketing purposes, the agency will likely ask for specific dimensions and formats, so this could be used as a teaching point.

> Please remember that images are subject to copyright restrictions and students will need to be made fully aware of this since it carries legal implications. It might be useful to introduce students to the idea of Creative Commons licensing. More details can be found here: `http://wiki.creativecommons.org/Before_Licensing`.

Image resolution settings

The resolution of the image in this example has been restricted to 800 X 600. It could be changed to 640 X 480 to save even more space if need be. The logic behind this is that it is best to go for the smallest possible denominator. Despite great advances in many countries, it is still the case that the digital divide is a reality and some people still do not have up-to-date computers with monitors capable of high resolutions, if they have computers at all. Therefore, making a smaller image size will ensure that everyone has a reasonable chance of being able to view and comment on the images. Many students these days use netbook computers, so a resolution of 800 X 600 would be a reasonable compromise.

Enabling comments on the images

In this example, we have enabled the ability for comments. Again, this is a decision based on how this is used for a teaching tool. As this will be a gallery to showcase Exemplar_Work, we would like to get some informal feedback from other students in the group to see if they agree. These comments, though informal, can be used as a means of assessment to see if they can pick up certain elements of good and bad design. If the students are instructed to do this and it is reinforced, it will become an excellent teaching tool.

Restricting access to images

This is similar to the option to make this gallery public. If you want others to see the work, you will need to make it public. If you enable this option, you will allow guest users to see the images, although they will not be able to add any comments. This may be a useful way to show local employers, such as restaurant owners, to see what students are capable of, without requiring the employers to be enrolled on the same course.

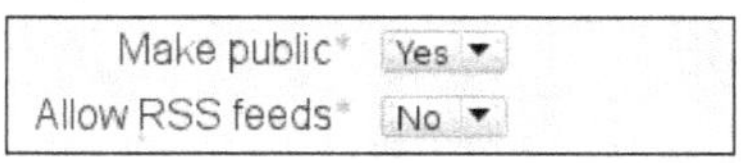

Allowing students to receive notifications through RSS

The RSS feed option allows you to apply a feed icon to the gallery and for students to subscribe to this feed. When new images are uploaded or images modified, the subscribed students will receive an update notification so that they are aware of the changes.

Displaying extended information

The final option gives some extra detail against the image, which may be more pertinent for design students where the construction and formulation of the image itself is important, though in most cases it will not be necessary. It does show the date it was loaded, which might be useful for informal work tracking. It also displays the image size, which may be useful for students on restrictive Internet connections so that they know whether or not it will download properly.

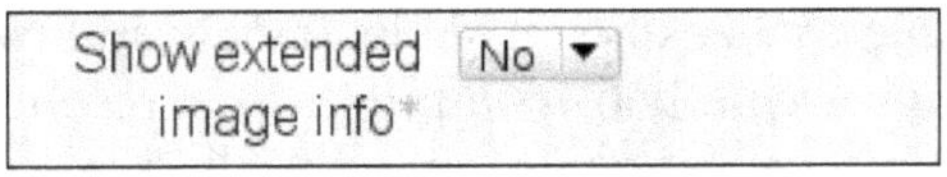

Adding images to the gallery

Once you have created and saved the gallery, it is available for use. As a teacher, you have permission to upload images to the gallery, and students are allowed to make comments. Therefore, with this option, you will need to take the pictures yourself or ask students to send them to you. Once you enter the gallery, you can then have a link to add some images. Click on the **Add image** link:

This will open the usual file management interface.

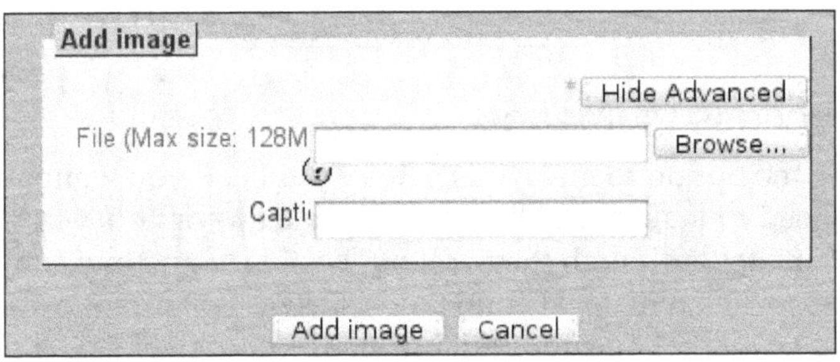

In this example, the **Show Advanced** button has been activated, which shows an extra field to add a short caption.

On this server, the PHP settings are set to allow up to 128 MB file uploads. The default on most servers will be 2 MB. You may wish to discuss this with the server admin to see what the optimum is and it will obviously depend on how much storage space you have on the server hosting your Moodle site.

Once you have chosen the image and added a caption, add it to your gallery. The caption would be a useful place to add a student's name so that it identifies the work.

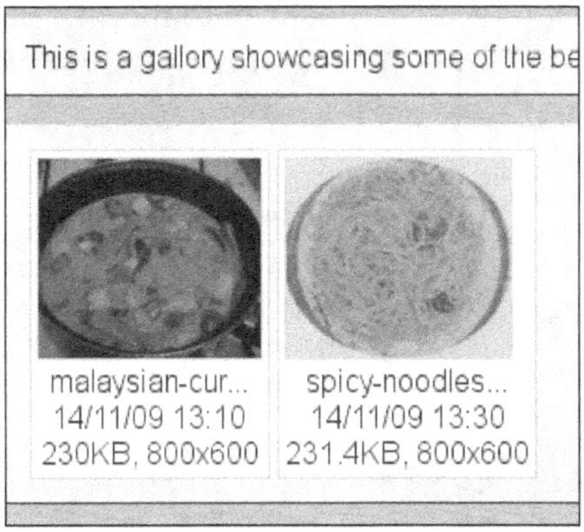

When students click on the images, they are presented with a larger image and can see any captions added.

As we have enabled the upload resize facility, all images are automatically set to a resolution of 800 X 600 regardless of the original image dimensions.

You can see the caption, which shows whose work this dish is. The **Next** and **Previous** navigation tabs appear when you hold the mouse over them.

Modifying images

The great advantage of this particular gallery is the ability to edit the images should they be unsuitable or if you want to modify the captions. By turning on editing in the gallery window, you have access to these options. Once you turn editing on, you have a drop-down box under each picture to modify aspects of it. Choosing one of these options opens up the different edit functions. For example, choosing the **Caption** editor will present the following screenshot:

In this case, you can add a bit more commentary to the caption and update it, but you can see that there are several other options in terms of modifying the image such as cropping or resizing, as well as a **Delete** tab. There is also a **Tag** function, which would allow you to organize pictures in the gallery in terms of a keyword search, which is the same as what we discussed with blogs earlier. Once you are in the gallery with the edit options, you can scroll through the images and make adjustments as required.

Creating individual galleries

In many cases, you may wish to create a gallery that the students can use individually for their work. This may not always be feasible given large class sizes.

The gallery itself has a standard set of permissions only for teachers, but as with all things in Moodle, there is the possibility to modify this and create an override.

Creating a folder to store images

The first step, as with a class wide gallery, is to create the folder for each student in the files area. Once this is done, it will be available in the image gallery options to choose.

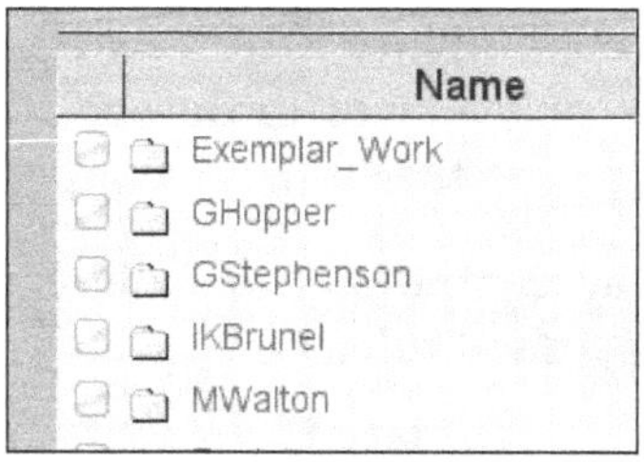

Once the folders are created, you need to create a gallery as normal, but obviously name it for your individual students and choose the correct gallery.

General option settings

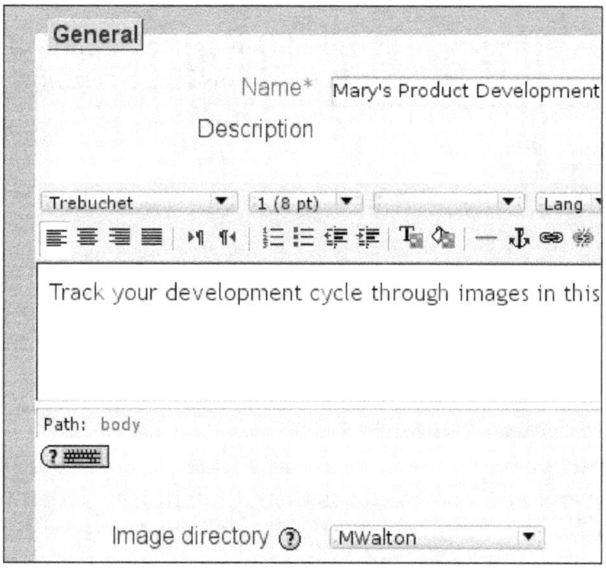

We now have a gallery created for this student. However, the current gallery will only be available for teachers to upload images to, although students will all be able to add comments.

Assigning admin privileges to a teacher

The next step may require admin privileges, as a teacher cannot, by default, create role overrides which is what is required, though there are various ways to achieve this. You could add the ability to upload images to galleries to non-editing teachers and then assign this role to this gallery for your student. The trouble here is that all non-editing teachers will have this ability, which may not be required. It is more efficient to assign it at the course level just for the specific student and just to this specific module item, thus allowing the students to upload images.

1. As admin, when you access the specific gallery, you will see the role override tab and the **Locally assigned roles tab**:

2. First, you need to add the student as a non-editing teacher to this gallery:

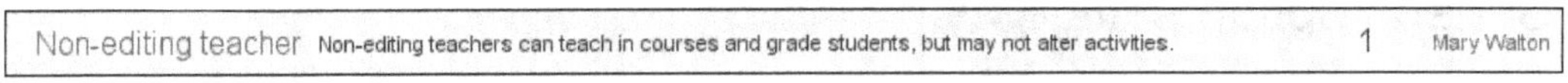

3. You can then assign the ability to add images to this role in this gallery only by the role override, as shown in the following screenshot:

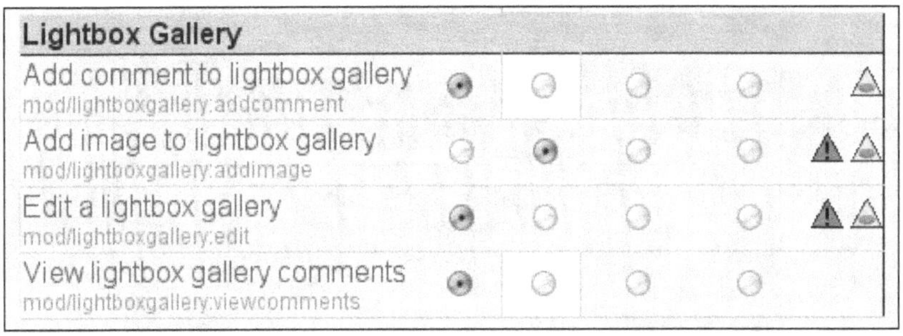

The non-editing teacher will have roles already inherited, but the student will be able to view the images and add comments as their student role. However, by selecting to allow the ability to add an image to lightbox gallery, this specific student can now control their own gallery of work. Other students will be able to see the gallery and add their own comments.

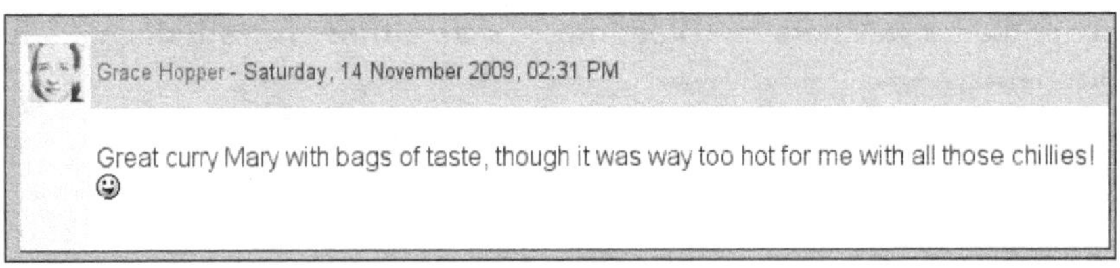

Examples of best practice

Now that students have their own gallery that they can control, you can set them some instructions to show the development of their work through images and captions to explain what stage the photo shows and what they were hoping to achieve. In the case of food technology, students could quite easily show every single stage of making a product such as cake, and other students and staff can make comments on this development and see if it makes sense. If they get positive comments, they can then use this sequence as the plan for their formal project write-up, which will then be assessed through the gradebook.

This is a great way for students to reflect on the way that they work and for them to have images to clearly show what they think is the right process. It also helps students who are more visual in their learning style. You could also create a gallery of sequences with obvious mistakes in the sequence to act as a discussion point.

Individual Learning Plan (ILP)

The final section of this chapter will deal with a system that will allow students to reflect on their own work through the setting of targets by staff and themselves. As with all things in Moodle, there are a number of ways to achieve this, but perhaps the most accessible is the third party module called the **Individual Learning Plan** (**ILP**) activity module, developed and maintained by ULCC and available at `http://moodle.org/mod/data/view.php?d=13&rid=1025&filter=1`.

The ILP module, once installed and activated, allows you to set some quite detailed targets within courses and to fine tune reports to and about students in order to better motivate them in their learning. This type of power means that there are quite a few options associated with the module and you will need to use the ones that are best suited to your needs. There is also the capability to tie the system in with your institution's own **Student Information System** (**SIS**) or **Management Information System** (**MIS**)) through a database abstraction layer. If you require this level of integration, you will need to discuss this with your network team or the company that provides your Moodle hosting service, as it will not be discussed in this book. In the UK, at least you can discuss this functionality with a Moodle partner that specializes in system integration with MIS. You can find out more about this at `http://moodle.com/integration/`.

The installation process will install two modules: targets and reports, as well as a number of ILP related blocks for your courses such as *Personal Learning Plan* and *Student Information*. The modules and blocks that are installed as part of this package have a number of related settings associated with them, which will need to be adjusted at the site administration level. If you are the site administrator, you can do this; if not, you will need to ask the site admin to make the necessary changes.

Module settings: Targets and Reports

The basic settings required are to be able to set targets and view reports, though there are numerous levels and complexities to this activity. Again, you will need to adjust these as required. The settings are in the site administration panel. You will see two new icons for the ILP modules, as shown in the following screenshot, namely, **Report** and **Target**:

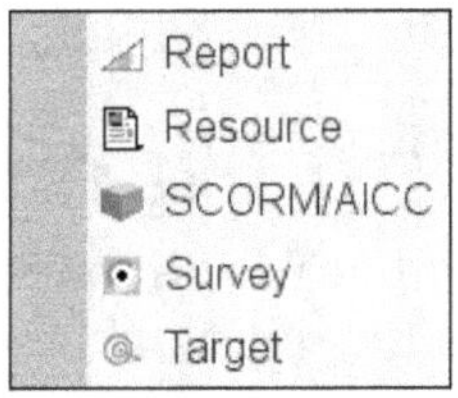

Each of these new modules has a corresponding settings link.

Report options

The settings for the report allow you to determine what reports are visible to staff and students, as well as what can be shared between students. Set the visibility and information as required by your particular course or institution. The first block of settings relate to how the reports are viewed and whether or not students are made aware of any interactions on the part of tutors, as shown in the following screenshot:

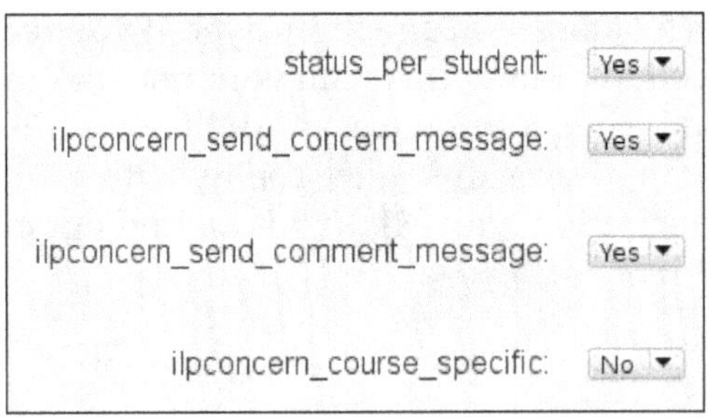

In this case, we are choosing to be able to see the status of each individual student and to send them messages when comments or concerns are posted. However, we have chosen not to show reports just within a course, as we are likely to teach students across the faculty. Therefore, it is more useful to get an overview of how they are working. The concerns we might highlight could be that a student has been missing key practical classes or has not attended their work placement.

The second block of settings determines what types of reports you would like to see. It may be that you are only responsible for a certain aspect of a student's learning, in which case you may not enable all of the reporting functions. In this case, we are choosing to see all reports, as shown in the following screenshot. This may be the case if you are a personal tutor for some students and wish to get a detailed overview of their progress and activities, as well as be able to talk to them about any concerns raised by other staff. For example, a student to whom you are a personal tutor might express an interest in Product Design and therefore you might consult with colleagues in this subject area to set key targets for the student to achieve. These targets and achievements can be discussed with the students or with the students and their parents, to make sure that they are working towards their desired goals in technology.

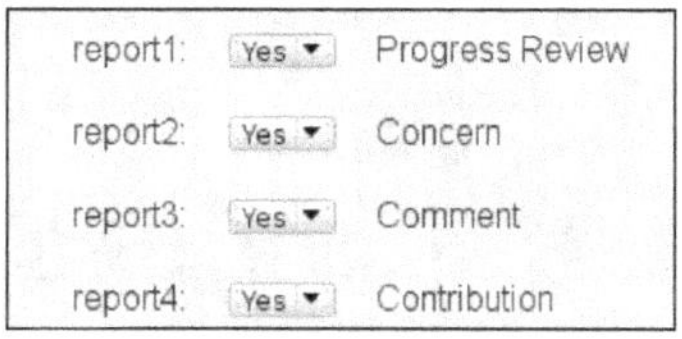

We can now save these settings in order to use all of these features on courses that we teach.

Target options

The settings for the Target module are similar—again the default for course-specific targets is disabled, which makes it easier to see student information across subjects. The main settings here, as shown in the following screenshot, relate to how messages are relayed to students about their targets. For example, there may be a modification to an exam board specification that makes a student's established target not such a high priority. If you are teaching students at a distance and do not see them regularly, then this would be a useful way to notify them of the changes.

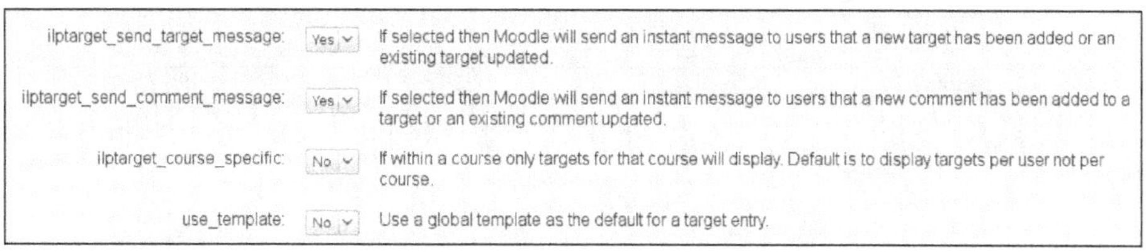

ILP blocks: Personal Learning Plan (PLP)

The block element of ILP has several more settings that allow some customization of the block once initiated on your course page. It is shown under the add blocks menu as the **Personal Learning Plan** (**PLP**), showing that it is something that students have more ownership of as they can add targets and concerns themselves.

Main options

The default settings would be "No", but in this case, we would like the students to be able to see a complete range of information in relation to themselves and their courses in design technology. If the user guide link is set to 1, then it will show a link to the online guide for the module. This might be something to set up once everyone is comfortable with the use of the ILP.

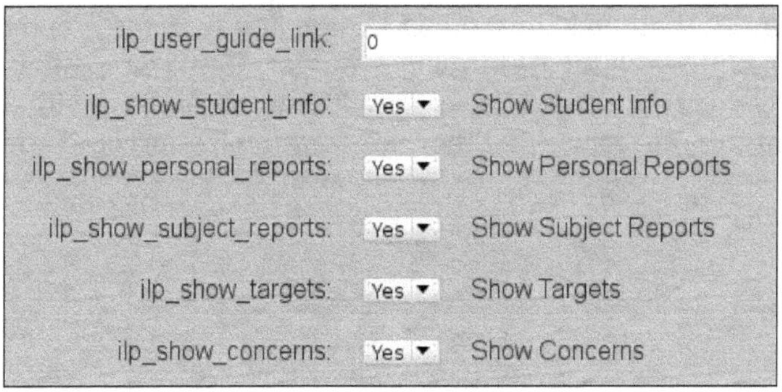

Student information block

The final settings on the blocks page are for **Student Info**. The settings here allow you to customize messages and instructions for students in relation to the information they put in the PLP, such as information about themselves that only they or their teacher can see, or shared information that all other students will be able to see.

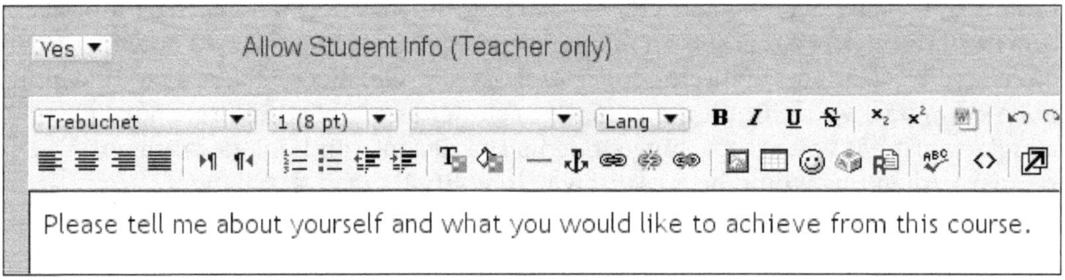

The student can then use this space to fill in information about themselves, which will tie in with their targets and concerns and give a full picture of them for staff and even potential employers. The student's view of this becomes available through the course, though it will also link in through their profile. We will look at this in detail now. The following screenshot shows the student's view of the above settings when initiated:

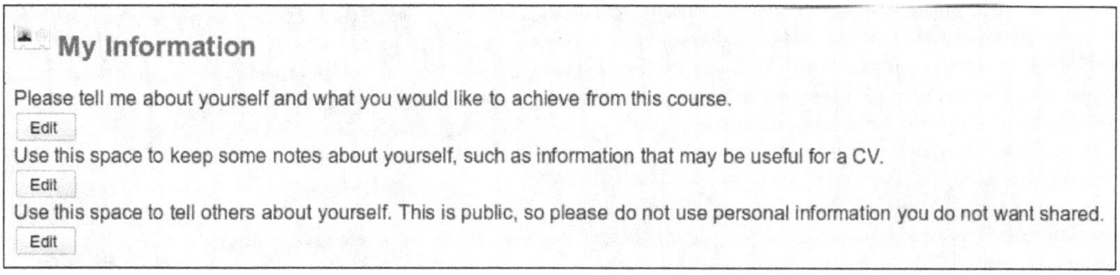

Once these settings under modules and blocks have been saved, staff can now create targets and modify reports, and students can get an overview of their work and learning, as we will see now.

Creating targets

The first task is to add some targets to your course for your students. The block will link to the area that displays the students so that you can see the targets, but the targets are added as activities. Switch on the edit function and choose a target for a section of your course where it is appropriate. This will be under the activities drop-down menu.

The target requires a basic name and a summary of what it is for, as with all other activities. Once it is set, you can then make more specific targets for each student in the group by clicking on the target link from the front of the course. The following screenshot shows the target named **Research Skills** that we have created:

Clicking on this link will open up a menu for all of your students. For each student, there is a link for targets and here you can add or modify targets for the students.

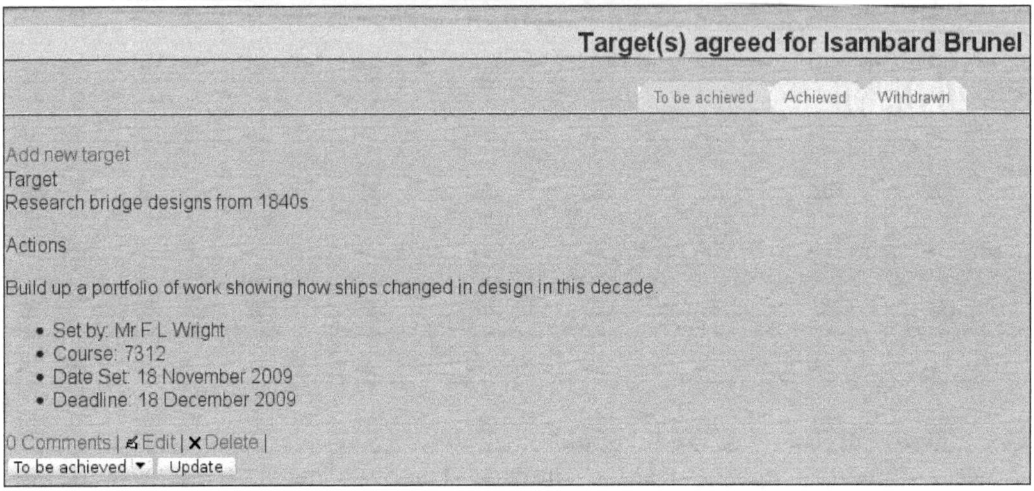

Here you can see that a target has been set with a deadline of one month after it is set. You can add comments as it progresses, and the drop-down menu allows you to modify it so that it is either achieved (in which case when, or withdrawn as not achievable).

The targets themselves can be general targets that need to be achieved across the range of the student's learning, or they can be tied specifically to a course by checking the **Course related** option checkbox, as shown in the following screenshot:

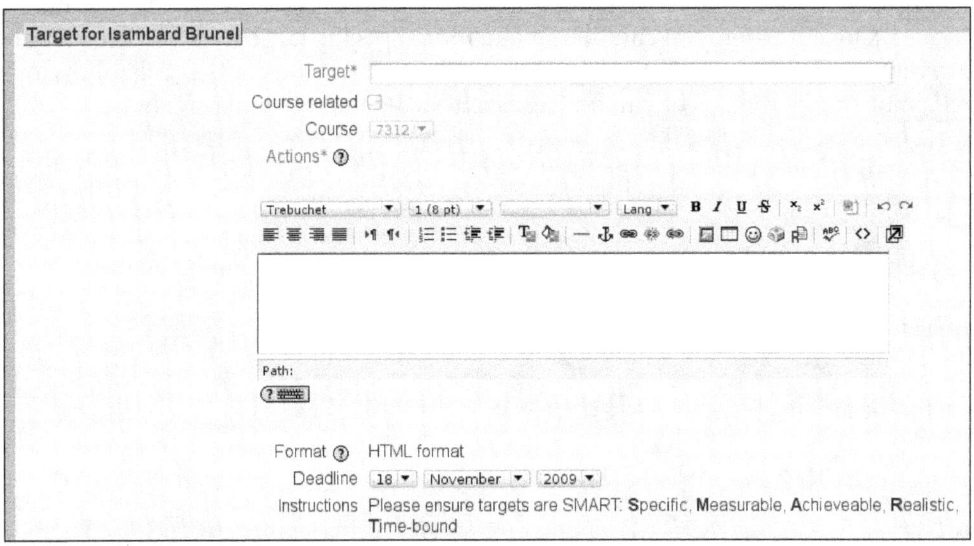

You can also see that we have the option to tie it to courses that the student is taking. If you are a personal tutor, you can work across the subject range and apply a number of targets. All of these can have a specified deadline. You now need to allow students to see their plans.

Accessing personal plans

As a teacher, you need to switch on editing for your course. This makes the block visible on the bottom-right margin of your course (assuming that is where you added the block). Choose the **Personal Learning Plan** block. This will then be added to your course and can be moved to where it is most suited to your layout.

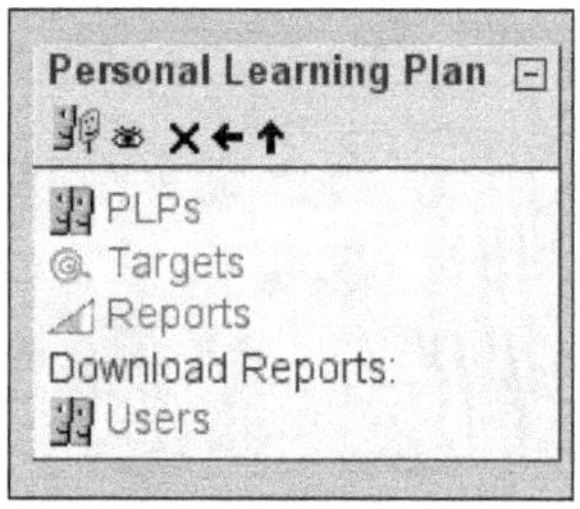

The preceding screenshot is the view that you will see as a teacher and will allow you to see and comment on a student's targets and reports as needed, as well as export those reports.

The students will have a more restricted view, as shown in the following screenshot:

When students will click on the link **My PLP**, it will open the interface showing them their personal settings as well as any targets, concerns, or reports related to them. The more settings you have enabled on the admin section, the more they will see, so it is down to decide what information they can access.

In this case, the student will be able to add some details about themselves for you and their class, but also see how they are faring in terms of targets. This can be used for tutorial sessions so that they can work on improving areas of perceived strengths or weaknesses.

In terms of the targets that are set, they can interact with staff through comments so that a clear dialog can be established and hopefully issues can be picked up on as soon as possible.

Once you have added various targets and worked with students through their concerns and those of other staff, you can then pull it all together through a report. The report can then be used to show their skills and aptitudes in their individual design areas and may show that they have a preference and an aptitude in one area such as resistant materials but not in food. This information can be used to provide clearer information for the students in the courses you design and the examples you use.

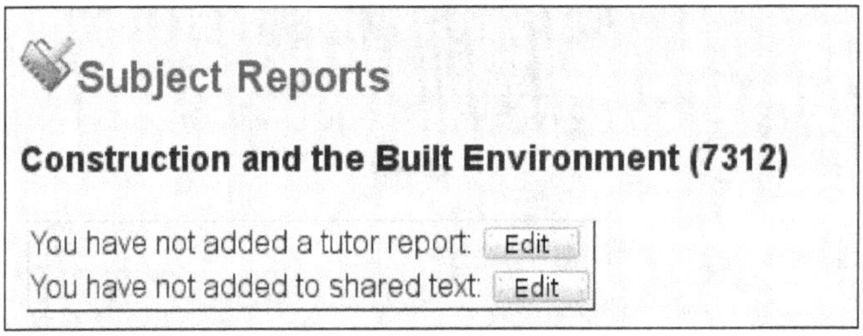

Summary

There are many tools in Moodle that allow you to support your student's learning and encourage them to take ownership of it through reflective practice. The key tools identified in this chapter, namely, forums and blogs, should create a framework for students to begin reflecting on what and how they are learning and also be able to share their thoughts and concerns with their peers and receive quality feedback.

Additional third party modules such as galleries and personal learning plans allow you to structure the student's reflections on the progress of his/her own development. In the case of galleries, this could be through showing and commenting on their design as it evolves. In the case of a personal plan, the students can tie key modules of work in the course to targets they would like to achieve, and they can then work towards these and receive the support where necessary to hit the targets. If they do not meet their desired targets, they can use tools such as blogs for further reflection. In the next chapter, we will investigate the use of electronic portfolios (**e-portfolios**) in order to structure a student's project work.

4

Exploring Design Portfolios

The subjects associated with Design and Technology, such as Construction or Resistant Materials, are very visual for the most part. Students studying these subjects have to amass a great deal of knowledge and information about materials in order to understand the various subjects. This knowledge then forms the basis of their product designs and evaluations. Moodle has some core tools to assist in this process of knowledge acquisition, such as forums and blogs, but in some instances, it is useful for students to have a greater level of control over how they construct and store their research and it is here that an e-portfolio comes into its own. An electronic portfolio (**e-portfolio**) is a personal space that students (and staff) can use to gather and organize their electronic materials. These could be files that are constantly useful such as health and safety documents that are generic to all subjects, or it could be images of certain materials that they have gathered while on work placements in industry. Either way, an e-portfolio is a good way for them to structure their own learning in a way that is comfortable and meaningful to them. In addition, if the portfolio is standards-compliant, it means that they can take their digital learning with them to their next phase; this could be a job or higher education. The other big advantage to portfolios, such as these, is that students can also share their work, which is not possible with many of the core Moodle functions.

There are a number of portfolios available to work with Moodle and they range in complexity and functionality. As they are a very personal thing, this chapter will try to give an overview of the most popular portfolios and a review of their main features in terms of supplementing Design Technology courses, as well as some examples of how they might be used to best effect.

In this chapter, we will look at three popular portfolio applications:

- **Exabis:** It is a small file manager-based portfolio that enables a degree of sharing and integrates as a block into Moodle courses
- **MyStuff**: It is a fully featured internal portfolio designed and maintained by the Open University, offering more sharing and collaborative tools
- **Mahara**: It is an external portfolio that integrates with Moodle using **Single Sign On** (**SSO**)

Exploring the Exabis portfolio

The Exabis portfolio is a third-party add-on that can be placed in your courses to allow students to store and organize their work and allow them to share it with others, for example, external verifiers. The code can be downloaded from the **Modules and plugins** section at the Moodle website (`http://moodle.org/mod/data/view.php?d=13&rid=1142&filter=1`).

Once the code has been installed, the site administrator will need to check the settings of the block for all users.

Site-wide settings

The first job, for an administrator, is to make sure the settings meet the institution's needs. These settings are available on the administration panel. You may need your site administrator to adjust these for you if you do not have these permissions. The following screenshot shows the two options available:

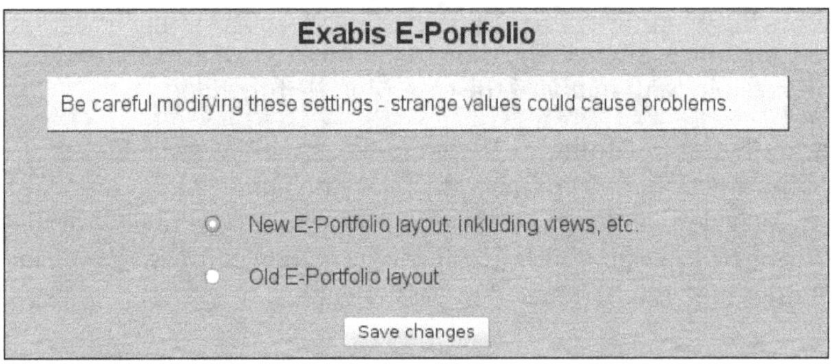

The settings will be determined by what version you have installed on your system, and in this case, the options relate to how the portfolio looks. The key feature of recent portfolios is the ability to create **views** that are customized web pages. Most students will be familiar with this activity through social networking sites.

Installing the Exabis block into a course

To use the Exabis block, you first need to enable editing within the course you are responsible for. To do this, you need to click on the **Turn editing on** button, as shown in the following screenshot:

This will change the view of your course, and a block will now be visible on the right-hand column to add further blocks to your course.

The **Add** button, as shown in the previous screenshot, is a drop-down list and will list all available blocks in alphabetical order. You need to scroll down until you find the Exabis E-Portfolio listing and then click to add this block.

Once the block has been added to your course area, you can make some more localized adjustments.

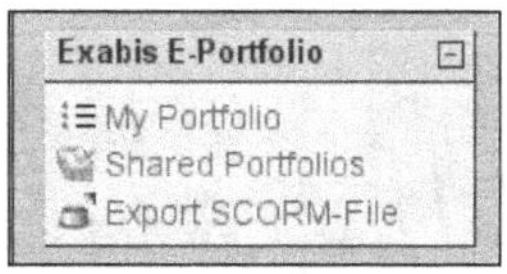

In the staff view, there are three options. However, the two lower options merely point to different tabs on the same menu as the **MyPortfolio** link. Once you open the portfolio, you can see the layout of the block and the functions that it supports, as shown in the following screenshot:

The personal information tab

The first tab allows students to build up some personal information so that they have a sort of limited resume or CV. Once students click on the **Information** tab, they will see one button (**Edit**), which will open an edit window to allow them to add some notes and details.

The Categories tab

After students have entered some basic information about themselves, they need to organize their material. This is achieved initially by establishing some categories under which the information they gather can be structured. In this example, using the Product Design course, the student may need to create categories for each section they are working with. In the UK, for example, this would be: Materials and Components, Design and Market Influence, and Process and Manufacture.

By clicking on the **Categories** tab, there will, as with the **Information** tab, be an edit button visible. Clicking on this button will open a window to create the required categories, as shown in the following screenshot:

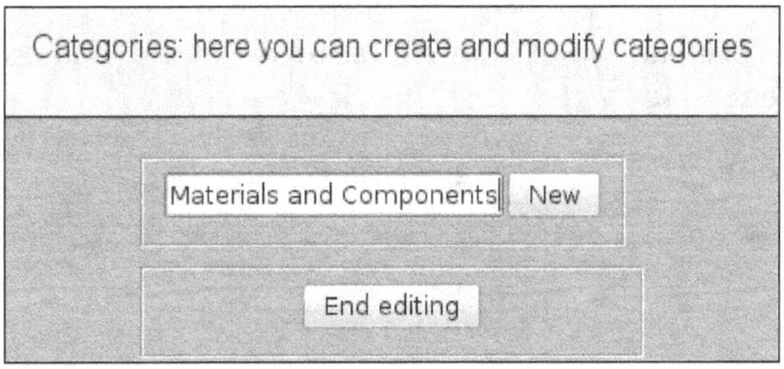

By clicking on the **New** button, as shown in the previous screenshot, the category will be created and you will then have the choice to add sub-categories or new categories as required. The layout of this edit window is as shown in the following screenshot:

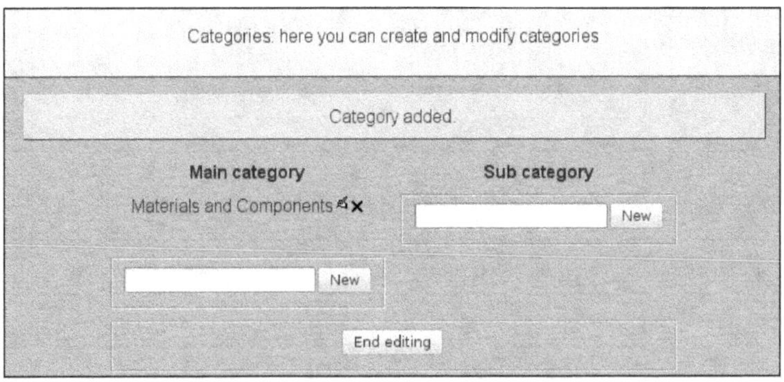

These can be further broken down into sub-categories that match the course specification. The process is the same as creating categories, and with each new category created, an additional field appears to add sub-categories, as seen in the previous screenshot. The resulting structure could look similar to the following screenshot, where each part of the specification has a corresponding category and sub-category.

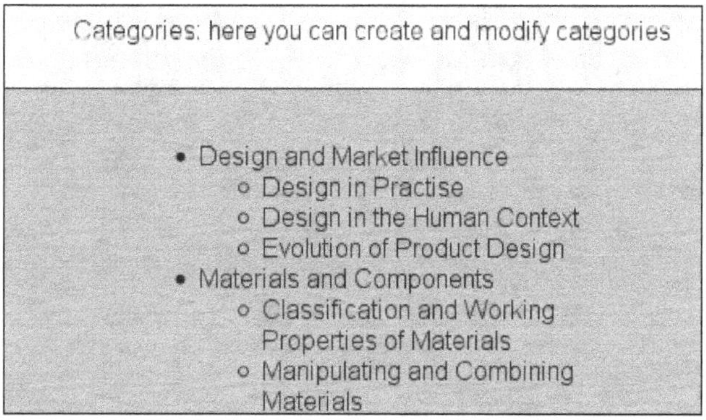

These categories will now be available in drop-down menus for the students to add various resources, such as files and notes, as shown in the following screenshot:

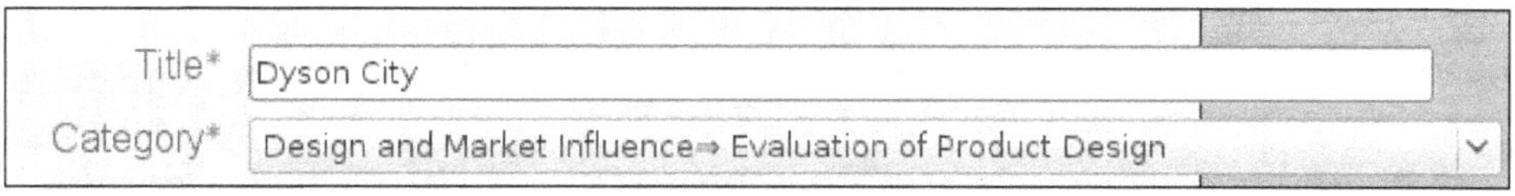

In the previous screenshot, you can see that students have a drop-down box under **Categories,** which lists categories and sub-categories for them to link their resources too.

Building up the portfolio content

Students can now build up their portfolio of evidence and can share this information, if they need to, with staff, other students, or external examiners. The information is organized through the main **My Portfolio** tab, as shown in the following screenshot:

Under this tab, there are sub-tabs that allow the students to link to websites, upload files, and also make notes about some of the material they have gathered. Each of these can now be associated with a category or sub-category to give some clear definition to their research work. The following screenshot shows a student adding some files to a sub-category related to design:

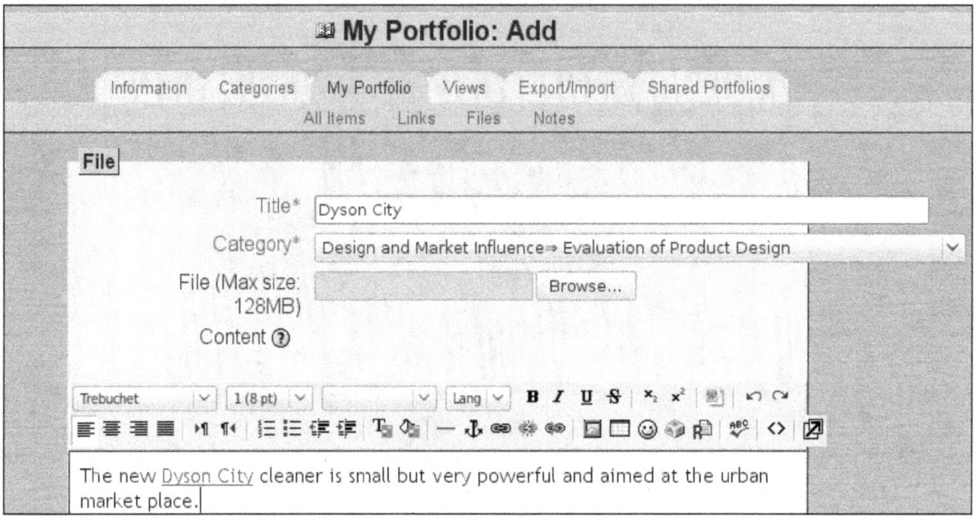

In the previous screenshot, students could attach a file which may be some notes they made on a factory visit that they have scanned.

Gradually, they can start building up a detailed folder of information and links to other useful resources. The following screenshot shows the **MyPortfolio** view as a student builds up some of their reference material and notes.

Category	Type	Name
Design and Market Influence	Link	Dyson's Vacuum cleaners Dyson has set the standard for the design of top end vacuum cleaners that all others now copy. Here is some more detail about his design.
Research	File	Metals Here is my research work on various metals and their properties.
Research	Note	Aluminium This metal, from my research, seemed to be the most useful in terms of how easy it is to work with, but also how strong and light it is.
		Link ▼ New

Each of the resources is clearly categorized and time stamped and the type of resources is easy to see.

Creating views

In the release under discussion here (version 3.2.3 release 168) there is a tab to create views. This is still under development and not fully functional, but may well be functional by the time you install it.

Clicking on the **Views** tab will show a button to add a view. Clicking on the **Add View** button will open an edit window to allow the student to organize their views, as shown in the following screenshot:

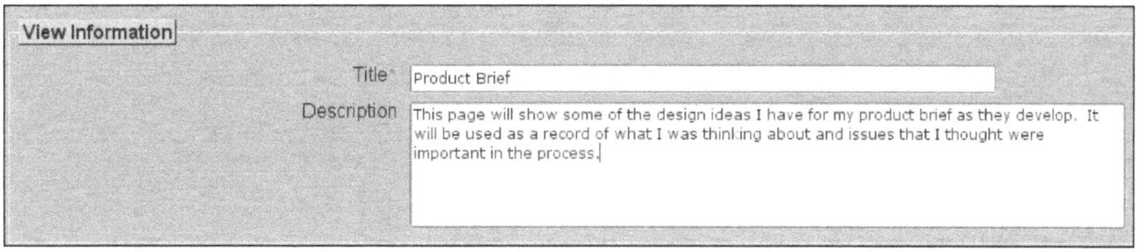

The views are quite basic at present, but will allow students to build up a portfolio of evidence in an easy and organized way.

Sharing their work and thoughts

If students would like to share some of their work with each other, then they can via the **Views** tab. This tab, on the latest version, has a link to allow sharing.

Once students enable the sharing function by clicking on the **Change** link, they can then choose what type of sharing they require and with whom.

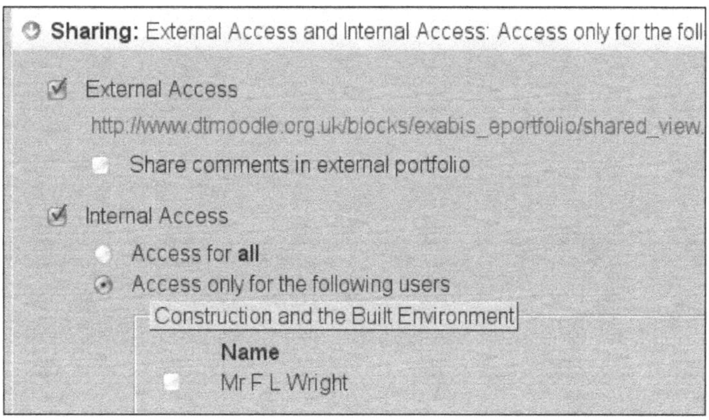

In the case shown here, the student can elect to share his/her work externally by creating a link to his/her folder from an external or an internal link. The **Internal Access** option allows them to further specify who can see their portfolio. In this case, they can share it with all of the staff who teach them in the design and technology faculty, or just some of the staff. In this case, when the product design teacher logs in and checks for shared portfolios, they will see this student's work.

Importing and exporting portfolios

Increasingly with e-portfolios there is the need to be able to take the entire portfolio with the students to other places of study or work. With the Exabis system, there is the ability to export the student's work in a number of formats. The two formats, currently available are **Shareable Content Object Reference Module** (**SCORM**) and **Extensible Markup Language** (**XML**). Both of these are file structures used to import and export groups of files from web-based systems such as Moodle. The import facility in Exabis will import a SCORM file, which is usually in a zipped format. The options shown for **Export/Import** are shown in the following screenshot:

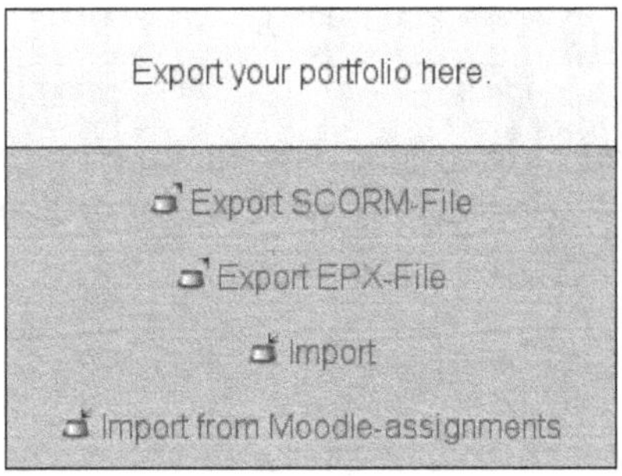

In both cases shown here, the export will allow students to save their work as a ZIP file, and depending on how they have structured their portfolio, they will have a range of choices regarding what to include in the export. The following screenshot shows the options for a SCORM export.

The student, as shown in the previous screenshot, has chosen to save his/her **Product Development** material in a SCORM file. Clicking on the **Create SCORM-File** button will open a download dialogue window where the student can chose where on his/her computer to save the zipped file.

An additional feature shown in the previous **Export your portfolio** screenshot is the ability to include Moodle assignments in the portfolio of evidence. This would be useful if students take the portfolio to a new job. Clicking on the **Import from Moodle-Assignments** link results in a screen where students can add their assignments, as shown in the following screenshot:

Under the **Action** column shown in this screenshot, the student can click on the **add this file** link. Clicking this link will open the **MyPortfolio:Add** window and the student can link this assignment to a category. The resulting link will then appear in their **MyPortfolio: Files** view. The assignment itself will be a hyperlink, which will open the word processed assignment when clicked.

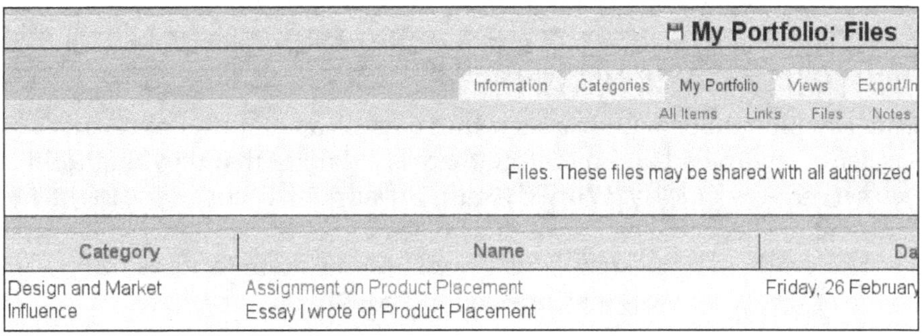

Opening the assignment link will create a full URL to where the assignment can be located so that external examiners or employers can also view the work. It allows additional notes to be added by the student, such as follow up comments, as shown in the following screenshot:

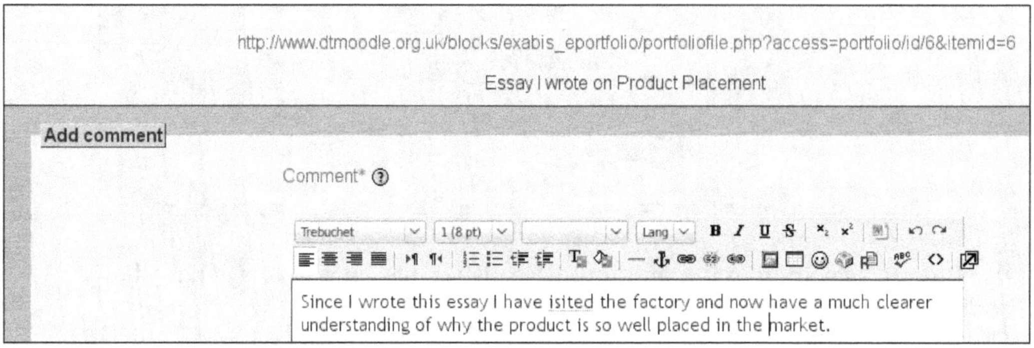

The additional commentary shows how the student has used the portfolio to track their learning process and to reflect on their earlier work. The whole process is therefore contained in an organized structure that the student controls and can be modified as their greater understanding dictates.

Future developments in Exabis

As mentioned, the views in this portfolio are not yet fully developed, but the current version is very usable. In order to have more flexibility and functionality, it is necessary to install a more fully featured e-portfolio such as MyStuff , which we will investigate in the next section.

Exploring the MyStuff portfolio

Like most e-portfolios, as they are quite a new feature, the **Open University** (**OU**) e-portfolio called **MyStuff** is heavily under development, though very feature-rich and usable. The latest download (currently codenamed Longmorn) can be found at: `http://www.open.ac.uk/blogs/MyStuff-info/?page_id=39`. At this address, you will find installation tips as well as support forums.

One of the key limitations with Exabis is that there is no real way to restrict how much students can upload and therefore there is a danger that they might fill up your web server very quickly. With MyStuff, the administrator user can set a limit on the amount of space that can be used as well as give the students some warning messages to alert them to this fact. This gives students more focus as they need to be more aware of what materials they are saving and why.

Configuring system-wide settings (Storage)

The settings, which control how MyStuff is used, are located under the **Modules** section of the administration block (**Site Administration** | **Modules** | **Manage Activities**), as shown in the following screenshot:

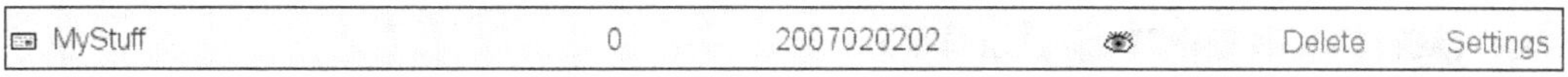

Clicking on the **Settings** link in the previous screenshot will open a configuration window. The configuration options are broken down into three tabs: mystuffconfig, mystuffexport, and mystuffimport.

MyStuff configuration

The first configuration tab relates to storage and usage parameters. There are also settings here which relate to the Open University's system called **eMTA** (**electronicaly Marked Tutor Assignments**), which do not relate to our system and so do not require any modifications. The settings we do require relate to the amount and type of storage we wish to allow. The following screenshot shows some suggested quantities for the maximum size of the portfolio per student, as well as warning levels.

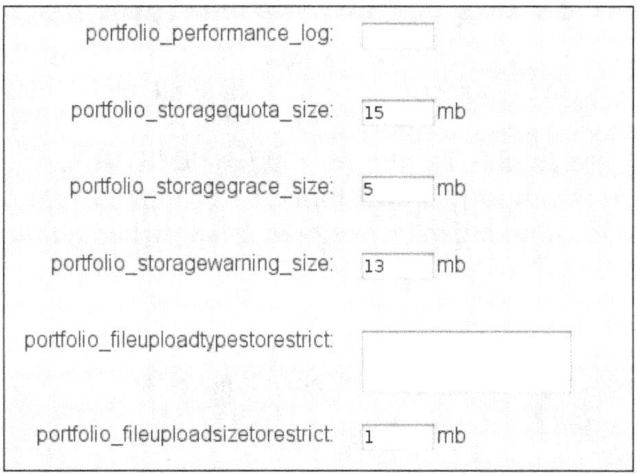

The main settings here are how much space should students be allowed and when should they be warned about it so that they can deal with the problem. Here we have settled for 15 MB, though we will allow up to 20 MB before they are frozen out. You may also wish to restrict the types of files allowed to be uploaded—**portfolio_fileuploadtypestorestrict**. As this is a student-controlled portfolio, the chances are that they may upload material that would be illegal under most country laws, such as MP3 music files, which they have not purchased.

[It is worth noting that the school is legally responsible for these files and the fines in the UK, for example, are huge. So it may be worth preventing them appearing, unless students can be trusted.]

MyStuff export settings

The next settings tab deals with the type and nature of allowed exports from portfolios. The first settings deal with the option to upload a list of users to be allowed to export material, assuming they are not currently in the list available. The list itself allows some choice between the available students. By default, they will all be selected since they are all part of the course.

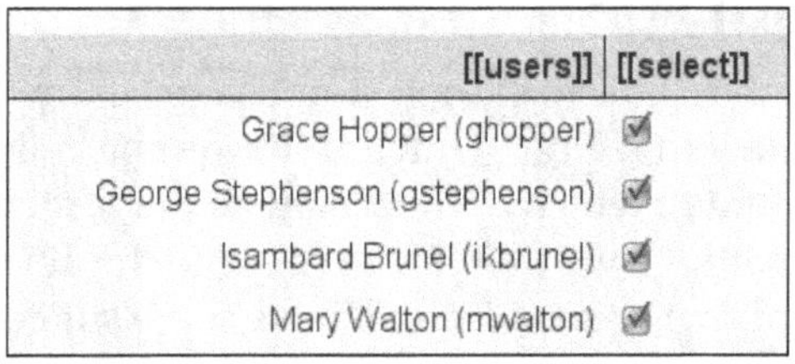

MyStuff Export Settings: File Export Type

The final settings determine the style of export allowed, such as files, **Information Management System** (**IMS**) structures, or no files at all. Once this has been set, the whole series of portfolios can be exported to another site. This may be useful when students are moving to another institution and would like to take their portfolio with them. Likewise with the import feature, though it is unlikely that most institutions will use these features, so they can be explored as and when required.

[The portfolio is designed by the Open University to work with their customized version of Moodle, so many of the features here are specifically for their system and will not be applicable.]

Using MyStuff in courses

Now that the settings have been applied, especially the folder size limits, the students can start using the portfolio for themselves.

With the editing switched on, choose the HTML option from the blocks drop-down menu. This will create an empty block on the course page. You can then click on editing to change the block and add the link you require.

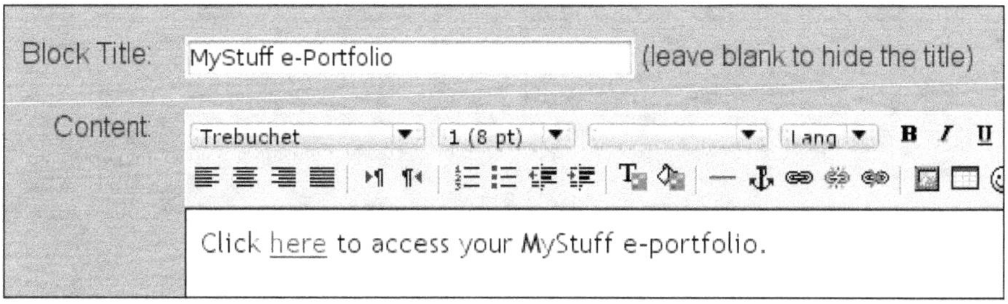

Select a word, in this example, the word **here**, and then click on the hyperlink icon to make it a link.

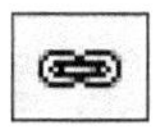

MyStuff is a module and is called **portfolio**, so the link needs to reflect this, as shown in the following screenshot:

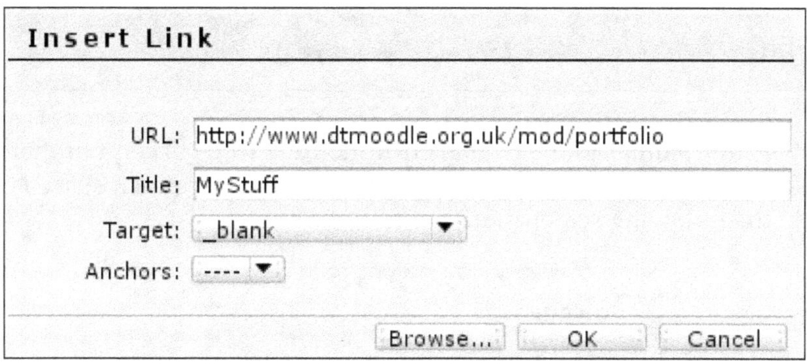

If you choose to open the module in a new page, it might make it tidier for students and easier to navigate. Either way, when students click on the link, the module will load and present them with their working interface.

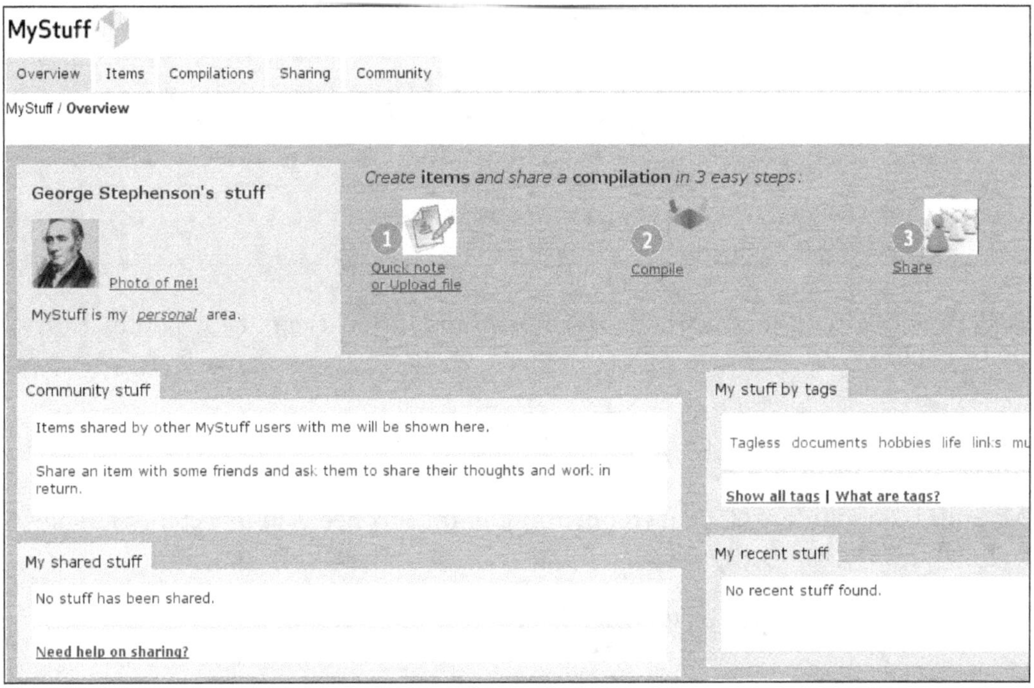

The layout is quite similar to the Exabis portfolio reviewed earlier, but there is more detail and options. There is also a clear indicator of just how much space is available, as shown in the following screenshot:

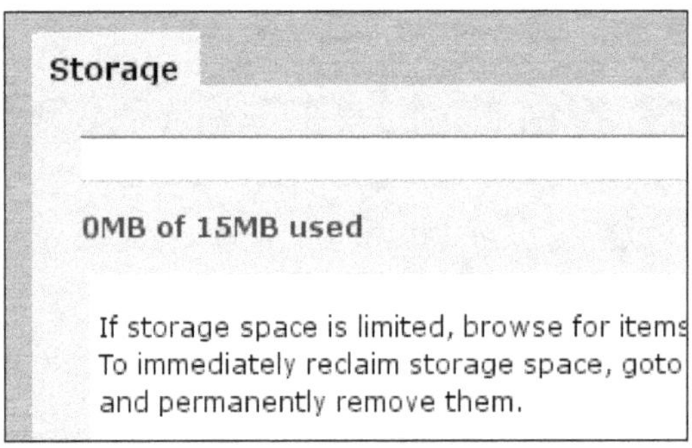

This feature will help students manage their space more efficiently. It could also be used as a discussion point in terms of storage and work towards some credit for students in the IT component.

Guiding students to use MyStuff

As the name of the module suggests, this portfolio is very much centered on the student's own ideas and resources. Over time, they will build up a digital portfolio very much akin to what would have been, in the "old days", their school bag contents. With this in mind, the students will need to be guided as to where to start and roughly what needs to be done.

Creating and using forms

A good starting point for this portfolio is the section describing the various forms and areas they need to compile. This is situated under the `/Items/Forms` directory and presents the students with an overview of all the areas they will need to use.

The first of these areas is information-specific to the student themselves and incorporates elements that will eventually lead to them creating an online resume or CV. The main components of this form can be seen in the following screenshot.

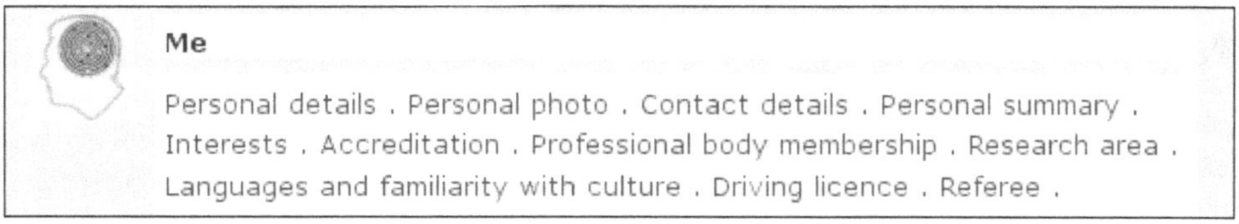

This module, as already mentioned, is developed and maintained by the Open University (OU), so some of the forms are geared towards this tertiary level of education. However, the basic details are relevant to students at all levels, and since the portfolio is mobile, it can be taken to higher educational institutions or jobs.

The forms are quite straightforward to fill in and students can soon build up a clear profile of themselves. Each form will vary depending on what information is required, but all forms can use tags, which will allow easy searching and reference at a later date.

Building a catalogue of information

In the forms section, there is also a personal library that students can use to build a catalogue of information to help them with their studies.

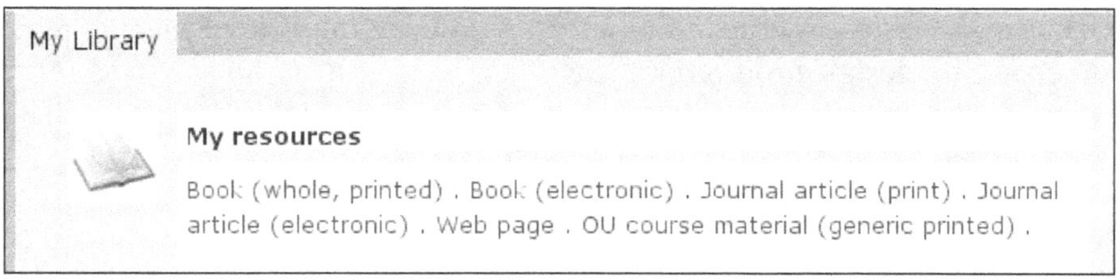

Each page gives some clear instructions about what is required to reference, but it will help students gain some good habits in organizing the material that they use in their studies and tie it to their courses in a very effective way. Information can be created and modified using the three main steps, as shown in the following screenshot:

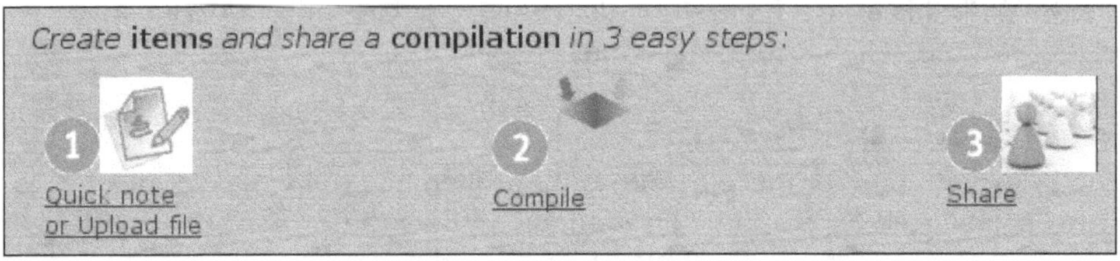

Creating notes

The first item that will probably be generated will be some kind of lesson note. It is assumed here that a student has taken notes during a lesson or a construction workshop on a notepad and needs to transfer them to their portfolio for electronic storage, perhaps as homework. They first need to create a note.

The form that opens is very much as any other form, which means that it becomes easy for students to get used to the way the system works. The form has five fields to complete:

- Title (name of the file or note)
- Notes (any notes about the item)
- Upload link (a browser to find and attach files)
- Alternative Text (an additional field for extra details)
- Tags (a field to tag the item for easy search and reference at a later date)

The student will need to create a title and then make some notes about the subject. In this example, it is lesson notes from a lesson on the evolution of plastics and their effect on changing design production.

> The key element to remember is to associate a tag with the item.

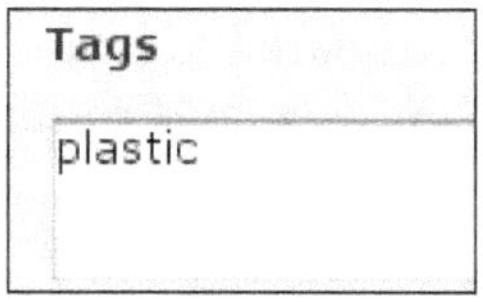

The tags will generate a searchable library of the student's information, which will make it far easier for them once they begin to revise for public examinations. The tags will also be more visible in terms of the amount of information, so the more the information, the larger the tag that will be shown. This will act as a visual guide to show students that these areas have been covered far more comprehensively and so are more likely to be key topics to revise. The overview page will keep track of the tags, as shown in the following screenshot:

Once the note is properly filled in, including any attachments, such as scanned notes from lessons or sketches, it can then be further edited and referenced.

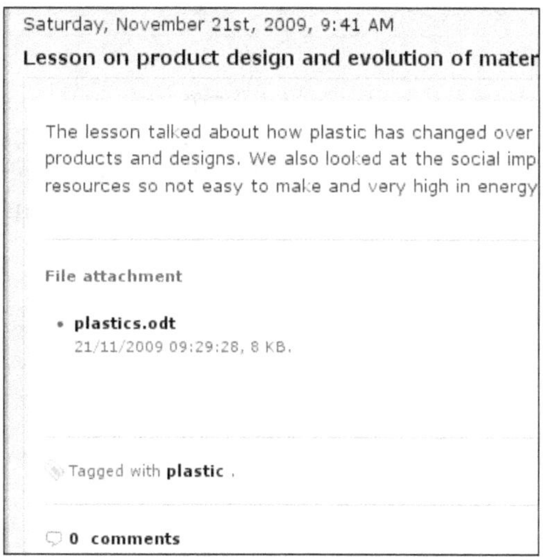

Any file attachments are also stored with the note, as shown, and likewise if it is shared with others. In addition, the note can store comments from the student themselves or from other people such as peers or staff.

Sharing the material with others

The key feature here is the ability to share the material with others. This can be view only, as with people in the group, or view and comment as for staff.

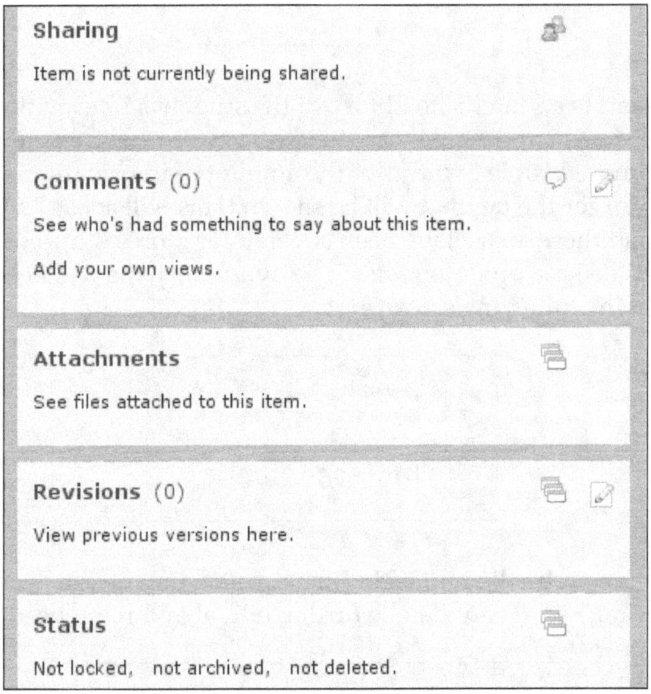

In the previous screenshot, you can see that there is an icon to show the ability to share this item. By clicking on the linking icon, you will be presented with an interface to set the options for sharing. The first part of this option screen, as shown in the following screenshot, allows you to select a whole group to share your material with.

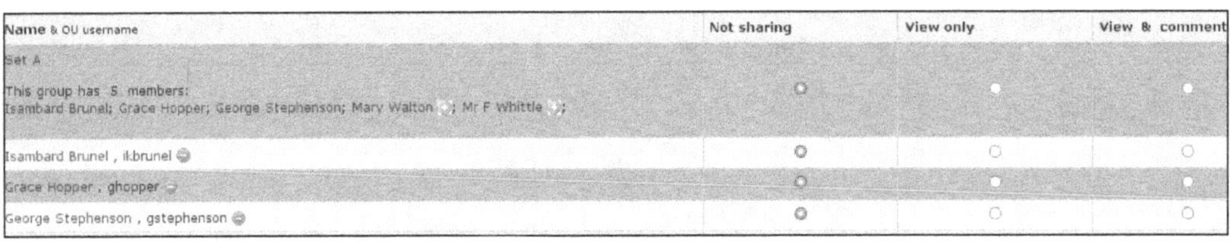

As you can see in the previous screenshot, you can select an entire group to view or write comments on your items or you can select individuals. This would be useful if you have a sub-group in a class such as four students working on furniture design. This group could share details with each other on their specialized subject, but more general materials with other students in Product Design.

> One useful feature for staff is the ability to see what and when revisions to the notes were made.

If they are used for formative assessment, this can be useful for tracking development and to make sure that students are meeting agreed upon deadlines with clear visual evidence to support it. If the note is to be shared, then it will appear on another user's system with the appropriate notes and status.

The people on the course will be listed in the share dialog, as shown in the following screenshot:

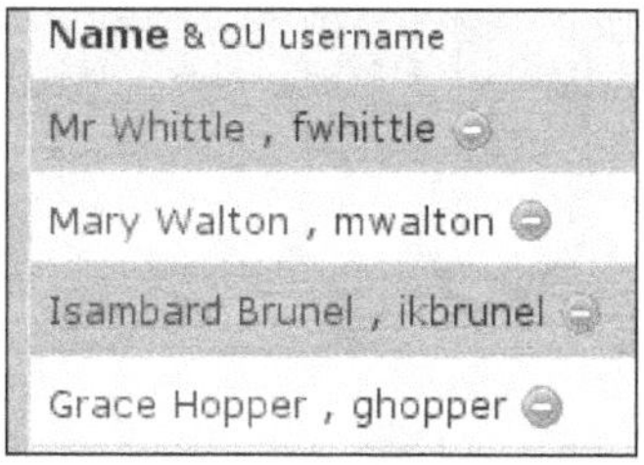

The student or staff can then select from the list of users the particular share permissions for this piece of work. As you can see in the following screenshot, the choices are: **Not sharing**, **view only**, and **view & comment**.

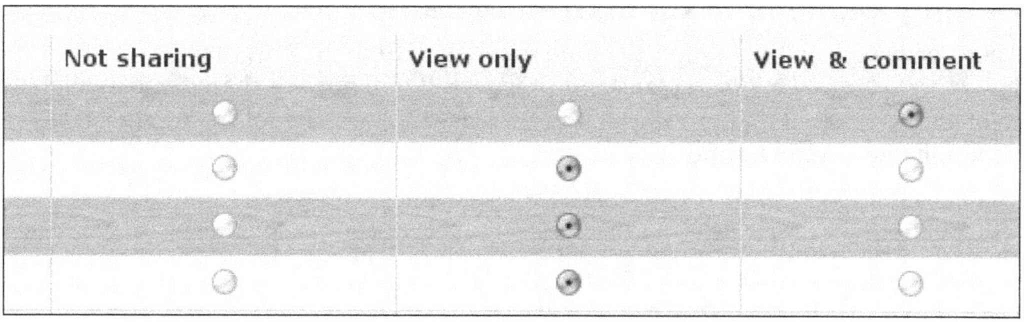

In the example over here, the teacher is allowed to make some comments on the work but others, such as students or a teaching assistant, can only view them.

Attaching a message to the submission

If the student needs to notify staff of the work, then they can choose to send a message, as shown in the following screenshot:

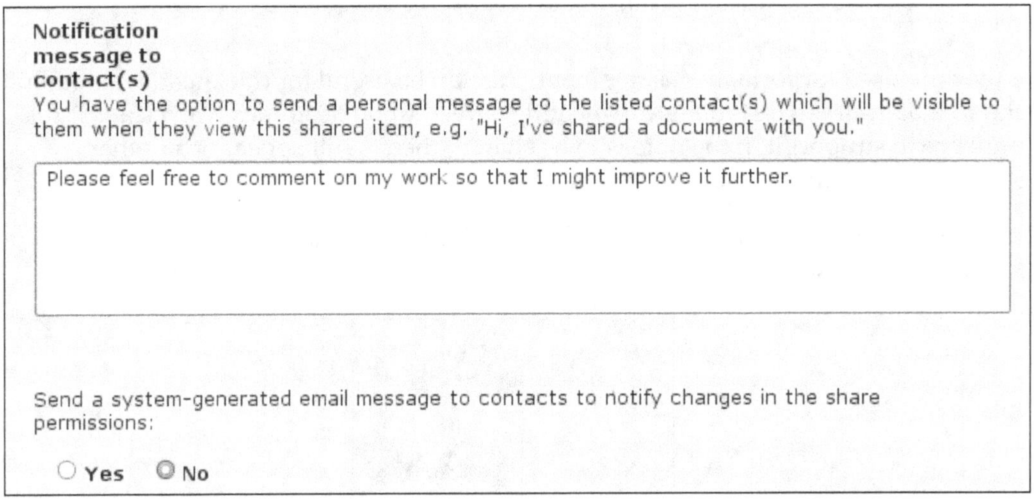

As shown in the previous screenshot, you can also set the item so that if any changes are made as to who can see the material, they will be notified. This could be useful as part of an external verification process where students can share their material with an examiner for a set period of time.

Setting a time limit on shared material

There is also the ability to limit the time that it is shared for. This may be incorporated into the lesson plans and practices. It will now be shared and available to other members of that group, such as the class teacher. The following screenshot shows the date setting options available:

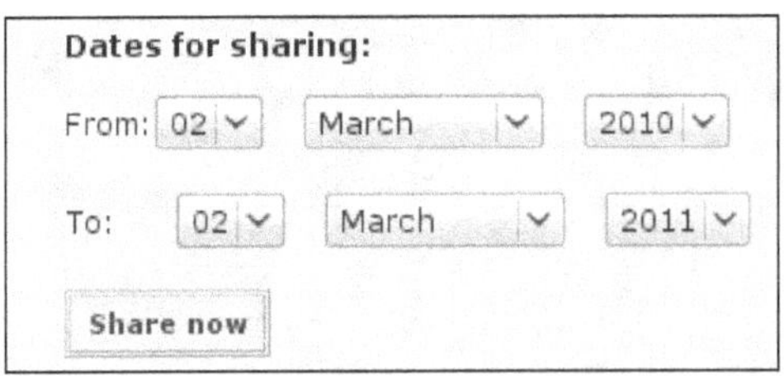

Commentary on shared work

The work can be commented on by staff once shared, as shown in the following screenshot:

This will allow some form of feedback and informal assessment, which could then be transferred back to the gradebook for tracking. The student will see the same comments when they log in to their portfolio.

Over time, the student will build up a detailed selection of items in their portfolio and can then export the portfolio when they move on to a job or higher education. The portfolio is fully **LEAP2A**-compliant, which means that it will be easier to transport between institutions and allow students to maintain throughout their professional lives. The LEAP2A specifications can be found here:

`http://wiki.cetis.ac.uk/LEAP2A_specification`

MyStuff development and limitations

The MyStuff e-portfolio continues to be developed and modified to meet student and staff needs, and new features are added as required. It is very usable and will allow students to develop a more holistic approach to their learning as well as make them more organized with their digital artifacts. One limitation of the current version of MyStuff is that it cannot be tied into assignments in Moodle. The next level of portfolio is to use an external one such as Mahara, as this can be used to assess a student's electronic work.

Mahara

Mahara is an e-portfolio developed and maintained by a New Zealand Moodle partner. It is designed to allow institutions to share information and best practices. It works through a method of **Single Sign On** (**SSO**) and is therefore seamless with Moodle. It is very powerful with a great many options, but will give students and staff a greater level of collaboration and design flexibility.

The installation of Mahara is a similar process to the installation of Moodle and is beyond the scope of this particular book, though there are many excellent tutorials on the Mahara website, `www.mahara.org`. There is also an excellent book on the portfolio.

`http://www.packtpub.com/mahara-1-2-e-portfolios-beginners-guide/book`

It is assumed that you have successfully installed Mahara and have integrated it with Moodle. This will create a new login box on the site for Mahara.

Students, when they click on the icon, will be taken to the Mahara site and automatically logged in with the same details as their Moodle account. Once they log out, they will be returned to Moodle. The layout they will see will be quite similar to other portfolios we have reviewed in this chapter, as they are attempting to achieve the same sorts of end results. The following screenshot shows a student's view once they have logged in to Mahara.

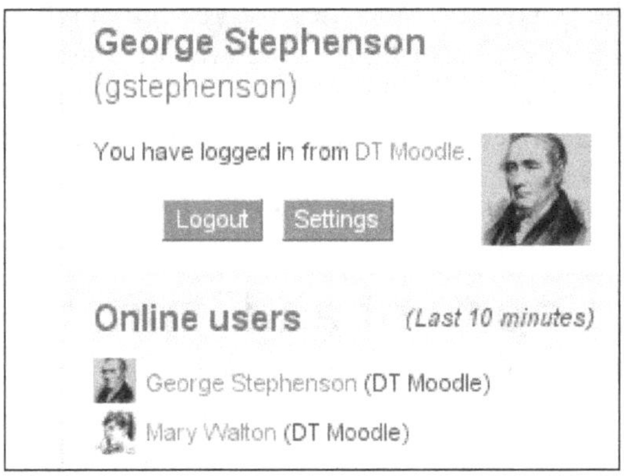

The left-hand column will give details about who else is online, so that students can interact with each other on topics. It also allows some account modifications through the **Settings** button. The settings or preferences are related to messaging and how the portfolio is presented to you, as shown in the following screenshot.

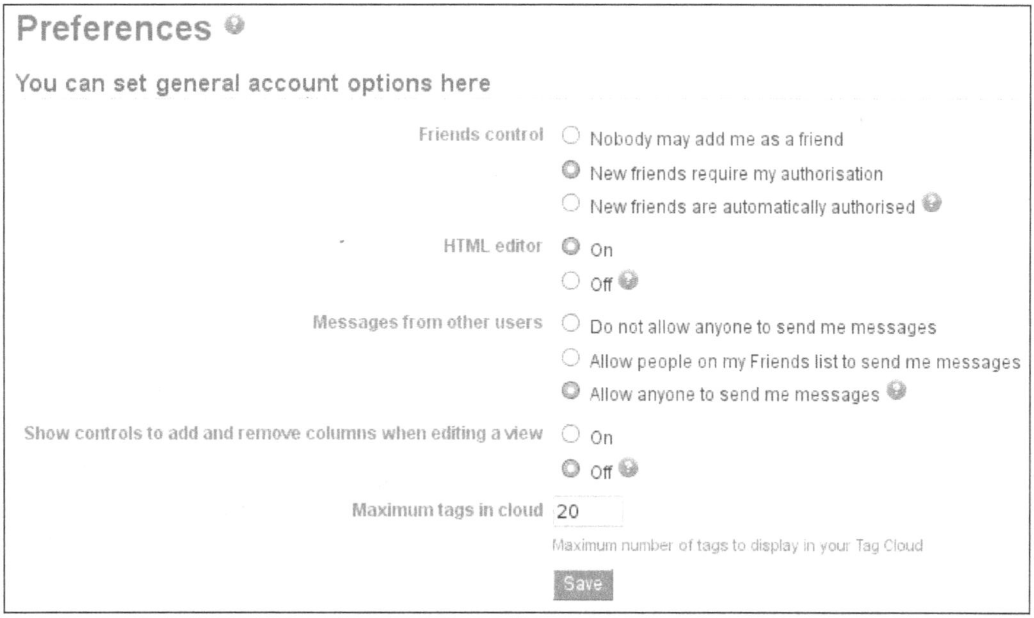

The five settings available here are as follows:

- **Friends control**: It controls whether or not you can be added by people as a friend
- **HTML editor**: It controls whether or not you wish to use the built-in HTML editor
- **Messages from other users**: It has control over whether or not other users who see your profile can message you
- **Show controls to add and remove columns when editing a view**: It controls whether or not to display options to add extra columns to your view layouts
- **Maximum tags in cloud**: It specifies the number of tags to be displayed in your main area

Mahara features

The main functions are located on tabs on the top left of the login screen, as shown in the following screenshot:

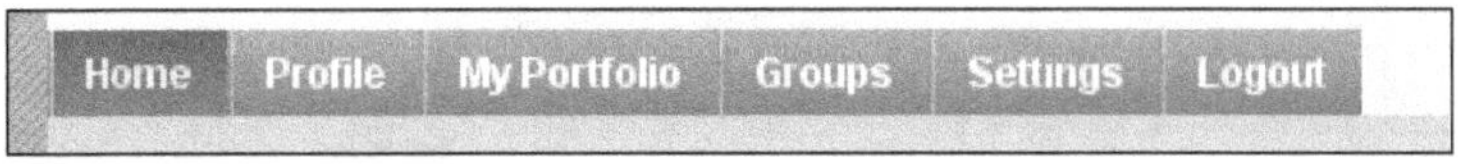

Adding details to your profile

The **Profile** tab allows for some detailed descriptions about the person to build up a digital application form for jobs.

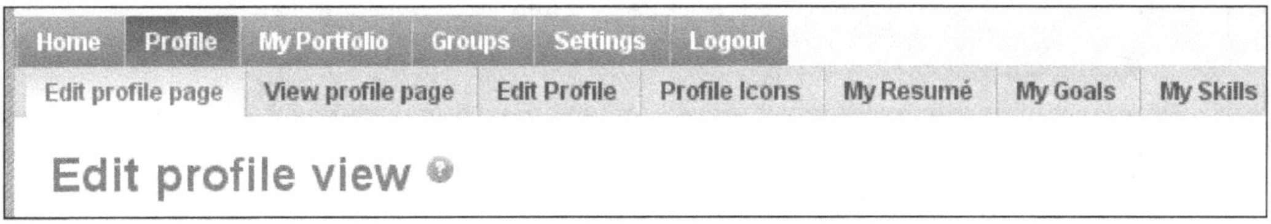

All of the sub-elements are highly customizable through dragging and dropping custom fields in, such as blog entries or text boxes. Every section that can be filled in is controlled through an HTML editor, which means that students can be as creative as they wish. In Design and Technology, this allows them to reflect their design skills and understanding of presentation and can act as a powerful employment record when submitting applications to employers. During the course of a student's education, they can gather a great deal of information such as useful web links, personal reviews of equipment they have used, or digital images of their work from conception to production. All of this digital information can be organized and stored with their electronic portfolio. When they go for a job interview at a local manufacturing company, they can simply log onto their e-portfolio and show exactly what work they have achieved and how they feel about the world of design technology. They can share some of the material and their most impressive work directly with potential employers. Even if they don't achieve formal qualifications, but are very competent in key areas of design, they should not be excluded from the opportunity of being employed.

Views in MyPortfolio

The central element of Mahara is views. These are very similar to notes in MyStuff. They are collections of web pages that contain links and files and are associated through groups and tags. They are created through the **My Portfolio** tab.

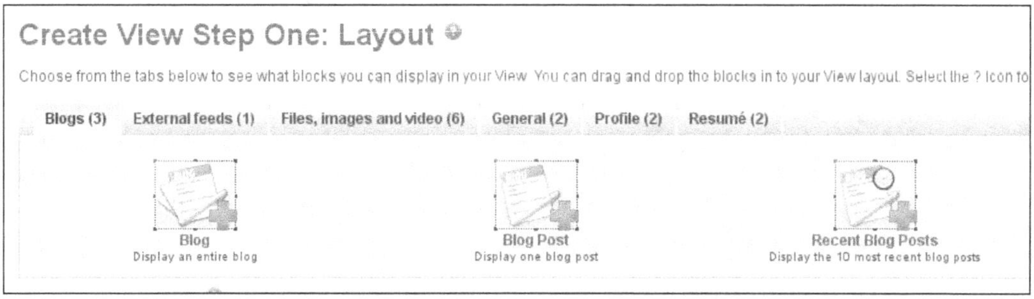

Each view can be composed with any number of elements from the selection, which constitutes all areas of the portfolio. For example, you may take some elements from the personal profile, some specific blogs, as well as from uploaded work of specific groups. As you can see in the previous screenshot, there are six tabs: **Blogs, External feeds, Files, images and video**, **General**, **Profile**, and **Resume**. Each of these tabs has elements that can be dragged into a view. For example, in the preceding example, we used the **Blogs** tab. We can select to add **Recent Blog Posts** to our view. This means that each time we add a new blog to our overall site, it will be updated and viewed in the view we created in this example.

Each item that is dragged into the lower box will require some basic configuration. For example, in the previous view, we added a textbox to store our lesson notes. To achieve this:

1. Click on the **General** tab.
2. Click and drag the **Text Box** element to the lower screen and place it where you would like it to appear. The configuration box, as shown in the following screenshot, appears:

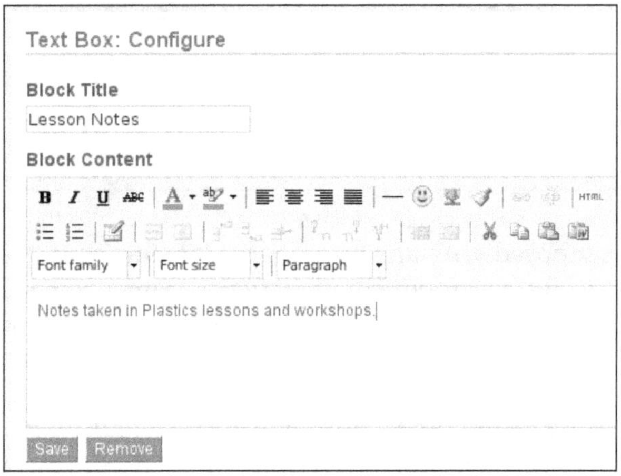

3. Save the configuration by clicking on the **Save** button.

Using live website feeds in views

There is a wide range of artifacts that your students can use to build up their portfolio. They may wish to incorporate their own live feeds from a design magazine website.

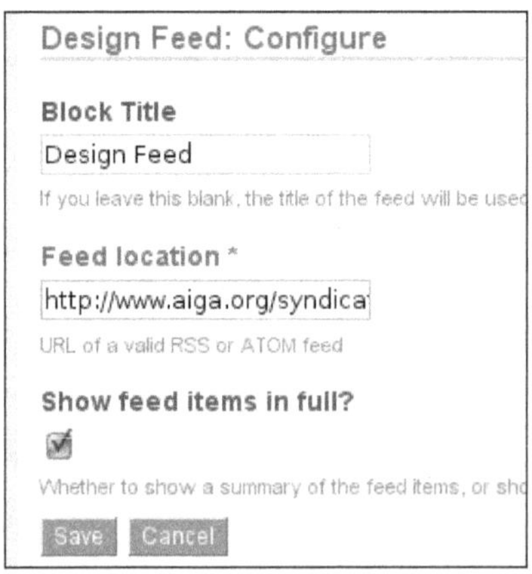

Inserting multimedia into views

They may use the multimedia tab to insert some links to some videos that they have found.

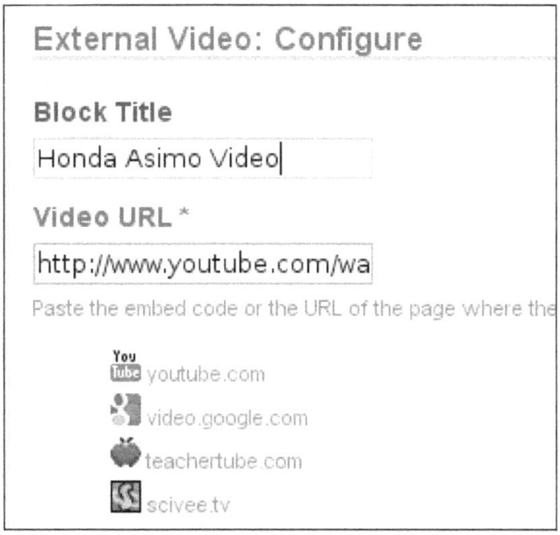

The feeds do not have to be the usual YouTube feeds as feeds can be brought in from TeacherTube (`http://www.teachertube.com/`) and other sites as well.

The range of media inserts should be enough to meet most student needs, as shown in the following screenshot:

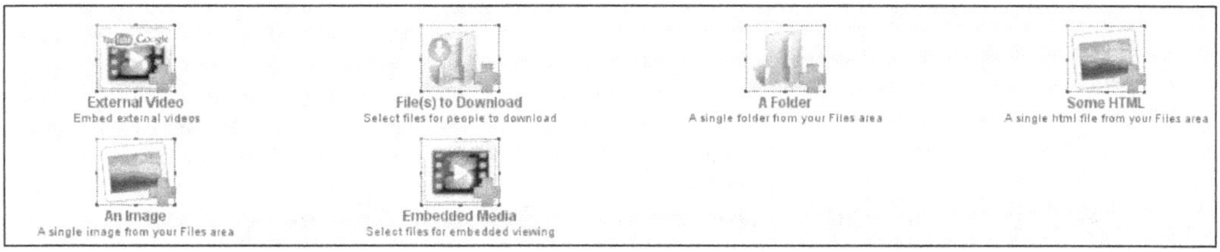

Once the view has been constructed, the students can then decide how and when the view will be available and if it needs to be shared with others. The other aspect is whether it can be copied. This will need to be discussed quite carefully in terms of plagiarism and legal issues such as the Data Protection Act and Copyright. The following screenshot shows the options available when sharing digital media and views with other people in the system.

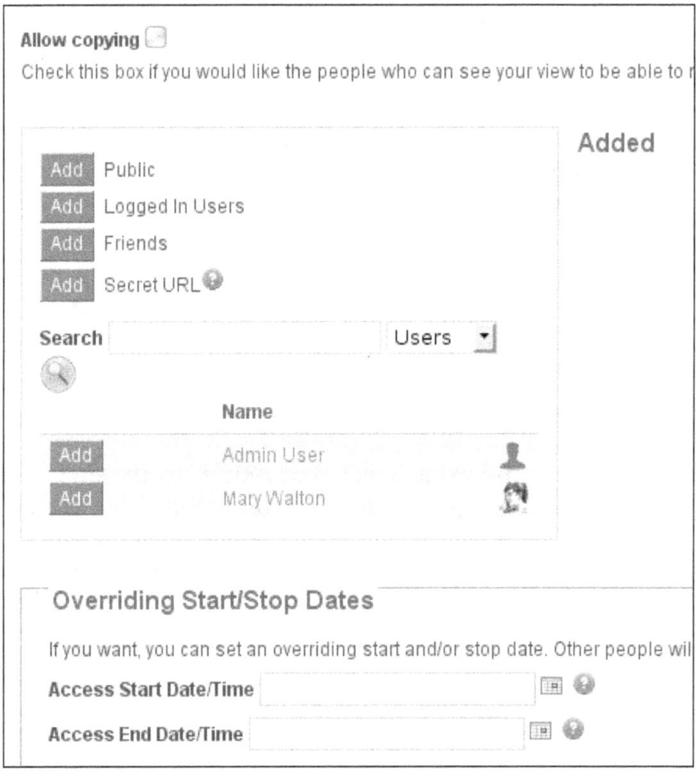

Students can share the material with people on the site in different groups. They can also use the Secret URL feature to allow external verifiers to see the work without logging in to the site, though for security purposes, it might be better to enroll external examiners on the site.

The view now becomes part of the student's portfolio and can be viewed by others in the site if so desired. The following screenshot shows one student's shared view incorporating a feed from a design magazine and a video of a robot running.

Using the MyFiles tab for file management

If students maintain digital images of their work as it develops, they can manage this under **My Files**. These digital files can then be managed in the views. The file manager allows them to create folders and sub-folders to organize their files, whether these are word processed documents or videos that they have recorded during work experience placements.

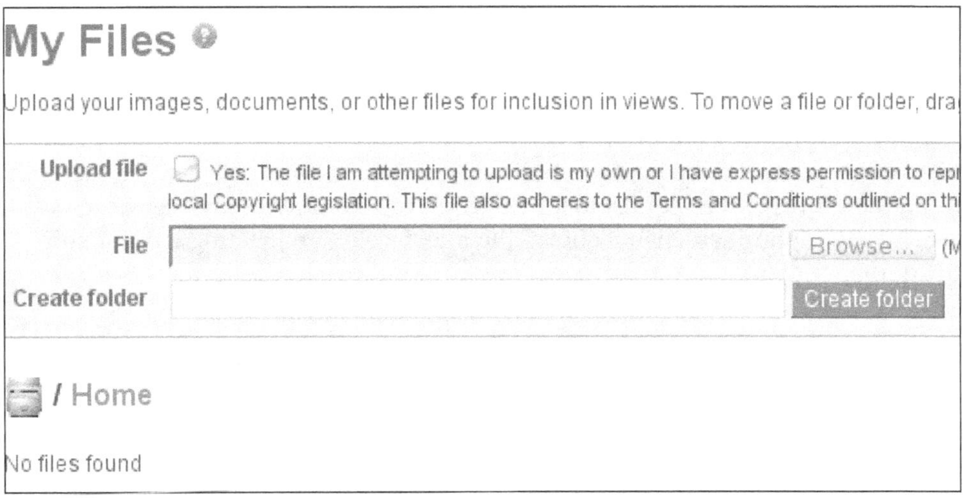

E-Portfolio advantages

Students can build a view around their product development, which can include videos that inspired them, websites which they found useful for their ideas, or also their notes and ideas in development. The whole experience can be stored in an organized way, as shown in this section, which is meaningful for the students and can be shared for feedback and commentary. This gives students far more control over their learning and caters to students who are less traditional in their learning style, which tends to be many students who are more able in design and technology subjects.

Throughout the portfolio, there are suggestions and information relating to legal requirements and it is quite important to stress this as often as possible to prevent issues of legality arising. Some of these issues can be avoided by using more open resources and qualifications such as those offered by organizations such as The Learning Machine (`http://www.theingots.org`).

Using Groups in Mahara

In Mahara, students have the ability to create groups, as with popular social networking sites, but they can also be assigned to groups by staff in their institution. The groups they are in can be checked on the **Group** tab, as shown in the following screenshot:

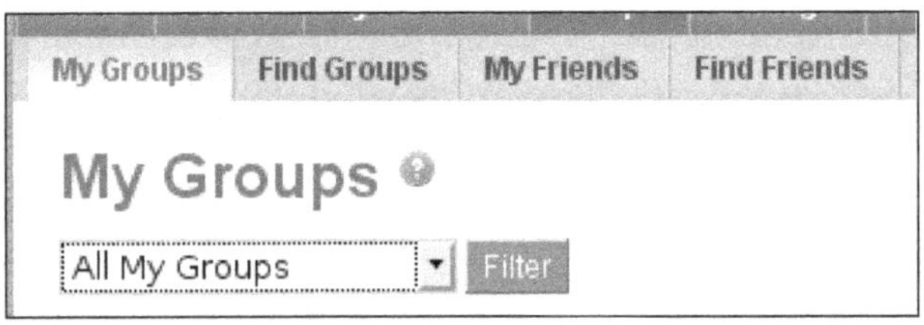

If no friends currently exist in their network (or if staff has not assigned specific ones), then requests can be made to build up a network. Students can see each other and can therefore send a request to join a group or to link with another user as a friend. The following screenshot shows the interface for requesting a friendship with another student.

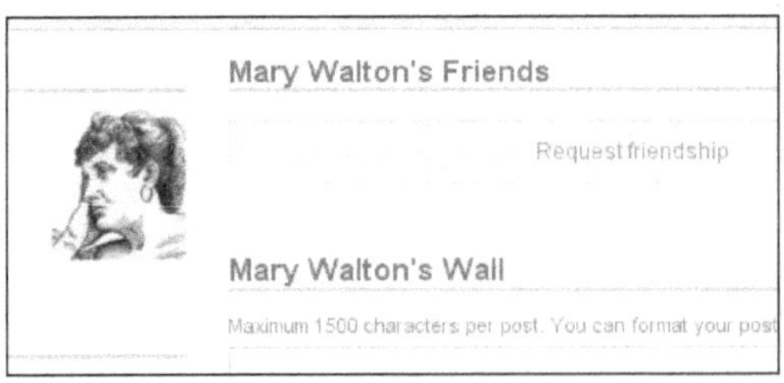

It may be useful to have a set number of formal groups that students participate in, but allow them to set up some informal groups so that they can discuss issues outside of the subject area. Since this is *their* portfolio, they need some degree of freedom to explore ideas.

Settings in Mahara

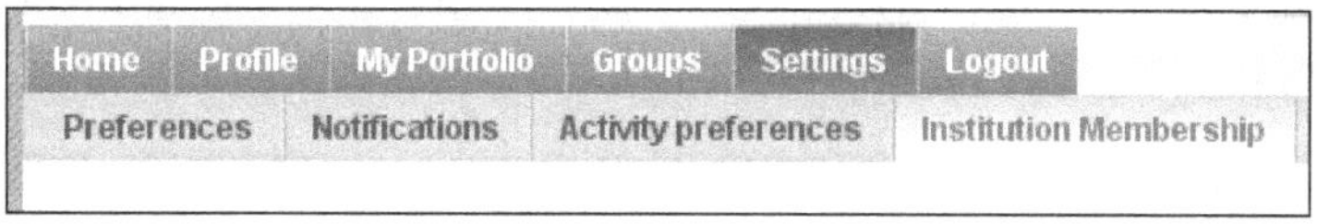

The settings allow students to determine how people can contact them and how their site looks and feels. It also shows them which institutions they are part of and allows them to leave this once they are completed. This helps with overall management and ensures that students can remove themselves from institutions once they are no longer enrolled in them such as their old school. The settings also allow them to check for notifications to make sure that they are receiving important notices.

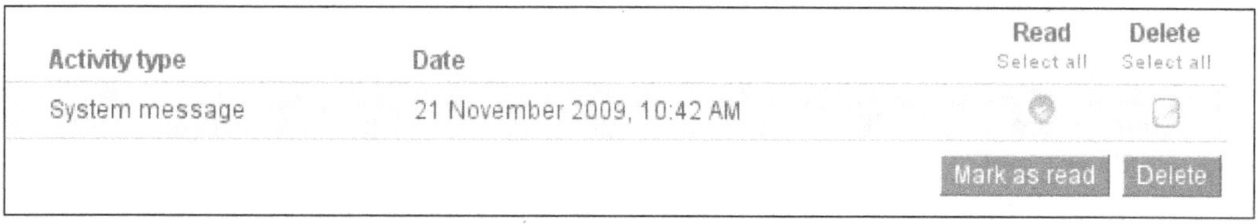

Students can now build up a detailed portfolio of views to share and interact with their colleagues and staff, as shown in the following screenshot:

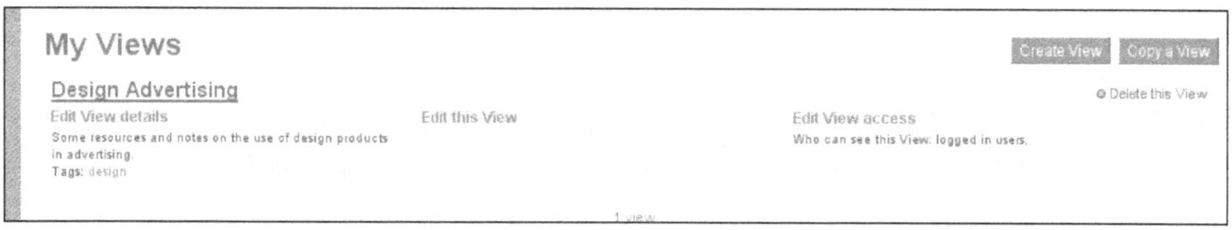

Setting up features of Mahara from the administrator login

It will be necessary to set up some features of your Mahara system such as creating and assigning staff and groups. This is all achieved through the administrator login. If the site has been set up to authenticate with Moodle, then students and staff will be added to the site automatically, though they will all be assigned as students, so you may wish to elevate your staff to staff positions so that they can control some aspects of the learning better.

As an admin, you will have access to the **User Management** tab. You can use this to add users to staff roles. The following screenshot shows the users currently available in the system that can be added to the **Current Staff** column:

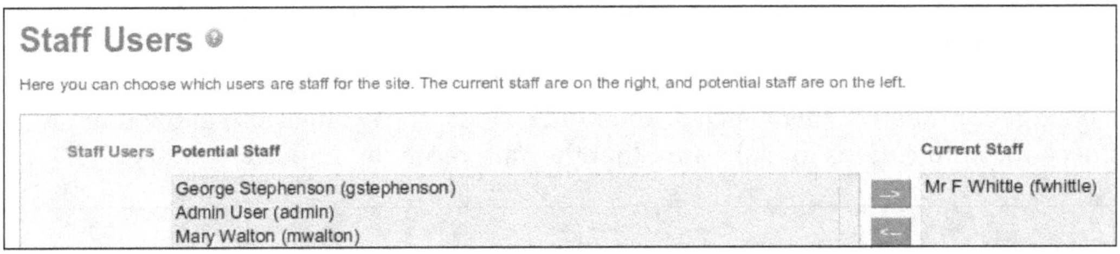

Next time, when Mr. F Whittle logs in, he will have extra rights and privileges to control his student groups more effectively. Once a group has been created, in this case, one which requires an invitation, students can join. The following screenshot shows the group created by the member of staff.

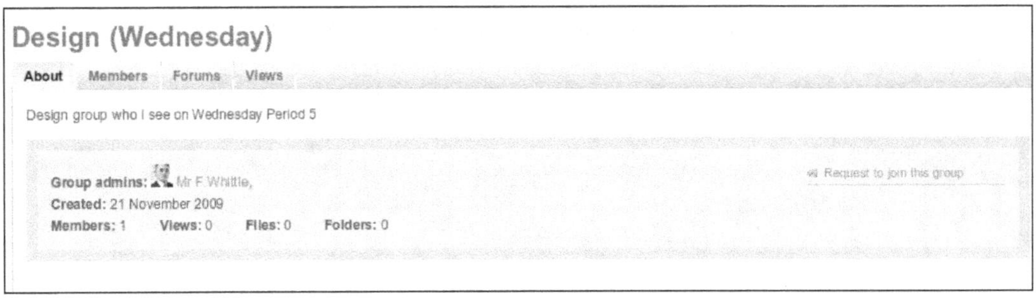

Requesting to join a group

All groups that are available to you as a student will be shown to you under your **Groups** tab. The following screenshot shows a group available and the link to **Request to join this group**.

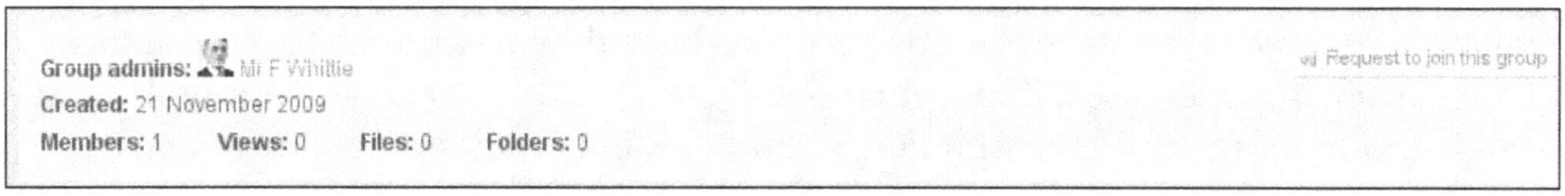

Clicking on this request link will open a dialog so that you can say why you wish to join as reference to the group owner, as shown in the following screenshot:

An invitation will be sent by the student, as shown in the following screenshot, and if they are part of the group, they can be accepted and enrolled.

Any views created by staff as part of this group can then be built up as a complete interactive lesson with videos and links to other resources.

Using Multiple institutions with Mahara

One excellent feature of Mahara is the ability to share resources and best practice with several institutions. These can be other Moodle sites or Mahara sites and all can be controlled through a SSO. In the case of tertiary colleges, they can have several local schools from early years to pre-college in a pyramid and all can share material and ideas. This allows students to see how they fit into the bigger picture of education. In some cases, it might be possible to make an arrangement with local design and manufacturing companies, so that students can interact directly with potential employers. The following screenshot shows the administration screen and a number of institutions that are part of the Mahara system in this case. If these institutions allow sharing and SSO, students can jump between Moodle and Mahara and have a complex and rich learning experience.

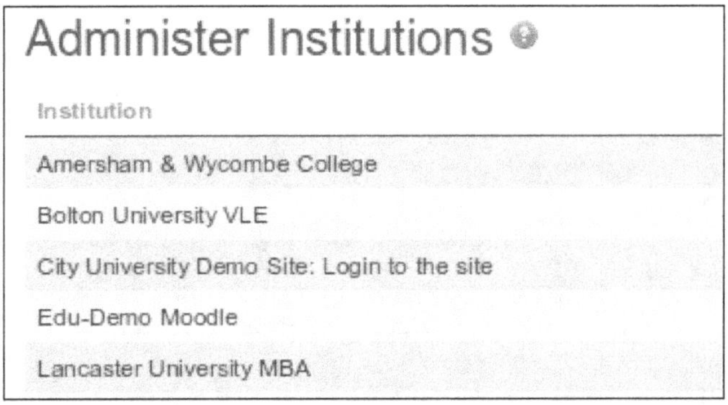

Exporting their portfolio

The material that students create can then easily be migrated to their new employer with Mahara's export feature. The following screenshot shows the export options available.

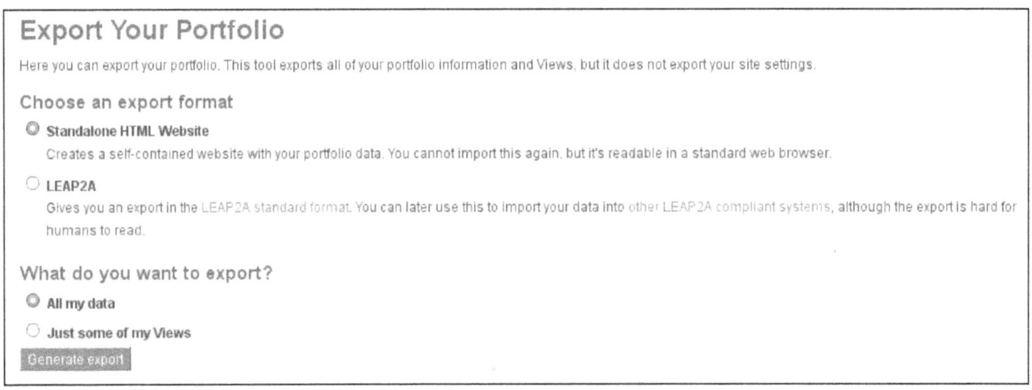

As you can see from this screenshot, there is the option to export a standalone website that would be a series of linked HTML files, which could be uploaded to a web server. Alternatively, you can export as a LEAP2A ZIP file, which can then be imported into a system such as Mahara that is compliant with this standard. The final choice is how much data you wish to export. Some students may only want to export their views which relate to their employability or academic achievements, but not the groups and discussions they were part of socially.

Summary

In this chapter, we have reviewed some, though not all, of the available portfolio modules. We have looked at Exabis that allows some basic tracking and sharing of material, through the more integrated MyStuff that allows storage limits and more complex views. The scope of this book cannot cover all of the features of Mahara, and as mentioned earlier, there is a book now available, but there should be enough detail here to start up some groups and begin creating some collaborative portfolios. If your institution can link up with local companies, there is huge potential for collaborative work and to give students a real hands-on experience of working with companies in the exciting world of design and technology.

Having spent some time looking at ways of researching and organizing the vast amount of information required for Design Technology, we shall now investigate ways to consolidate this information.

5

Testing Students' Knowledge using Moodle Modules

If you have followed the preceding chapters and implemented some of the suggestions, you will be at a point in the development of your DT Moodle site where the students will have a great deal of material that they will be working on. You will also know about their portfolios and reflective practice techniques. The key requirement for them now, and for you, is to find out how much information they have consolidated and can, therefore, use in their work. There are a number of tools in Moodle to find out the students' depth of understanding—some formal and some informal. There are also some tools that allow the students to assist themselves in their own knowledge consolidation. We will now investigate these tools in more detail.

Implementing a glossary

The **glossary** is a well known and commonly used module in Moodle, but it may not always be used as the effective teaching and learning tool that it can be. Given the jargon-rich nature of design and technology, it is also an important glue for the whole subject area.

Checking the settings

The key options here relate to the functioning of the glossary and how you use it as a teaching and learning tool. The first thing that needs to be done is to check the overall settings for the module in the administration section of the site. The settings are divided into three key areas:

- Default settings for the glossary module
- Settings for the entries in the glossary
- Format of the display styles

The previous settings can be found on the administration panel in the **Site Administration** | **Modules** | **Activities** | **Glossary** section.

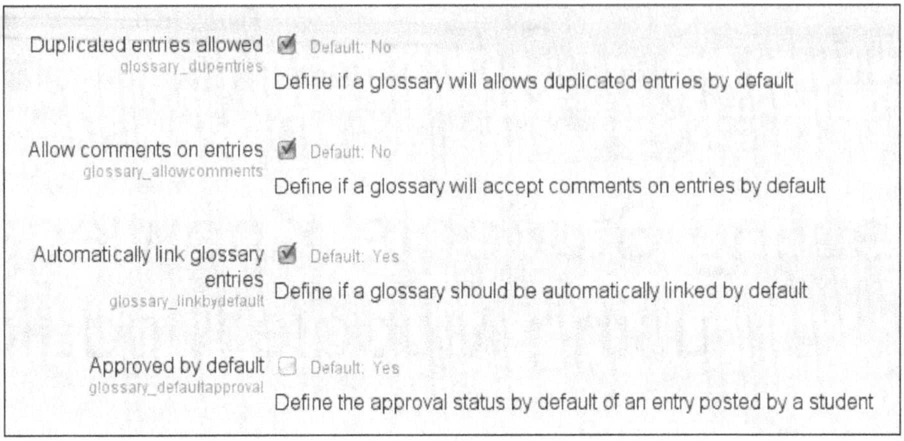

Default settings

The first section determines which functions of the glossary are generally available to the users of the module on the site. In the previous screenshot, the main options relate to the linking functions and comments on the entries themselves. For example, do you want to allow students to comment on the glossary entries? For a subject such as DT, you might wish to allow students to add their own understanding of terms. In some cases, there may be regional terms for some things which are different from the "formal" definition of a term, such as the term used for certain woodworking tools. As woodworking is an ancient craft, there are many different local terms to describe some of the equipments used. The glossary would then reinforce the social nature of the design as a part of a teaching method.

Preventing duplicate entries

As you can see in the previous screenshot, the default setting here would be to not allow duplicate entries in the glossary—although it can be enabled to perhaps show the nuances in a term or allow the term to be defined in another language, if your school has a partner school in another country. In some instances, you might have a definition that is the accepted definition, but also one that students might come across such as a building term. Likewise, you might have a definition relating to a usage as opposed to how a manufacturer might determine an item. Allowing duplication gives students a sense of how terms change, depending on how they are used and by whom.

Allowing comments

Allowing comments on the entries is useful for students to build up an internal dialog whereby they may be able to add examples of best practice to the definitions in the glossary relating to their on-the-job work experience. This is useful because students who had previously worked in a company and gained some experience of the job can leave a historical record to help the students who have just started the course or work.

Automatically linking comments

The linking of the glossary terms is useful if you use a consistent approach throughout your course design; in particular, if you use the **Compose a web page** function under **Add a resource**, as discussed earlier, rather than uploading the proprietary word-processed files, then Moodle will be able to link the terms through the database. However, please bear in mind that the linking function will add some load to your server and may not be appropriate in all cases, such as when using a server on a shared system. Linking definitions throughout the site allows students to have a better understanding of all the elements, as they work through them and when they forget some key terms. However, you need to remember that this links across an entire site and some definitions may clash across curriculum subjects. Therefore, there is a need for the duplicate entries. The ability to create a glossary for all the users on a site is only available to site administrators.

Entry level default settings

The following screenshot shows the options that are available for the entries, which are added to the glossaries. If enabled, the options shown in the following screenshot will automatically be enabled when the entries are made. Users still have the choice to disable the options like the automatic linking shown as follows:

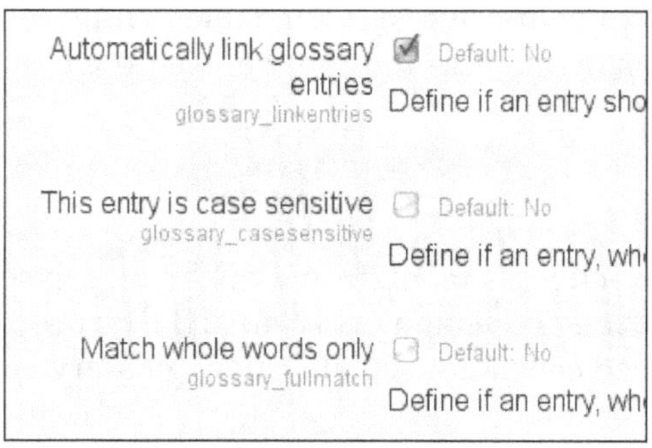

Again, you can link terms in the course to the glossary definitions, and if necessary, make the terms case sensitive. The case-sensitive option as well as the matching of whole words allows some fine tuning of the glossary. For example, you may make an entry for a law, which is *HAM*. If you enable the case-sensitive option on this entry, then a link will be created in the database when the specific term *HAM* is entered on a page in the course and not for every instance of hammer. This may be more useful with younger students when it is important for them to learn the key terms, but perhaps not so with older students.

You can now save the settings you have chosen. If the changes have been applied for you by your site administrator, you can move directly to your course to begin using a glossary.

Creating a glossary

Once you or the site administrator have set up the module in the way that is most appropriate for your institution, teachers can then begin to apply them to their courses. We are assuming here that you have other subject areas on your Moodle site, therefore, we will focus on the course-level entries, but the principles are same.

Enabling the glossary

For this example, we will add a glossary of terms to our construction-based course. Younger students may be unfamiliar with this subject in many cases and they will, therefore, have a greater need for some ways of understanding the wealth of the terms. The same is true for Food Technology or Resistant Materials, but it is more likely that they would have at least encountered food-based products or materials in their lives. It is less likely that they had been involved in the construction of their environment or have working knowledge of these key terms.

As with all the modules, the first action is to enable editing on the course to activate the activities drop-down menu. This requires clicking the button that follows:

This will then show the activities menu from which you can select the glossary module **Glossary** from one of the many **Add an activity'** drop down menus, as shown in the following screenshot, to create a new glossary activity module.

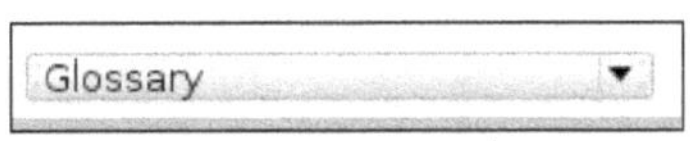

Editing the glossary

Once enabled, added, or created, you can then name the glossary and determine some of the functionality you want in it to be available. Like all the other modules, these are related to time and display elements. The following screenshot shows some of the key settings such as the type of glossary and the display format.

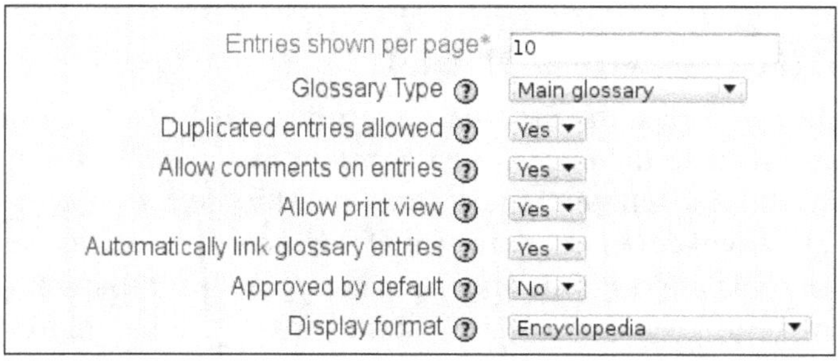

Most of these settings were determined at the site level, such as allowing duplicate entries or comments, but they can be changed by the staff as required. The key point here is that we make one glossary—a main glossary for the course. We make all the subsequent glossaries secondary, which means that we can export the terms into this main one, but this is the overall glossary for the course. We might have secondary glossaries for the human aspects of construction or health and safety, as opposed to the material elements for example. As this is a very graphical subject, we have enabled the display to be like an encyclopedia. This will allow staff and students to add images and video files to explain the terms they are defining in a better way.

Rating entries

If you are going to use the glossary in a more formal way, it would be useful to allow the students to rate the entries, so that they can peer assess each other's terms. If you set each student a number of terms to define as a homework exercise, you can allow the students to research and populate the glossary and for the other students to award marks. This makes the terms far more dynamic and real for the students. You might also invite your contacts from local companies to rate the students' definitions and give them feedback to help develop their understanding on a deeper level. This is enabled through the grading option, as shown in the following screenshot:

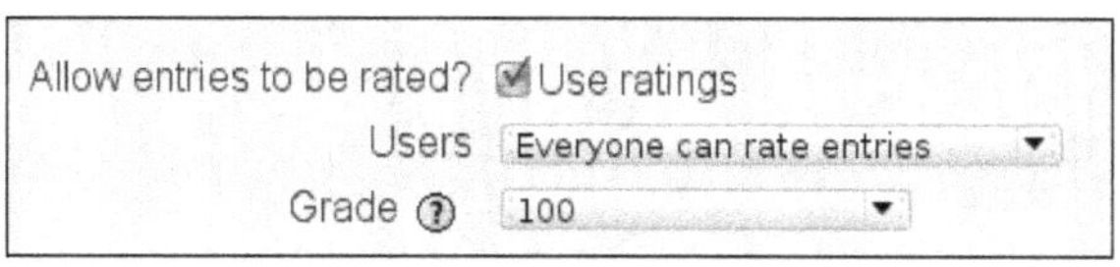

In this example, we are using the standard 0-100 scale for ratings, but you could devise a custom scale such as confusing, not completely clear, clear, very helpful, and so on. The creation of custom scales is covered in detail in *Chapter 9, Tracking Progress with the Gradebook*.

The glossary can now be saved.

Adding entries (categories)

When we are adding entries, the first real requirement is to create some categories in which you can organize the terms. A category in this instance is a group of terms such as tools or techniques. If we had created one Moodle course to cover all the DT subjects, we might have a main glossary for DT and secondary glossaries for Food and Construction. This makes it more organized as well as making it easier to search for items. In this example, we are creating some glossary items relating to the term 'carpentry'. We need to create an overall category for this area. This is achieved by first adding a new category item by clicking on the **Browse by category** tab and then on **Edit categories**, as shown in the following screenshot:

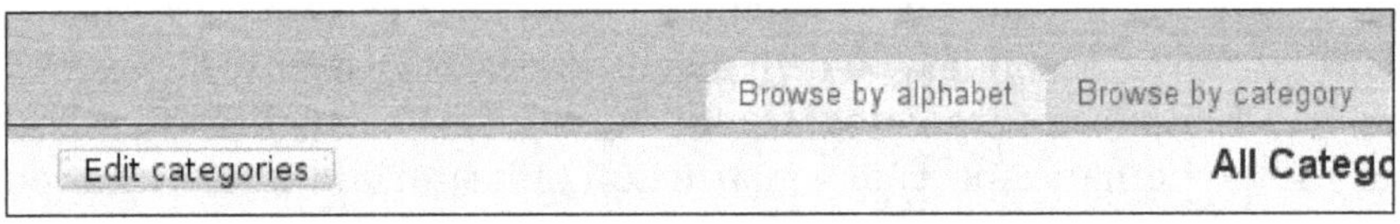

This will open the dialog window to create a new category for this glossary, as shown in the following screenshot:

If you select to link the category, this whole sub-section will be revealed by a hyperlink to this term, which could be useful for newer students.

Adding entries

If the course you are managing incorporates all of the DT subjects, then you may wish to create a main glossary for DT and secondary glossaries for Food or Resistant Materials and so on. In this example, we have a course for Construction and the Built Environment, which is the main glossary. We are going to create categories to group the terms in the glossary for areas such as carpentry or electrical. With the categories set, it is now possible to add and organize the definitions for your course. This can be managed entirely by the staff or can be an exercise that allows student participation, such as a homework exercise as mentioned earlier. In this example, we are building up a definition for a particular woodworking joint. Once we have set the name and basic details, we can then categorize the entry and add some keywords for searches, as shown in the following screenshot:

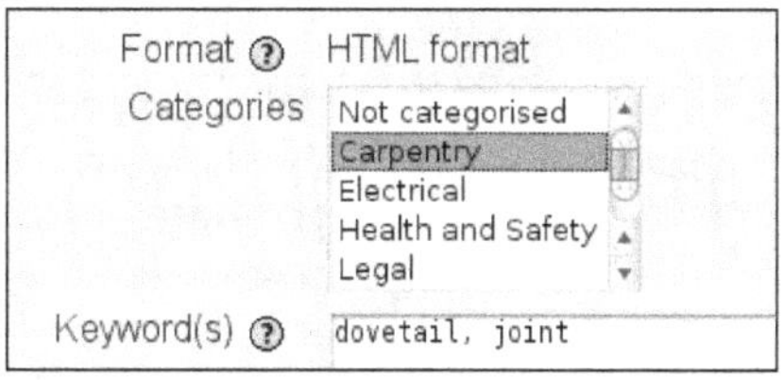

The entry can now be viewed by students as well as rated and commented upon. In the following instance, the student has not only rated the entry, but also added a comment with a link to a website they have found, which further illustrates the particular woodworking joint.

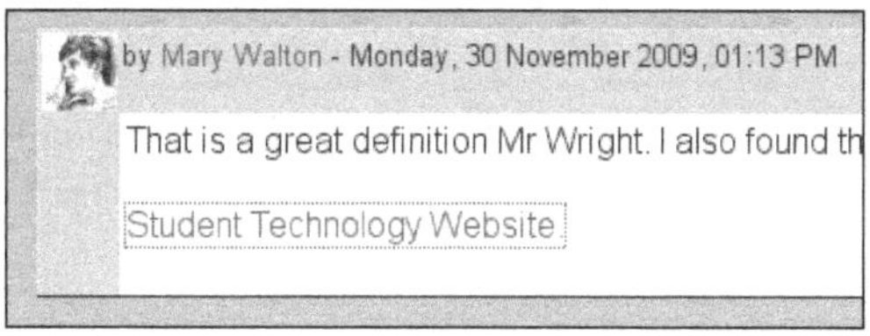

Students could also embed a video stream from a video site, which would also help to explain the process more clearly. This level of collaborative learning is immensely powerful with this type of kinesthetic information.

Students can now add their own entries as part of a homework routine or teaching strategy.

As shown in the following screenshot, items added to the glossary are linked to other pages through the database. The terms are highlighted by Moodle and clicking on them will take users to the glossary page, which defines them.

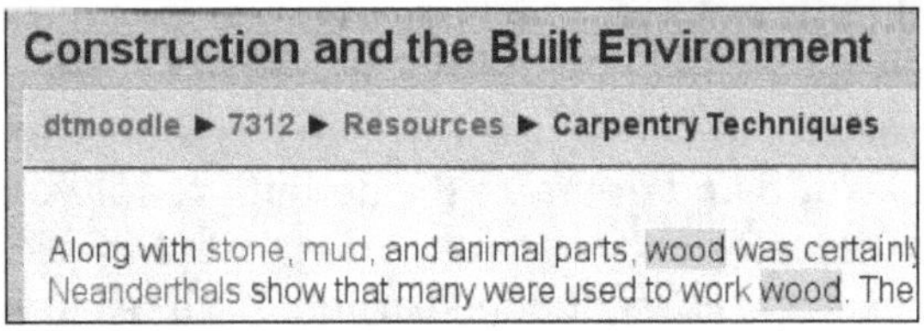

In this example, the word 'wood' is highlighted in green. When you click on this link, it will open the corresponding entry for wood in the glossary, as shown in the following screenshot.

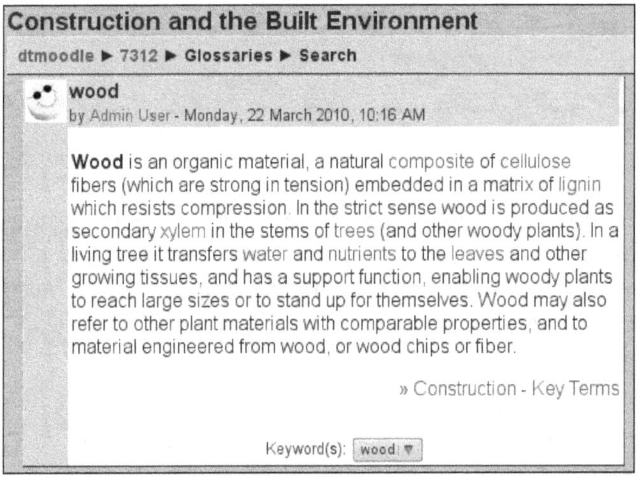

Mapping their minds

Many aspects of design require students to sketch out their ideas in a graphical form in order to get to grips with the complexity and the various components. These sketches could be scanned and uploaded as formal assignments, but they could also be incorporated into the Moodle site through the use of an add-on called **Mindmap**. This is a third-party module that allows the students to map out their ideas using a basic interface and permits them to link and label the items on a screen. We had covered the installation of third-party modules in *Chapter 2, Organizing Information Using Moodle Modules*. It can be saved by them in their area and can be viewed by the staff for guidance and support. The **Mindmap** module can be found at:

`http://moodle.org/mod/data/view.php?d=13&rid=1628&filter=1.`

Once the module has been installed, it is added to a course in a similar way as we add any other module, by turning the editing on.

After choosing the drop-down activities menu, you can then add the **Mindmap** module, as shown in the following screenshot:

This will activate the dialog to set up the name and settings for the **Mindmap** module for the course.

Making a map

Students can now log in to the course and create a map of their ideas and plans in a pictographic form, which may be easier for them to grasp. It might also be easier for staff to understand what they are trying to achieve and therefore to help them.

The interface is quite basic and allows objects and sub-objects to be added and labeled, as shown in the following screenshot:

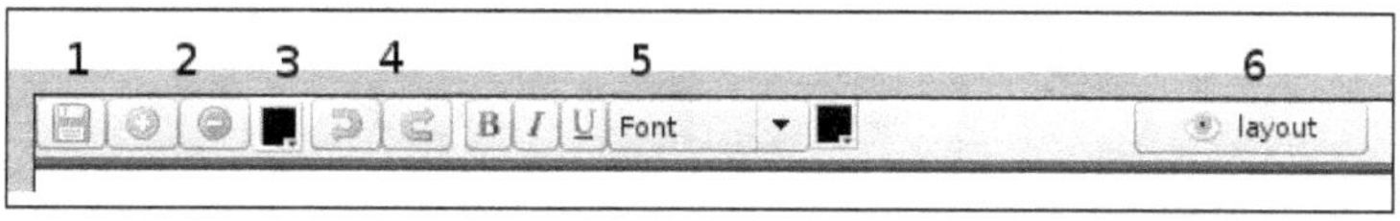

The function of the toolbar icons is described in the following list:

1. Export the image as a picture or PDF file.
2. Add or remove blocks or sub-blocks.
3. Change the block colors.
4. Undo or redo any actions.
5. Edit the text on the boxes, as well as color.
6. Auto layout to fit the screen.

The module opens with a central shape that can be renamed (defaults to Moodle). Sub-items can be added and pressing the *Insert* key will add sub-items to these items. The design will end up as complex or as simple as required, such as the following image that shows a basic plan for a project:

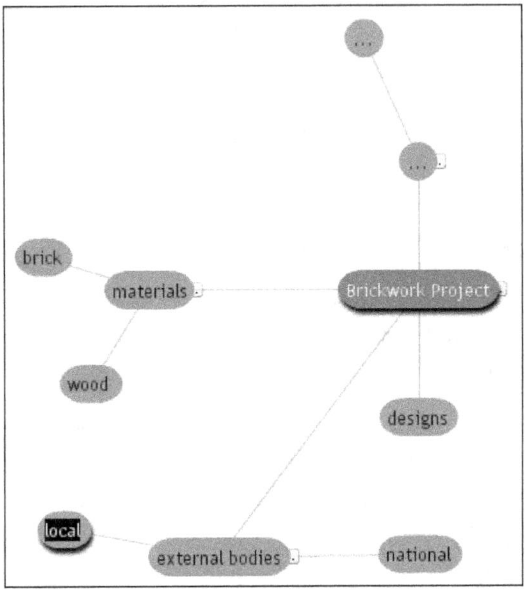

By default, each map that is enabled can be used by the course participants. This may be useful to create one instance for each student on the course in order to make it easier to track their work. For example, you might name each instance for your students, such as, "Mary's Mindmap for understanding circuit board construction", maybe using your own design for reference material or a special localized method of practice or building method, as shown in the previous image. All the users on the site can, however, edit the mindmaps, so you will need to instruct your students to only modify the reference maps that the staff creates if they ask in advance.

Quizzing their understanding

One of the most effective ways of assessing a student's progress, both formally and informally, is through the use of the **Quiz** module. The **Quiz** module is very flexible and has a great number of styles and options to suit most requirements. Once it has been set up, it can be used over and over again through a quiz bank and can be set for multiple attempts or just one. Students can access the quiz at their convenience and the reporting tools associated with the quiz. When used in conjunction with the gradebook, it can give a clear indication of which areas of a course are most accessible to your students, and which areas still need work.

Developing a quiz for Food Technology

For this example, we are going to develop a quiz for Food Technology. One aspect of food technology, which is vital, is an understanding of ingredients and equipments. In most cases, it would be best to supplement more kinesthetic activities with the quizzes. However, the quiz will only act to show how much of a class-based practical demonstration the students have retained. It will also help them before they attempt any formal examinations by drilling in any unfamiliar terms and items.

Site-wide settings

As with all the other modules, it may require some basic settings at the site level to make sure that the quiz performs the way you would like it to, or at least have a set of common functions, by default. The following screenshot shows the settings page with some of the options available:

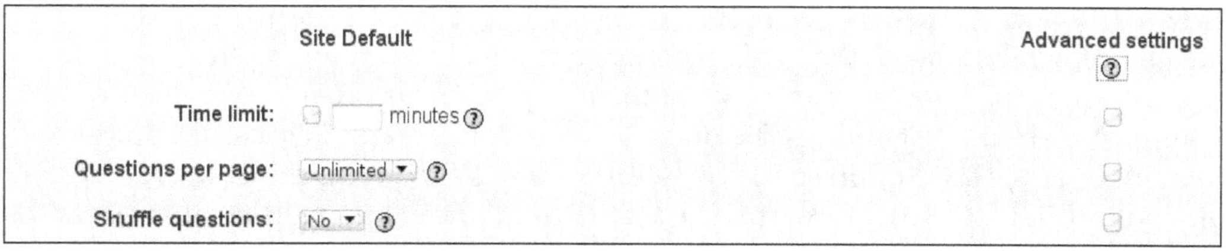

If you are a head of the DT department, you may wish to tick the advanced settings box to hide some features to make a cleaner interface. Once your staff is comfortable with the setup and using quizzes, you may then wish to introduce other features.

Preparing the work surface

A requirement for an understanding of food technology and production is to have a basic understanding of the composition of food. Most countries have food course specifications. For example, in the UK, this is termed as an understanding of the physical and chemical properties of starch, sugar, protein, and fat. Students need to be aware of the characteristics of the food they prepare in order for them to do the best possible job in its production. Making a good Béchamel sauce is not entirely down to good technique and timing; it also relies on an understanding of the properties of the ingredients and the interaction of fats and starches.

As with all the modules, the first task is to enable the edit state on the course.

From the resulting drop-down menu, choose the **Quiz** option, as shown in the previous screenshot.

Choosing ingredients

The quiz options will be available once you choose the module. The first two options are common to all the modules and have been described in the previous chapters and require you to name and describe the quiz. The remaining options are related to how the quiz is displayed, to whom, for how long, and so on.

Setting the quiz timings

The first group of options is the **Timing** of the quiz. If it is a quiz that is testing the students' knowledge and requires a start and an end time to make sure that the students are meeting deadlines, then you can set the start and the stop dates for when the quiz can be taken, as well as how long the quiz is visible for the students when they take it. This may be useful for trying to get students to work with tight deadlines, which is what they will experience in a real restaurant. In this example, we will leave the quiz open as we want them to practice as often as possible to reinforce their understanding. The quiz can be taken as many times as the student requires and the style of presentation, with penalties for wrong choices, will hopefully allow students to learn the questions and the corresponding answers at a pace that is comfortable to them. The following screenshot shows some settings such as when the quiz will be available (the date it opens and the date it closes for students). The quiz also has settings for delay between attempts. In some cases, a student may take the test multiple times and learn the pattern of answers in order to get a better score. In this case, they are not really learning the answers. Setting a delay between attempts allows student's time to reflect on their wrong answers and possibly time to go to the library to do some more revision.

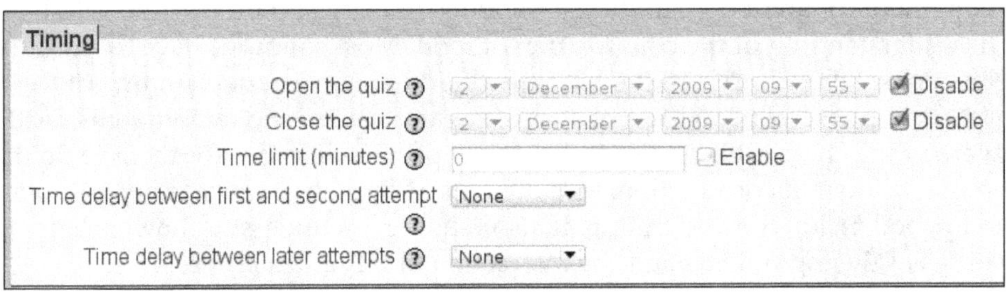

Setting the quiz display options

The next set of options relate to the way the questions are displayed to the students. If you have questions that have images in them or quite a lot of supporting text, you may choose to limit the number of questions viewed per page. In the following screenshot, we have chosen to have just one question viewable at a time. If the question contains a large amount of text and pictures, such as a detailed description of a process with some terms missing, the students will need to focus on that one question. If it were a part of a series, it may be distracting.

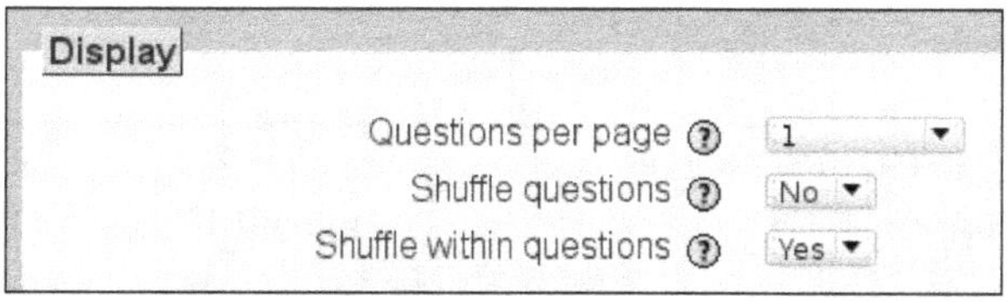

Setting the attempts allowed

The next couple of options relate to how many times students can try the quiz and what grade is stored. Again, if it is to be used as their mark towards a government-controlled qualification, you may limit them to one or two goes and only keep the highest score, or allow them to keep the score from the first or last attempt. In the following example, the students have three attempts at the quiz. In addition, we have chosen to enable that each attempt builds on the last and that the answers are adaptive. In this case, each time the student retakes the quiz, they will see their previous answers and can, therefore, concentrate on why they gave the wrong response. The adaptive mode means that they will receive a penalty for each wrong response, but they will have the chance to try the same quiz again.

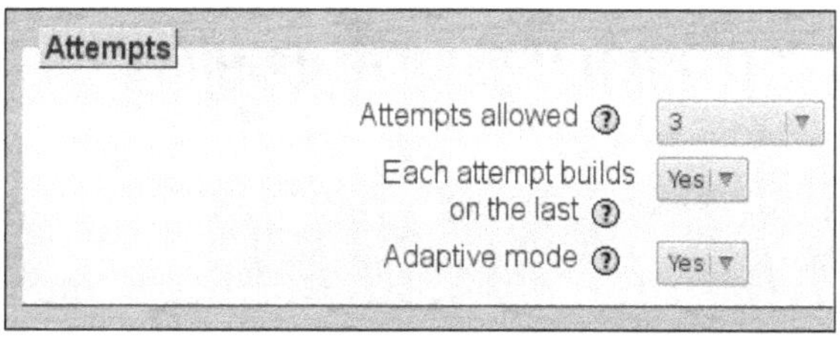

The default review options will be fine in most cases, unless it is used for a public examination where you may decide to hide any feedback until they have all completed the quiz.

Setting common module settings: groups and categories

The security settings can be used to restrict the examinations to a specific set of computers, which is good for the examinations. This could help in conditions where the staff can monitor the students taking the quiz to cut down on cheating. The common settings are for specifying which groups will see the quiz. If you have also enabled groupings, you can set the quiz only for a small group. The groupings function is useful for advanced groups or groups that need additional help in some areas. If you have set up your gradebook already (see *Chapter 9*), you can also specify if the quiz is for examination practice or coursework related, as shown in the following screenshot:

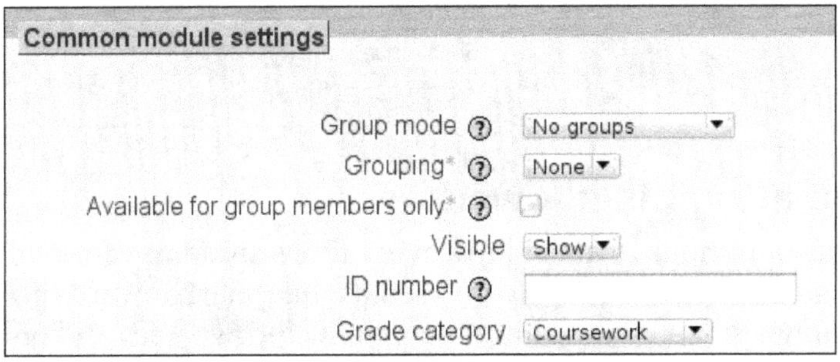

Determining feedback options

The overall feedback option, as shown in the following screenshot, is what feedback the students will see once they check their scores. You can set some default comments here, or you can customize them for the nature of your course, which makes it more real for the students by incorporating the feedback related to the food industry for which they are trying to gain knowledge and understanding.

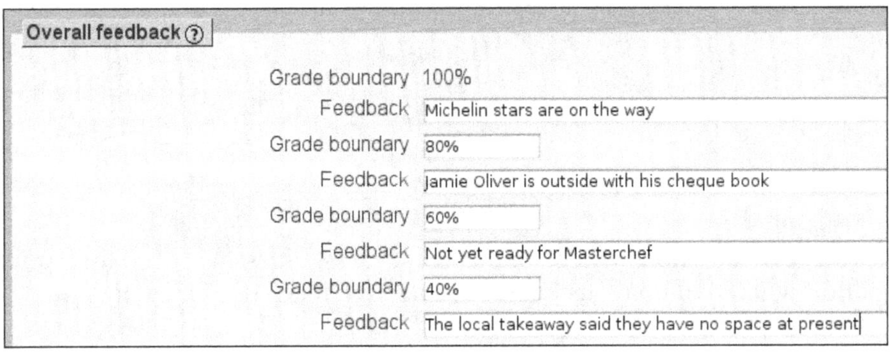

You can now save the quiz and start preparing the questions. The quiz will appear on your course, as shown below. You need to click on the link, in this case Food Properties, to add the questions.

Mixing ingredients

Once you click on the link to the quiz, it will open the main editing window showing all of the options available for the new questions, as shown in the following screenshot:

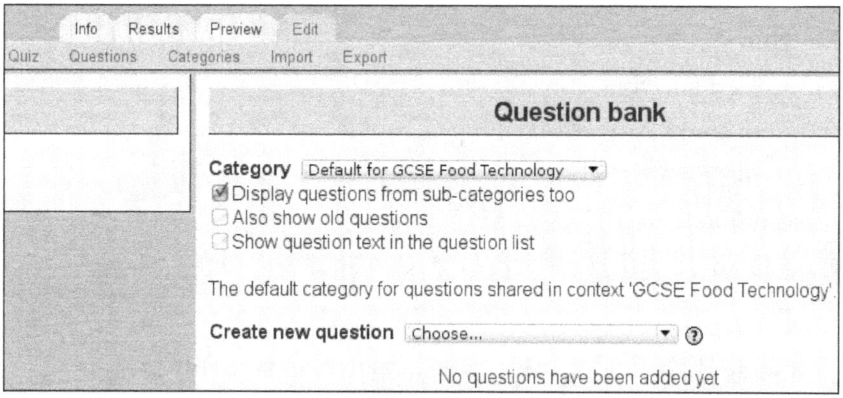

The module, by default, will create a category for the course, but you can also elect to use a category specific to the topic you have chosen as well. If you have created questions in another system or program, you may also choose to import these questions into your course. The following screenshot shows the current systems from which you can import questions into Moodle:

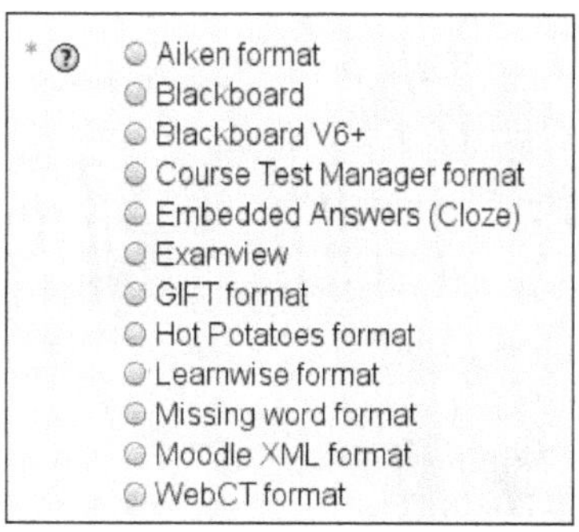

You can also click on the **Categories** tab and make some more categories. In this example, you might have categories for equipment or ingredients, or possibly for elements such as fats, starches, proteins, and so on.

With the category selected, you can now make the questions on your own. From the drop-down menu for creating new questions, you can see that there are several types to choose from. These are:

- Multiple choice
- Short answer
- Numerical
- True / False
- Matching
- Embedded answers (Cloze)
- Random short-answer Matching
- Random
- Description
- Calculated
- Essay

This gives a wide variety of possible questions to help students in their understanding. In most cases, the multiple choice and essay questions will be the most familiar and widely used. For this example, as the process is the same, we will use the multiple choice question type.

The following screenshot shows the name of the quiz and its actual question:

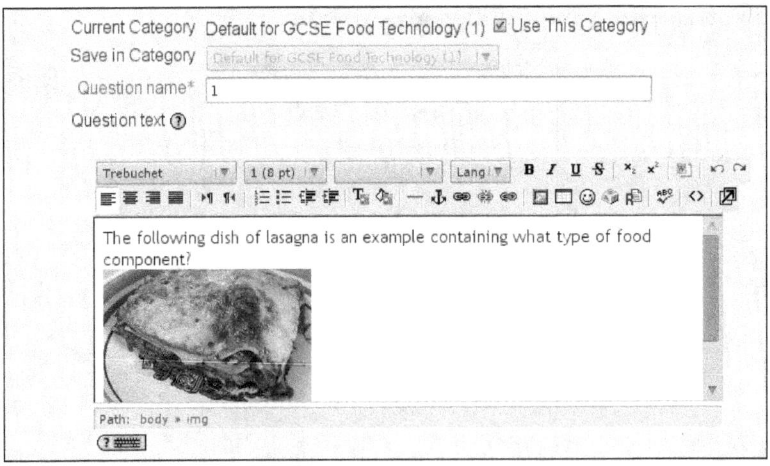

In this instance, an image has been uploaded and inserted into the question for reference. This is achieved by clicking on the insert image icon as follows:

If the question has multiple answers, you need to select the option, as shown in the following screenshot:

Also, you can enter whether or not to apply the penalties for multiple attempts. The following screenshot shows these options:

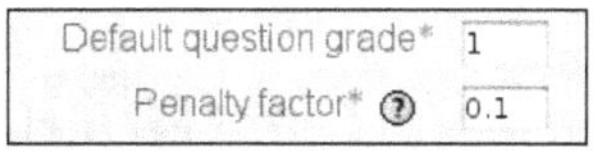

The following sections are the answers themselves. For the correct answer(s), you need to apply the resulting grade. If you have set a default grade of three, then three answers can have 100 percent. If the default is one, then each correct answer will be 33.333 percent and so on. The following screenshot shows the basic setting for a correct response:

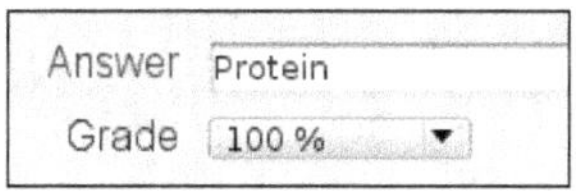

With all of the answers filled in and any specific feedback, the question can be saved.

Once you have built up a bank of questions, you can select them from the list, as shown in the following screenshot, and click on the arrow to add them to the quiz.

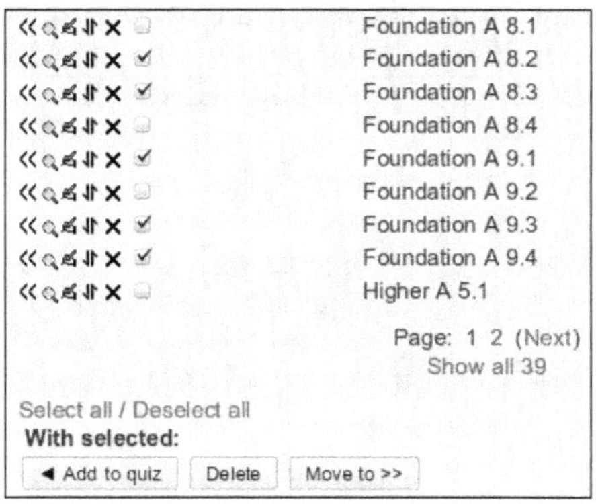

The number of questions can be used as the total, or if you have a series of 10 quizzes, which collectively make up the entire formal assessment of the course, you can make them each out of 10 to get the 100 percent total marks. Here, we have made the grade 15 to equate to 15 percent of the course formal marks.

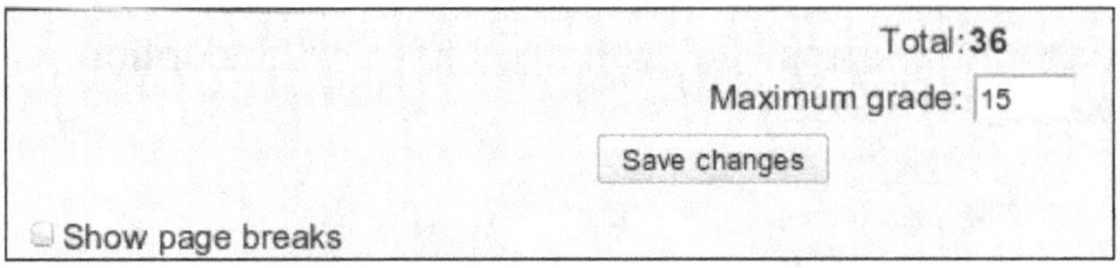

You can preview the quiz to see what the students will see and to make sure that it is presented in the way you want, as shown in the following screenshot:

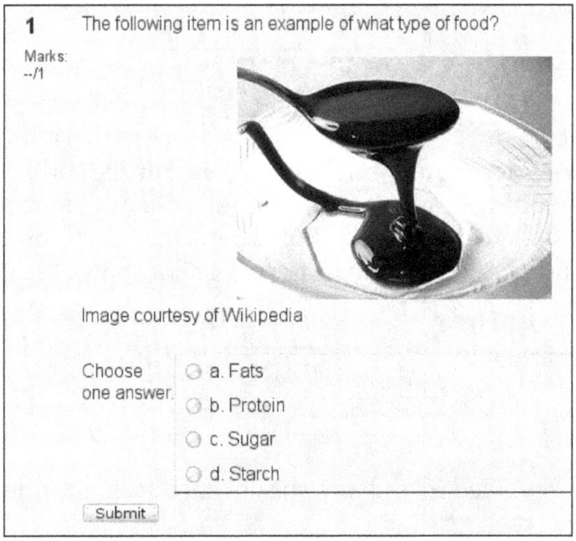

You can also test the responses to make sure that the feedback is how you would like it to be, as well as any penalties, as shown in the following screenshot:

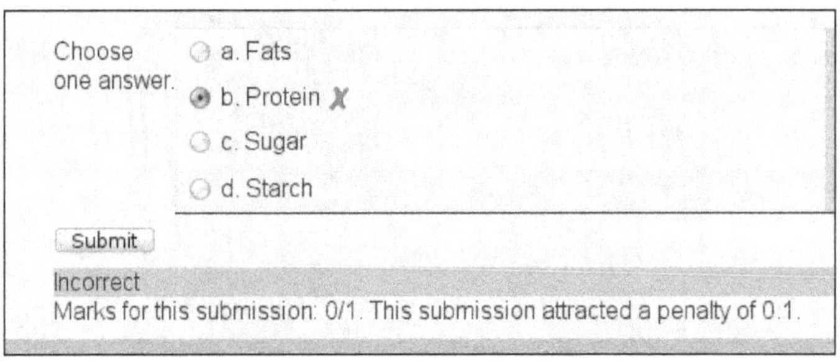

The results obtained from the quiz will be stored in the gradebook and can be further interrogated, as we will see in *Chapter 9*.

Summary

The activities outlined here—the glossary, the quiz, and the Mindmap—will allow the students to test their understanding of the material that they have studied and give staff a clearer idea of where their groups are, in terms of knowledge. This sort of information can help you design better courses and materials for the students. In the next chapter, we will investigate the Feedback module and the DimDim module to show how the students can gather information about their intended market of users.

6

Helping your Students Gather Data about their Potential Markets

One vital element in all aspects of design technology, given that the driving force behind the discipline is bringing items to the market, is the ability to understand and gauge reactions to ideas and concepts. Students that you teach really need to engage with potential customers and people outside of their discipline to see if their proposals are valid or desired. They also need to find out, once the products have been developed, how closely they meet the target audience and their own stated objectives, which they hopefully set out at the beginning of the process. In order to meet these requirements, there are a number of tools in Moodle that you can use to assist the process.

Encouraging students to perform SWOT analysis

Students in business studies, leisure and tourism, and geography will be busily analyzing the factors that make up aspects of the marketplace, but nowhere is this more necessary than in design technology. A failure to carry out some type of SWOT analysis could lead to lots of problems. To remind ourselves, SWOT stands for Strengths, Weaknesses, Opportunities, and Threats. This gives students a clear picture of where their designs might fit into a crowded marketplace, but also what competition they will face and how well they might overcome this. Once you have reinforced the ideas behind carrying out a SWOT analysis with your students, you can set up a series of modules within Moodle to help them gather the necessary data. A powerful combination of modules that can be used to gather this data are the Questionnaire module and the Feedback module. Both of these modules are third-party modules and will therefore need to be installed by an administration user before they can be used. The process of installing these modules is covered in previous chapters. The modules can be downloaded here:

Feedback module:
`http://moodle.org/mod/data/view.php?d=13&rid=95&filter=1`

Questionnaire module:
`http://moodle.org/mod/data/view.php?d=13&rid=84&filter=1`

Gathering data using the Questionnaire module

The quickest and most effective way to gather some data from a range of people is a questionnaire. The questionnaire can be designed to gather data and opinions on all of the issues relating to your student's product design including the usage and factors such as concern for the environment. It can also be used in a more general way to find out what is required from a potential product before your students begin the first designs. If you have good communication channels with the local community, it would be good to find out if there was a need in the local area that could be met, such as furniture for a local youth centre or care home.

Setting up a Questionnaire

The first action, as with all modules, is to enable the edit function on the course to be able to add an activity.

This will enable editing, and you can then select the **Questionnaire** module from the resulting **Add an activity** drop-down menu, as shown in the following screenshot:

This process will open the basic editing window for the creation of the questionnaire, including when and how data is collected. After the questionnaire has been named, the next section relates to its visibility. You may want the questionnaire always open for all respondents, or you may be more restrictive and set an open and close date for it. In this case, we are setting a time limit, as we need students to gather the data and move forward quickly, as shown in the following screenshot:

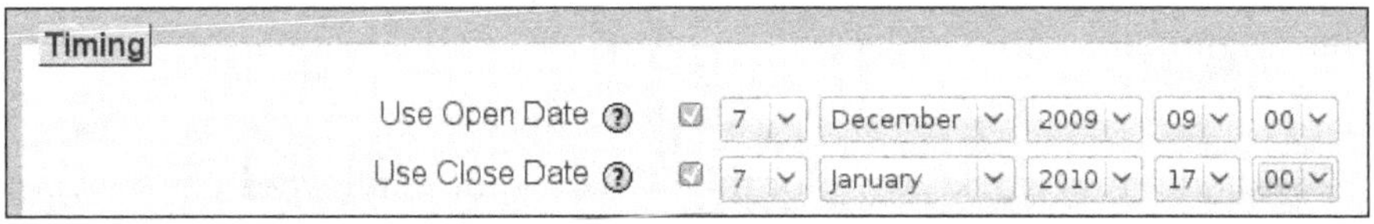

As long as you discuss with your students in advance the importance of these time constraints, they should be willing and able to work within the deadlines. The use of deadlines is also not a bad thing in this discipline.

Setting the Response Options

The next section relates to how we reference the respondents and whether or not students can see how it is progressing. You might change this once students get used to the module, but for speed, it is best to minimize the ongoing output they see. They don't need too many distractions. The following screenshot shows some possible settings to achieve this:

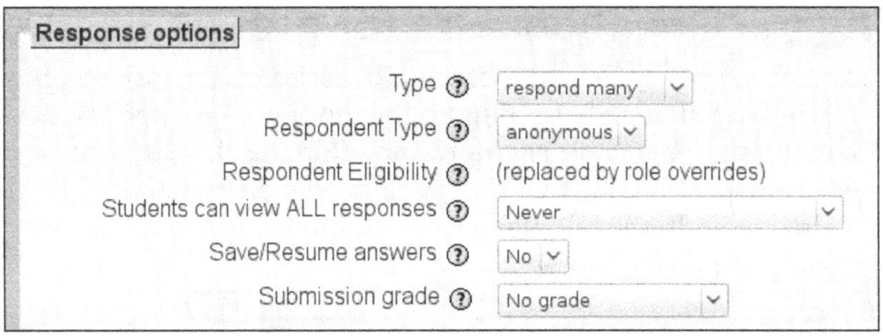

In the previous screenshot, there are a number of settings that can be set for the responses available to respondents.

Type

There are five choices for the type of responses available on the questionnaire and the type you choose will depend on the nature of the data you want to gather or perhaps the audience participating in the activity. Out of the five types, three of them are date related:

- Respond many: Each participant can have multiple attempts at the questionnaire
- Respond once: Only one attempt will be allowed
- Respond daily, weekly, or monthly: One response allowed per day, week, or month respectively

If the questionnaire is being used to gather very general responses to student designs, then you may wish to allow multiple responses to get as much data as possible. The data can be used to find average responses over time, as many people may well change their mind as a project develops. Students can incorporate this changing mood as part of their reflective practice. If the questionnaire is being designed to gather a snap reaction to a design proposal, then one response should be allowed from each student and students can write about the range of reactions in a specific audience. This type of response may be useful for a construction proposal. Once the response has been taken and the project is under way, it may be too late to gather more opinions from a sample.

Enabling the Questionnaire for groups of students

The final group of settings relates to more micro control of the module, in particular, on the use of groups. You may be setting up the module as part of a wider policy on gifted and talented students or as a sub-group within the class, so you would assign it to a specific group of students. Likewise, you may wish to make it a homework exercise for extra credit. In the following screenshot, we have made it part of the overall course requirement.

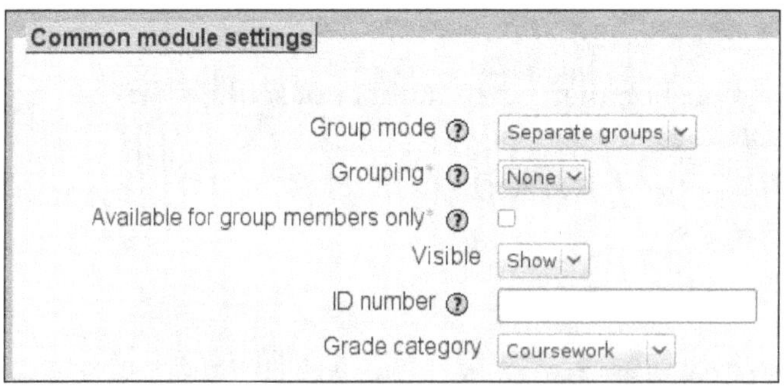

The questionnaire structure can now be saved and will appear on the course to use. In this instance, we have created it for our student so that participants know that the data will be part of her project.

Configuring the Advanced settings

With the structure in place, we can now add some questions to the design. Once you click on the questionnaire, you will see the following screenshot that shows four main headings to edit the questionnaire, as well as a button to update this questionnaire which will take you back to the main settings discussed earlier.

The first thing to do is set the advanced options, as shown in the following screenshot:

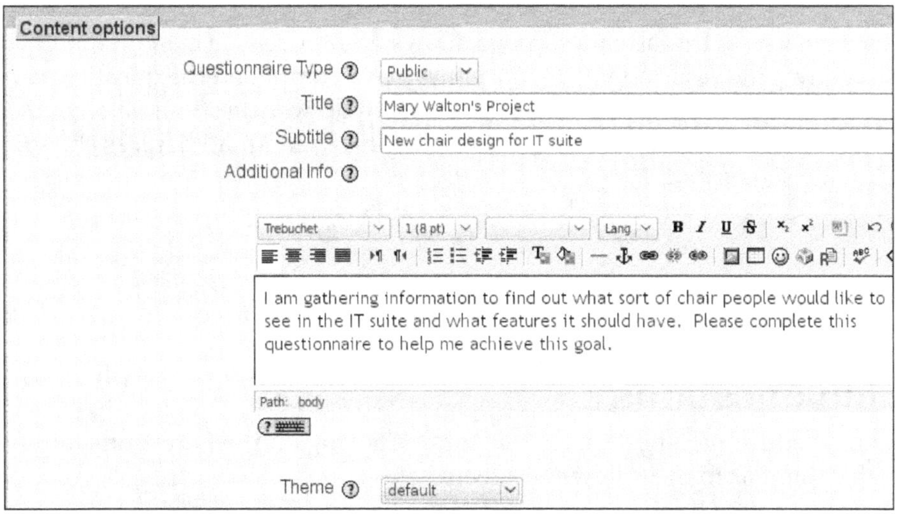

In the example here, we have decided to make the questionnaire type **Public**. This setting allows the questionnaire to be used in other courses. If we are teaching design technology, it is likely that we teach several subjects such as Food Technology and Resistant Materials and therefore we do not need to keep on designing the same questionnaire for each instance. If we set the questionnaire as Private, it would only be available in this course. All responses, even if the questionnaire is in other courses, will always come back to the original creator. Depending on how you set up your site and where this is placed, we could gather data just from our own institution, or we could open it up to the public to get more responses. If the questionnaire is set to take anonymous responses and is placed in a course which has guest access, this would be possible. In this sample case, the target audience is quite specific, as it relates to a school IT suite so it would only be students and staff responding, although parents may also wish to get involved.

> If you have added the Create Parent Account block to your site, parents can participate in their children's courses and therefore, this questionnaire. The Create Parent Account block would need to be installed by your site administrator and is available here:
>
> `http://moodle.org/mod/data/view.php?d=13&rid=2221&filter=1`

The other section on this advanced page allows you to create a custom thank you page to redirect the respondents to, once they have completed the questionnaire. In this case, we will not require one. However, we do want responses to go to our student for his/her coursework file, so we place his/her e-mail here, as shown in the following screenshot:

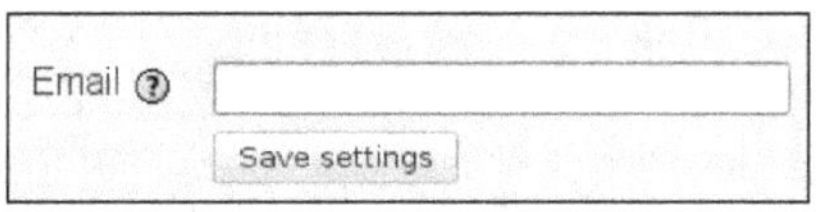

Adding questions

We can now add some questions to our form. Clicking on the **Questions** tab shows an interface similar to the following screenshot:

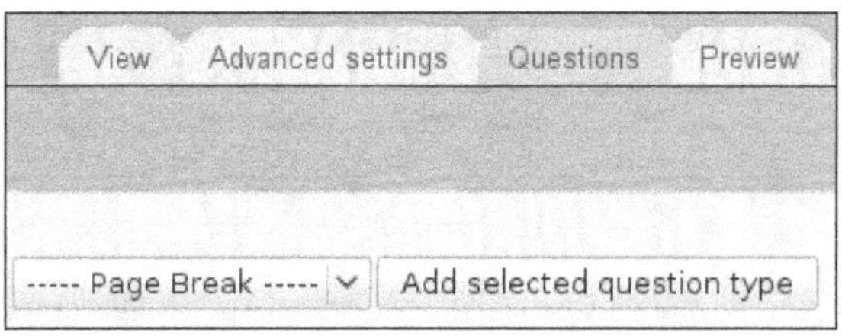

Examples of the types of questions are clearly shown in the help dialog box with some examples of usage and can be accessed by clicking on the help icon, as shown in the following screenshot. To summarize the questions that can be used:

Question type	Options	Possible use
Checkboxes/ Radio buttons	Can include an Other field Possible to display horizontally or vertically	Gathering opinions on designs or proposals such as taste choices in a food product.
Date		Useful to gain an idea of when someone might want a product that you are designing.
Drop Down		Useful on large questionnaires to save screen space. Also for restricting choices to items you are working with.
Essay Box		Useful for longer and more open answers. Asking respondents what their opinion is on a style, for example.
Numeric	Number length	Useful for getting specific numbers, such as how much they might pay for something.
Rate (scale)		Creates a grid of options for respondents to rate items. Good for finding out respondents' feelings on items, such as desirable to not desirable.
Text box	Length of response	More structured than the essay box.

In addition to the main question types shown in this table, there are also Yes/No question types and formatting options such as adding information labels or breaks.

Once students have designed the form and the questions they require, you can use their design and build it on Moodle. The range of question types should be sufficient to gather all of the data they require to be able to build a product, which suits a great number of users' needs.

Analyzing the results

As people take the questionnaire, the data will be gathered and eventually it can be viewed and discussed with the student to see which aspects of their design are the most important or equally, which aspects are not worth pursuing. The following screenshot shows the output summary from a questionnaire, following a number of responses.

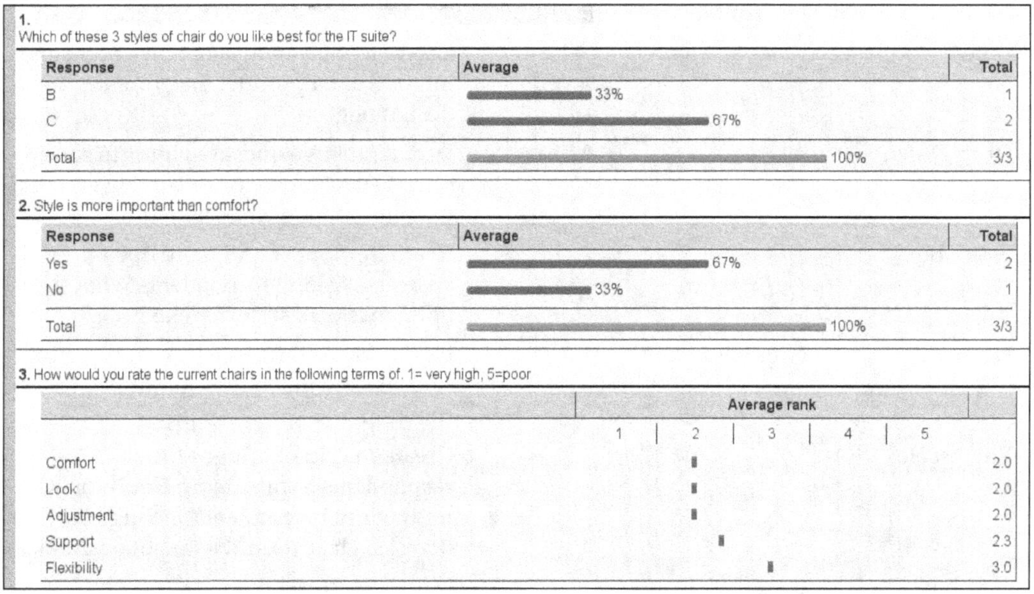

As a member of staff, you can also export the data into a spreadsheet for more detailed analysis and manipulation and give the file to your students for their project files. You can access this function from the output summary window by clicking on the **View All responses** tab or by downloading the data in a Comma Separated Value (`.csv`) file using the **Download in text format** button, as shown in the following screenshot:

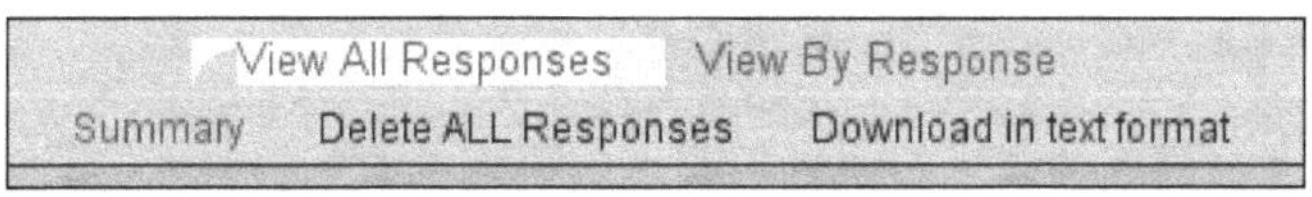

If the questionnaire is a generic questionnaire covering all subjects in design technology, it can be saved as a template and then reused by other members of staff.

Collecting user feedback with the Feedback module

During the design process, and after the completion of the project, it is useful for students to gather information from potential users on certain aspects of their work. This feedback is very important in making sure that the design stays within the initial objectives and has some possibility of meeting sales targets. If the students receive some negative feedback at the right moment in the process, they can adjust the design and make sure it is more suitable, before wasting too much time on dead ends.

The module to assist in this process would be the Feedback module. As with the Questionnaire module discussed already, this is a third-party module, which would need to be installed by your system administrator.

Adding the Feedback module

As with all modules, the procedure requires you to first switch on the editing function by pressing the button shown in the following screenshot:

This will allow you to choose the **Feedback** module from the resulting drop-down list in the **Add an activity** drop-down menu, as shown in the following screenshot:

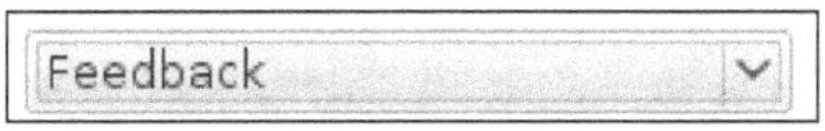

Changing the settings of the Feedback module

Once you have added the feedback module, you can begin to adjust the basic settings to suit your needs. After naming and describing the feedback instance, the next settings relate to the time and date that the feedback is open to participants. You may wish to set a time limit here as with the questionnaire, depending on how strict your deadlines are for the student's project write-ups. The next settings are about how information is displayed and notifications. The settings are down to your policy in this instance. The following screenshot shows some possible settings for anonymity.

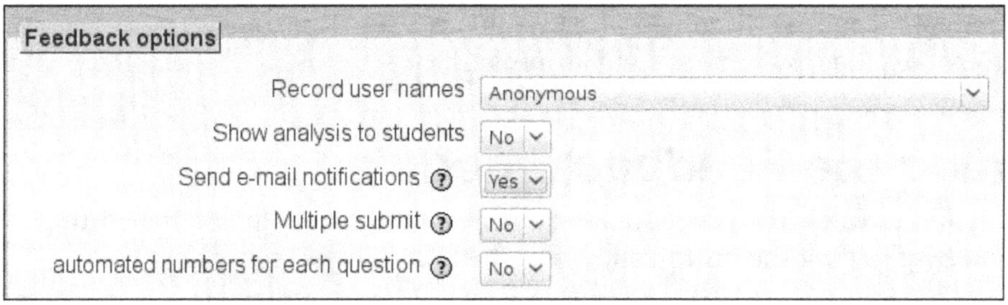

The previous screenshot shows the general options available.

Feedback options

The options available on the **Feedback options** screen are as follows:

Record user names

The first option allows you to choose to show all respondent's names in the analysis or to keep the names hidden. You will still be able to see responses, but the names will not be displayed to other participants. This may reduce respondents copying their friend's answers.

Show analysis to students

You may wish to allow students to see the analysis as they respond to the answers if you are using the feedback module to inform the group about general design principles. If the feedback is enabled on a course, that is, open to all students, the respondents can get a feel for overall opinion trends, and this might be useful for ongoing classroom-based discussions.

Send e-mail notifications

After the respondents have completed the feedback form, the course administrator will receive a notification.

The final two options relate to how many times each respondent can submit an answer and whether or not the questions in the feedback are automatically numbered in the responses.

In most cases, it may be better to have anonymous users recorded, unless you specifically are teaching students about how they respond to questions, though you will still be able to see who responded, but the respondents will not be displayed to each other. You may use a test feedback in the first instance to show students' possible responses to discuss with them the impact. In this case, you might keep their names in the responses as discussion points. In this example, we have elected not to show the results to students. This would be something that can be changed later when there is enough data to warrant more in-depth discussions.

By default, the respondent will be shown a thank you response at the end of the feedback they provide, but this can be customized if you feel it is appropriate. The next block on the settings page labeled **After Submitting** is for this purpose.

The form design can now be saved.

Adding the feedback questions

Once the feedback options have been set, the feedback itself will appear as a link on the course, as shown in the following screenshot:

Clicking on this link will open up the window to add the questions for the feedback form. The main edit functions are available in tabs, as shown in the following screenshot:

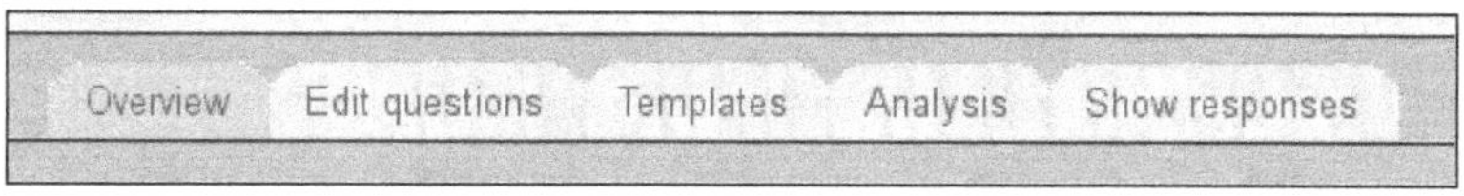

In this case, we only need to add questions to the form, so we need to click on the **Edit questions** tab. This will open a dialog window similar to the Questionnaire module, as shown in the following screenshot:

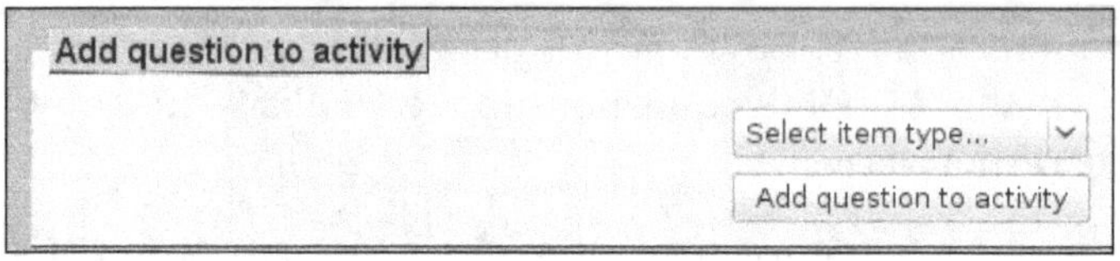

The question types available in the feedback module are listed below. Some are more self-explanatory than others and some you may not use at all. More detailed descriptions can be found on Moodle docs: `http://docs.moodle.org/en/Adding_Feedback_questions#Available_question_types` in the appendix on the Moodle site.

- Captcha
- Multiple choice - multiple answers
- Multiple choice - single answer allowed (dropdownlist)
- Dropdownlist (rated)
- Label
- Numeric answer
- Picture
- Multiple choice - single answer
- Radiobutton (rated)
- Longer Text Answer
- Short Text Answer

The only option which may be unfamiliar is the Captcha type. A Captcha type question creates a response window that requires some intelligence and is designed to ensure, as much as possible, that a person is completing the feedback. The following screenshot illustrates the completed question and how it would look.

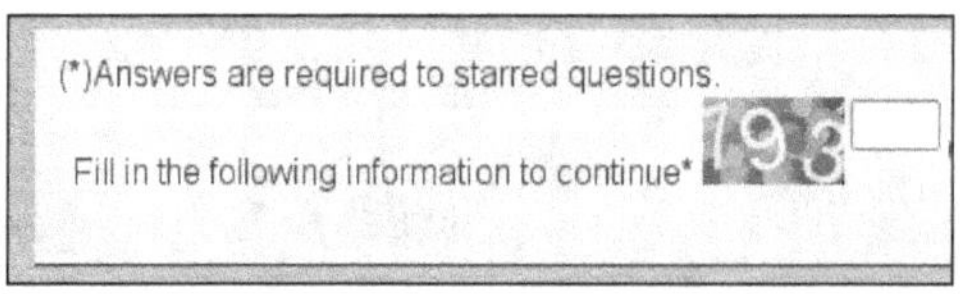

The Information and Label types of question are for design purposes. You may wish to give participants a set of extended instructions about the purpose of the feedback form and how it is going to be used. If a set of questions within the form is different than the bulk of questions, you may insert a label to differentiate them.

The rest of the questions are what you might expect in a feedback form. Each one will have settings specific to its type. For example, adding a multiple-choice drop-down list (rated) will allow you to set the options for the ratings that will be given as choices ranging from desirable to not desirable in a design. The following screenshot shows the option settings for the list:

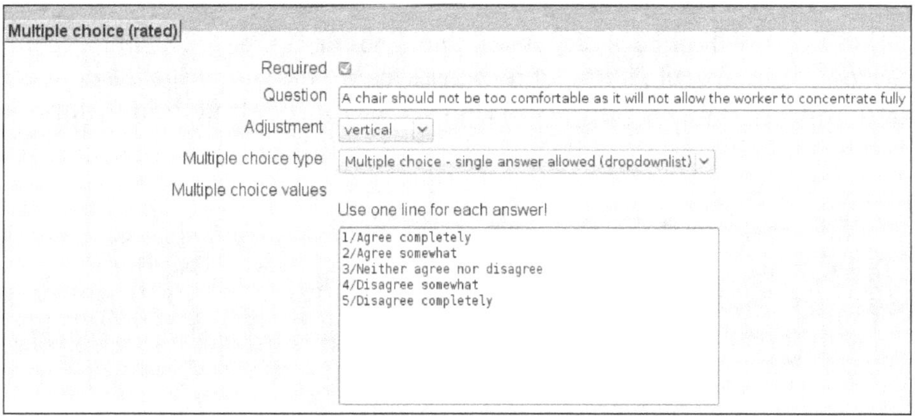

The resulting question, as it appears to the respondent, is shown in the following screenshot with one choice being made.

As with all data gathering that requires some quantification, it is best to stick to closed type questions that gather specific responses such as numbered responses or yes/no responses. Most of these would be covered by the multiple-choice type responses. However, much of design relates to more aesthetic and therefore not easily quantifiable responses and these would best be handled by a more detailed response such as the **Longer text answer** type.

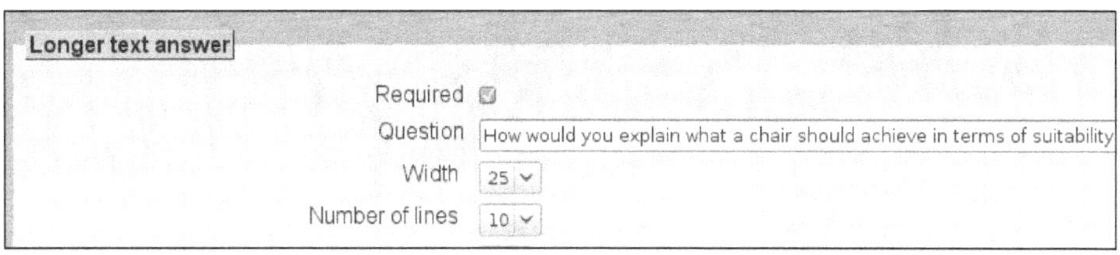

The options, as shown here, allow you to customize how large the box is for the response and therefore how much information the respondent can proffer. The resulting response box from the above settings is 25 characters wide and 10 lines high. These can be adjusted to suit and may be determined by the needs of the students. If you have many of these types of responses, it will mean a great deal of subjective data for students to work through, but if they are trained to deal with this, it could be an invaluable resource for making the exact product they need for the demand.

Analyzing the results

The output from the Feedback responses is very similar to the Questionnaire module. You can look at an overall pattern of responses, as well as individual responses to specific questions. The following screenshot shows some output from clicking on the **Analysis** tab.

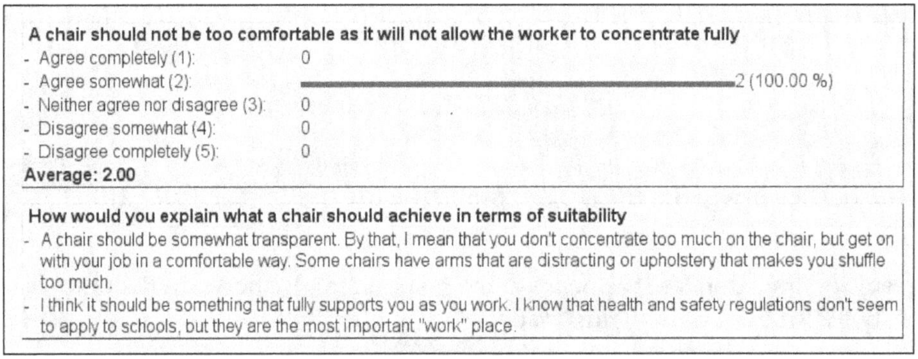

You can see here a mixture of quantifiable data and subjective material that can be used for making informed decisions. All of this data can also be exported by clicking the **Export to Excel** button, as shown in the following screenshot:

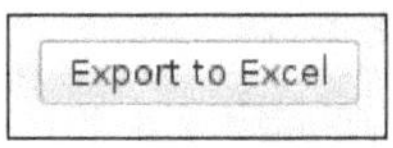

The resulting data will open in a spreadsheet ready for more detailed manipulation, bearing in mind that most of the data would need to be number-based. The following screenshot shows the exported result:

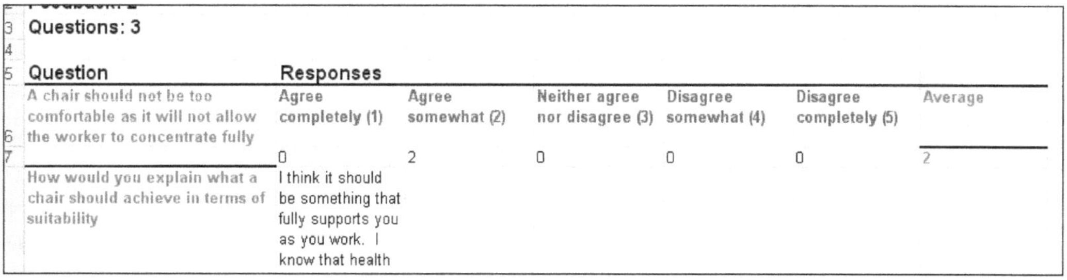

	Questions: 3						
5	Question	Responses					
6	A chair should not be too comfortable as it will not allow the worker to concentrate fully	Agree completely (1)	Agree somewhat (2)	Neither agree nor disagree (3)	Disagree somewhat (4)	Disagree completely (5)	Average
7		0	2	0	0	0	2
	How would you explain what a chair should achieve in terms of suitability	I think it should be something that fully supports you as you work. I know that health					

Widening the response

The two modules highlighted earlier are useful tools in order for you and your students to maximize research time and gather all of the data required to make a product that suits the needs and tastes of potential buyers. They also allow students to micro manage their development by gaining insights into each stage of the process. In some instances, it is useful to appeal to a wider audience and in a more interactive way. The following module will address this need.

Using the DimDim interactive tool

The DimDim module is a third-party module, which will need to be installed by your site administrator but will allow you to set up remote teaching environments using an interactive whiteboard and desktop sharing facilities. More details about the system can be gathered from their website:

`http://www.dimdim.com/`

`http://moodle.org/mod/data/view.php?d=13&rid=932&filter=1`

These days, thanks mainly to the scope and features of the Internet, it is possible to participate with a much wider and more diverse audience. For students, they have the opportunity to use Moodle to present their designs and ideas to a huge audience and gain invaluable feedback.

System settings

The module itself, once installed, requires very few settings at the system level and these are shown in the following screenshot. By default, the software will run from the DimDim server and all materials created will be stored on that server. However, some companies, such as Moodle Partners, can set up a server for your own site and this will allow more control. The default DimDim site, for example, will not record sessions and play them back to users.

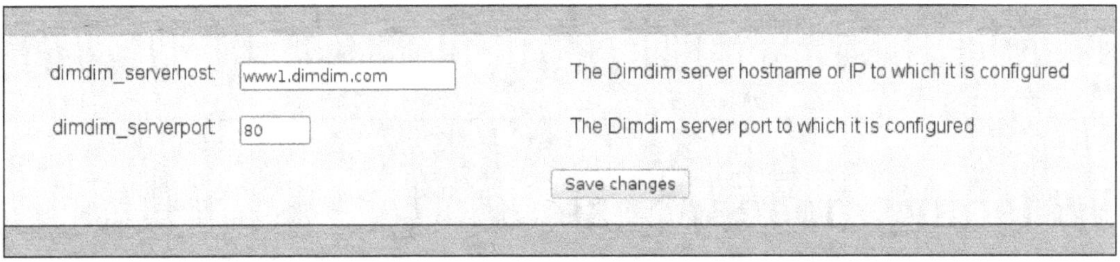

Setting up the DimDim module on your Moodle site

As with all modules, you first need to turn on the course editing button.

Then choose the **Dimdim Web Meeting** activity from the drop-down list as shown in the following screenshot:

This will open the menu to set up an instance of DimDim to configure. The first part of the configuration is to name the meeting for the link on the course page and to give a summary agenda of what the meeting will be about.

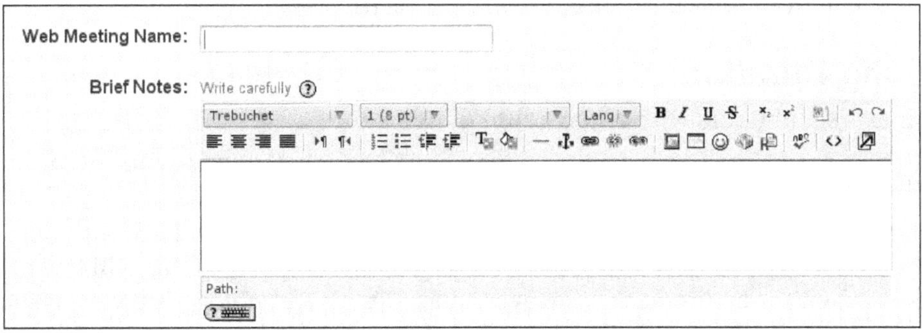

In this example, we are looking at sharing ideas about recipes with schools around the world. But it could just as easily be looking at how other cultures use raw materials or their specific construction techniques using local building materials.

Customizing the meeting settings

Once we have the name for the meeting, we then need to set the numbers and style of the meeting itself. The following screenshot shows the options available for sound and video as well as resource sharing:

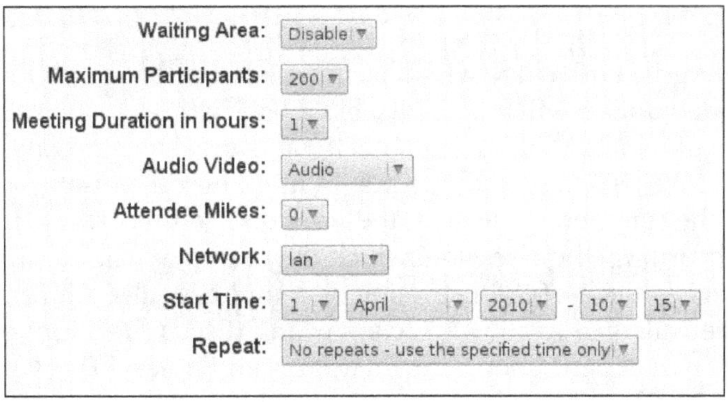

Waiting Area

The Waiting Area option, if enabled, allows participants to chat with each other in a chat window, if they have entered the meeting area before it is scheduled to start. This may be a useful way for people to introduce themselves more informally before a meeting begins.

Maximum Participants

The number of people who can be involved in the meeting can be set here, though bandwidth issues may be a consideration and having too large a group may exclude many people from their input because of time restrictions.

Meeting Duration

The time is set in hours with a maximum of five hours.

Audio/Video

In cases where you are working with institutions who do not have fast Internet connections, it may be better to restrict the data to audio only, as this will have a lower bandwidth requirement. However, since design technology is a very visual subject, a video setting would be more desirable.

Attendee Mikes

If you are using the meeting to demonstrate a design and do not require any audience interaction, then you may disable the attendee mike, which means they cannot request to talk and so interrupt the meeting.

The remaining settings relate to the local connection options, such as dial-up or LAN (Local Area Network), as well as the ability to set the start time/date and whether or not this meeting will repeat. If you are using it for a weekly teaching session on using CAD software, then you can set this to repeat each week on a certain day with a certain time.

The options for Audio and Video will determine what is loaded on the participants' desktop. The video option will only be usable if both parties have webcams at their disposal. You might want to allow students to have break out private rooms for chat or keep it public. We have a specific agenda in mind here, so disable any chat going on. If you have the commercial version and have enabled recording, it will send all participants a recording of the session, which they can play back as a flash video at a later date. This is quite useful for revision or complex issues. All resource sharing options have been enabled to allow us to show and discuss desktops either way, as well as having a whiteboard to do some diagrams and notes. With the current free version of DimDim, there is no function to save whiteboard sessions, so you will have to instruct students to take screenshots and save them if important. The Pro version, if purchased, does have the ability to record sessions.

Having a meeting

Once the options have been chosen and saved, you will then be taken to the meeting interface in Moodle itself. Other users will be presented with a similar screen but will be participants and not the moderator. If you have set the meeting in the future, you will be presented with the following screen to tell you when the meeting will take place.

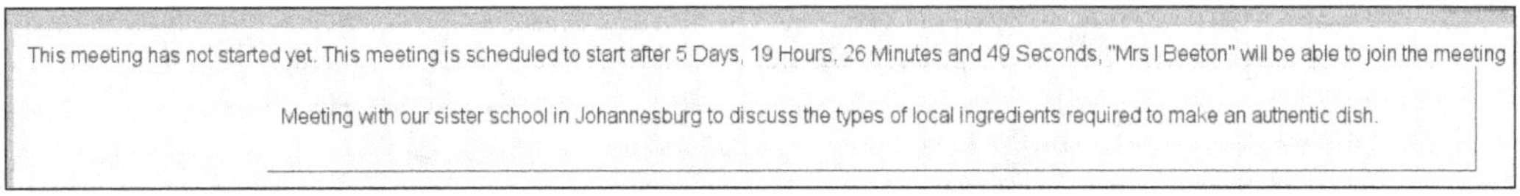

If you set the meeting up to run immediately, or if you have reached the required start time, you will see the following screen:

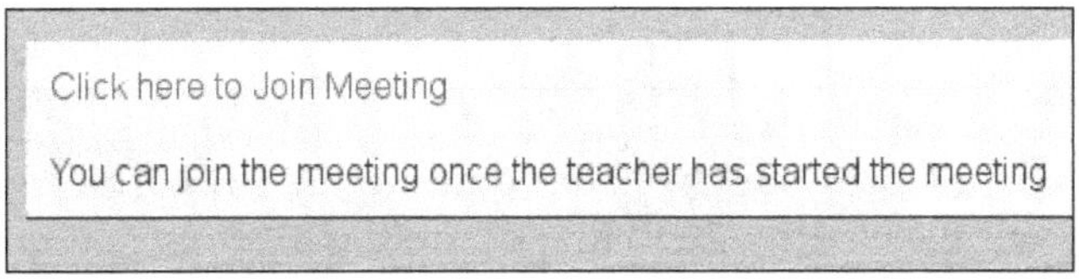

As a teacher, you can start the meeting by clicking the link (for staff, it will say **Click here to Start Meeting**). If you are using DimDim's server, you will be taken to the meeting welcome screen with a default name for the meeting. As you are using DimDim's servers, you don't have the option to change this, but it is only for reference. The login will appear, as shown in the following screenshot:

If you have set up your own DimDim server or are using one from a hosting company such as a Moodle Partner, you will be taken to the system check screen to make sure your system is compatible with the interface. You will see a number of checks run on your browser as in the following screenshot:

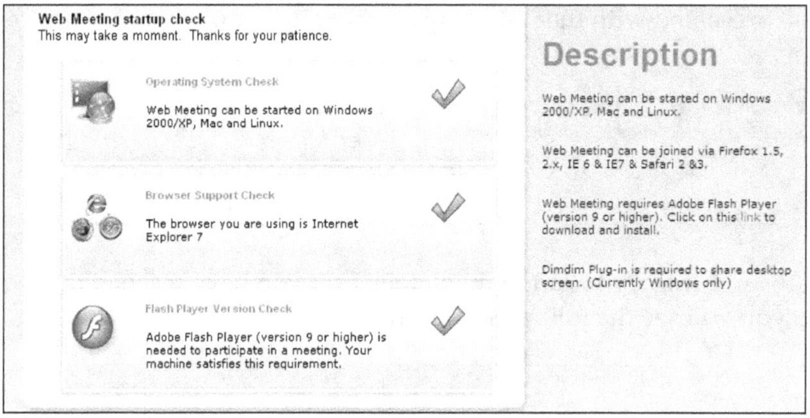

As you can see here, the browser check has determined the correct operating system, browser version, and flash software to make sure the meeting can take place. If you see any red cross marks, you will need to address these. It might be worth doing a test run with both parties before you proceed with an actual meeting.

Meeting facilities

Once you have passed the browser and flash requirements, the DimDim meeting User Interface will load on your desktop, as shown in the following screenshot. The screenshot shows that it has detected a working camera and therefore needs to allow this to be used.

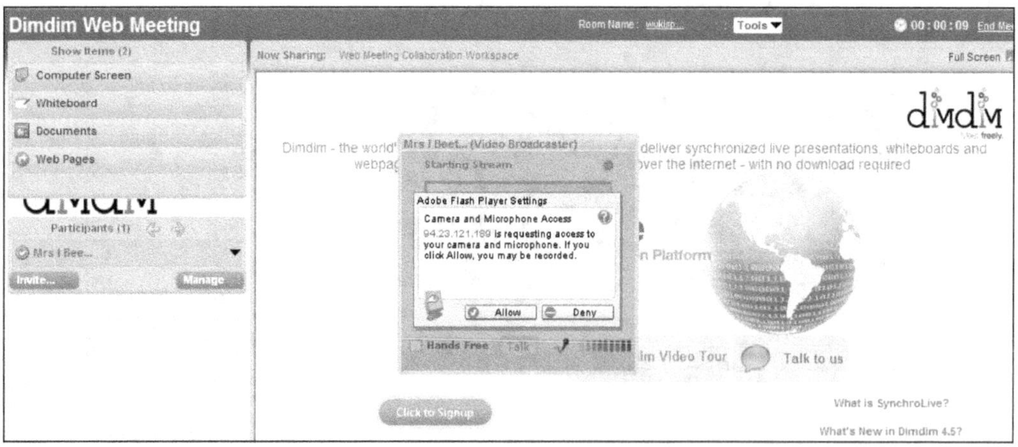

By allowing the webcam interaction, both you and your participants should see each other's face and be able to interact better. Your camera window can be moved to where it is convenient for you and the same for your participants. The video window is shown in the following screenshot and can be turned on and off as required.

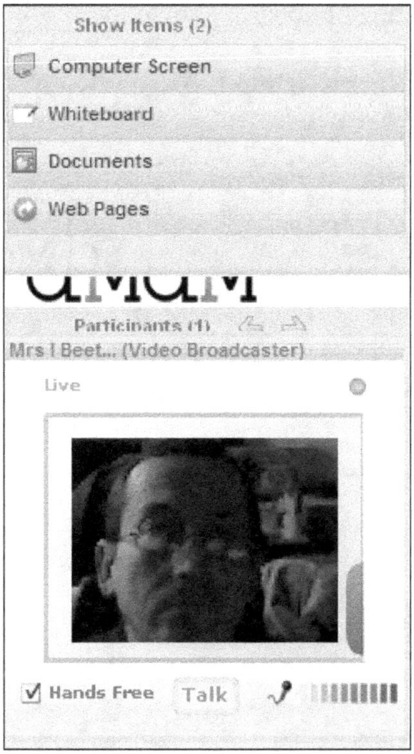

You can also see in this image the various resources that can be shared with users in the presentation, such as files and websites. You can also share your own desktop. This would be very useful in product design, as you may share some proprietary software system such as Desktop Pro.

Setting the meeting preferences

The bulk of the settings were made when you set up the meeting in your Moodle course, but you can also adjust them in the meeting itself. You might choose to modify some of the meeting functions and settings, such as extending the meeting. To do this, you need to select the meeting options, as shown in the following screenshot:

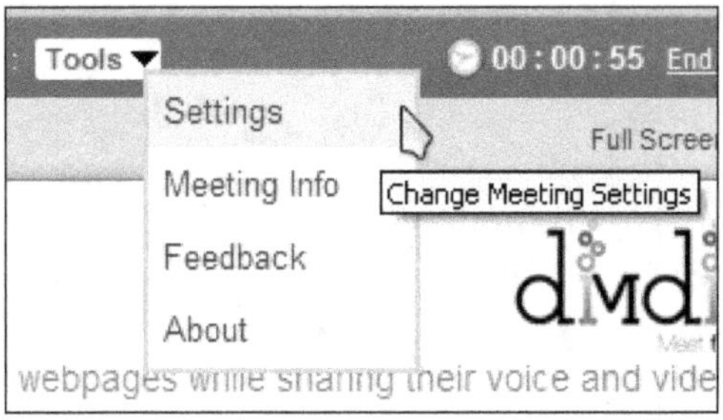

This will open a dialog window and allow you to change a few settings as shown in the following screenshot:

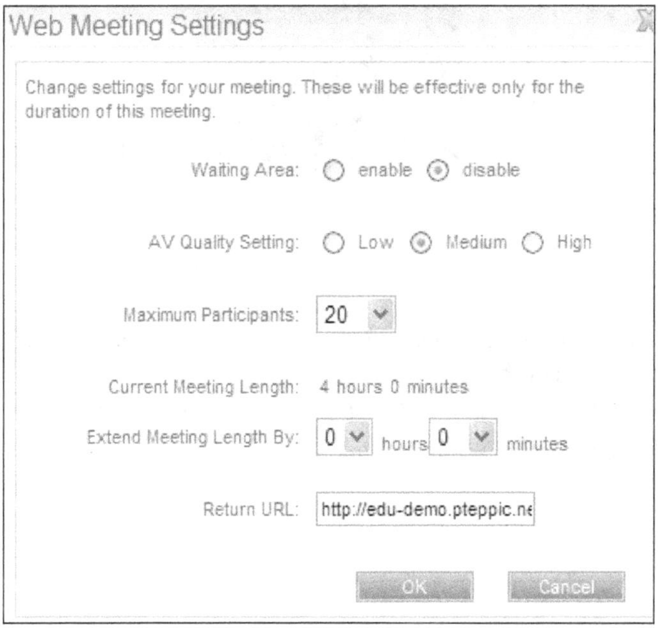

In this case, we can increase the numbers allowed in and change the video quality if their link is not fast enough.

Sharing ideas using the whiteboard

Now that the meeting is set up how you want it, you can begin sharing ideas and resources. The system comes with a built-in whiteboard that can be shared. The view that you have is the same for all other users, so it closely resembles your existing classroom setting. As you draw diagrams and notes on the whiteboard so that they can be viewed by your attendees, they can discuss the ideas and also draw on the board themselves. The whiteboard has most of the basic settings required such as text boxes and shapes, all of which can be modified in terms of size and color. The following screenshot shows this in operation:

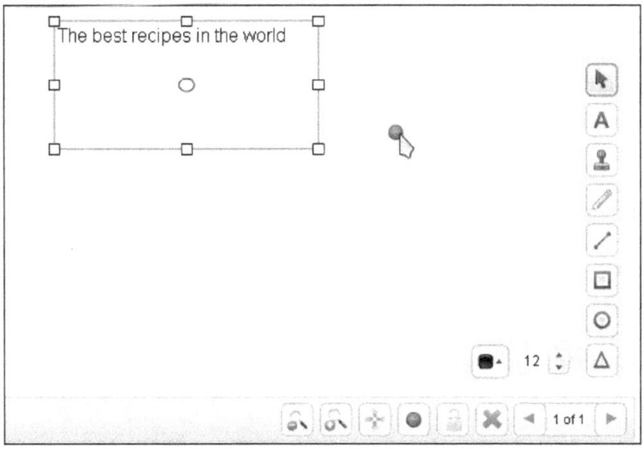

Sharing your desktop

If you need to show the attendees what you are working on in terms of your own desktop, you can share this with them as well. In most cases, you will need to download and install some software to allow this to take place. As shown here, you will be notified of this action. There are a number of products that can carry out this function such as ScreenToaster or Jing.

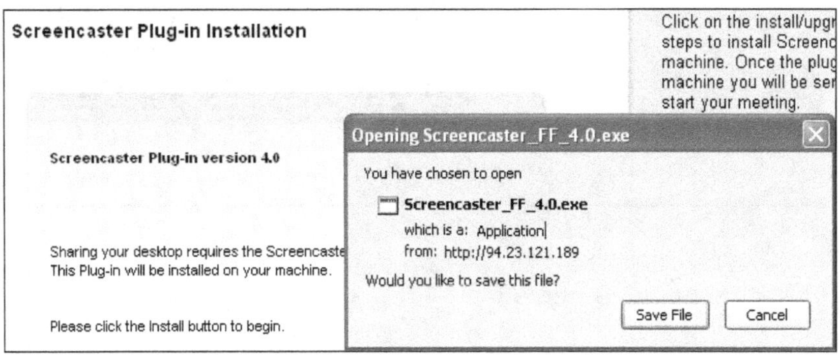

Once this has been enabled, the users can then see what you are working on and you can interact with them. This may be a useful way for local experts to give students some guidance on the best ways to use certain software products effectively, especially if you don't have the in-house expertise. The following screenshot shows you the students' view of a graphic design package:

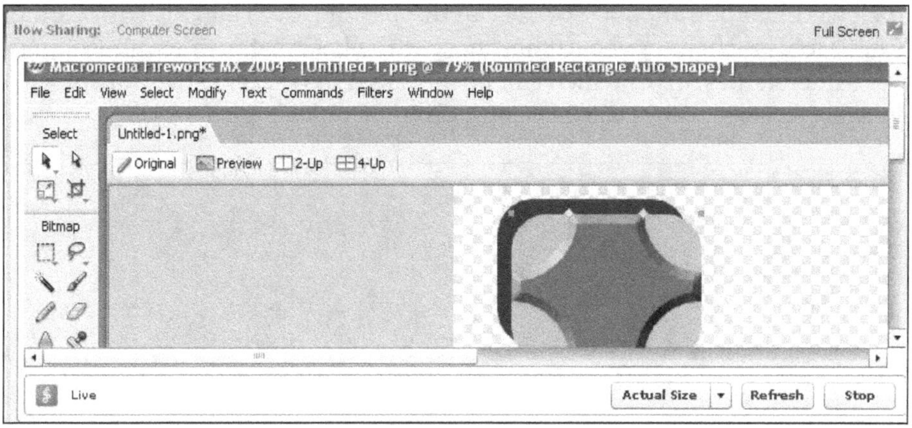

From the main menu, you can also share websites and presentations. In the following screenshot, the students are sharing and discussing the teacher's development of a presentation. This could equally be students pitching their ideas to local companies.

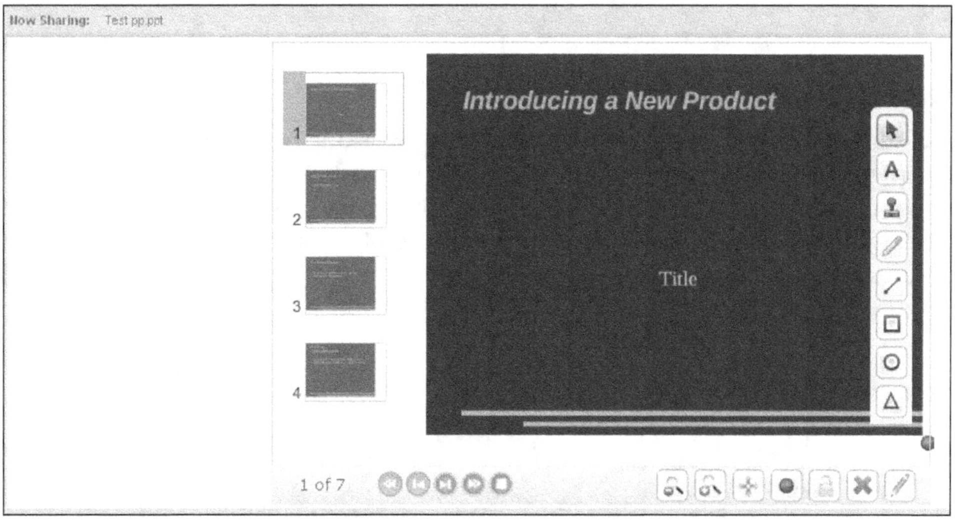

During the presentation, if it was a joint meeting, you could pass over the control of the presentation to someone else. This may be useful where vocational students are working collaboratively with mentors in companies locally. The following screenshot shows the option being enabled.

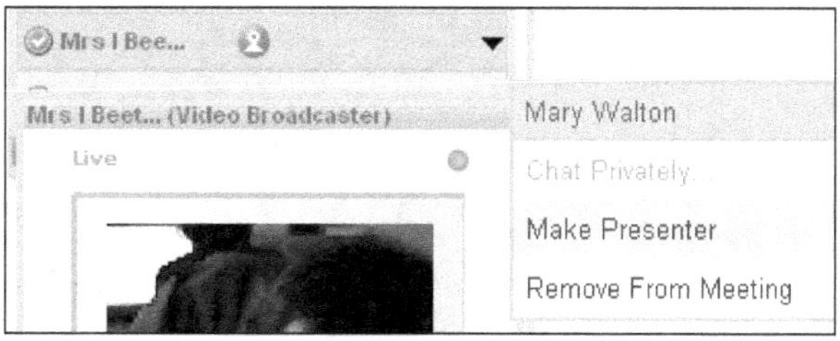

Students can also interact with emoticons and general feedback if they don't want to participate more verbally, as shown in the following screenshot:

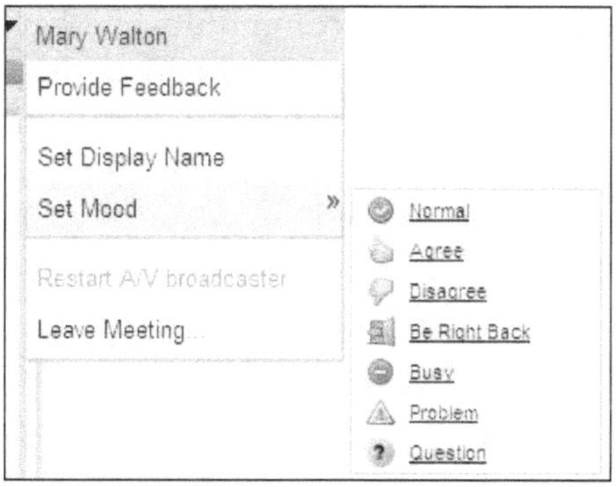

Reminding users about a meeting

There are a number of interactive software systems in the market, but DimDim is (for now) open source and has a module that ties it in closely with Moodle. When you create a meeting in a course, it automatically adds it to the course calendar and upcoming events so that students are reminded of the event. This is clearly shown in the following screenshot:

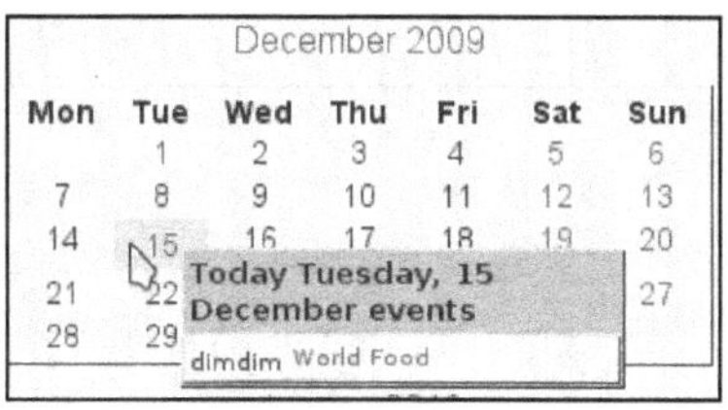

However, if you do need recordings to take place and have the budget, you might also consider something like Elluminate. Elluminate is a fully-functional web-meeting software that allows recordings and has many advanced features. Although it is not free and needs to be paid for, there is a Vroom, which allows five users for free and does integrate with Moodle.

`http://www.elluminate.com/`

`http://moodle.org/mod/data/view.php?d=13&rid=2198&filter=1`

Summary

There are a great number of tools incorporated into Moodle to allow your students to test the views and attitudes of their potential customers, as well as ways for you to gauge how well they are understanding the material via questionnaires and intermittent feedbacks. There are also some more powerful tools to allow you and your students to reach out into the local community and beyond and really share their ideas with a global audience. This type of interactivity really brings home to students the world at large and allows them some real-time experience of users and producers, so that they can understand their own work and the consequences of their choice to study design and technology better.

7

Adding Multimedia Resources to your Moodle Site

The construction of interesting courses using Moodle is greatly enhanced by the use of interactive materials and media files such as videos and audio sequences. Many students studying vocational subjects such as technology will likely be more kinesthetic learners and respond better to pictures and image sequences than to more didactic methods. Fortunately, Moodle is equipped to cater to these needs and can deliver media-rich content to students with varying levels of interactivity. Many of these resources are made available in self-contained packages, which will run inside Moodle and collect useful data about the students' responses and levels of interactivity. These packages are created as **Shareable Content Object Reference Model** (**SCORM**) packages—effectively, they are mini courses within courses. The SCORM packages can be used to enhance the learning within your courses to add extra detail, or they can be the whole course itself.

In this chapter, we will look at some of the available resources that can be added to your site such as those produced by government bodies and commercial companies. However, we will also look at how to make your own SCORM materials with free and open source options, as well as using the Lesson module to construct your own structured learning resources with media-rich content.

Using the Lesson module to construct media-rich content

The built-in Lesson module is a comprehensive learning package, which allows you to create media-rich content and structured learning in order to target specific learning outcomes. The package incorporates some of the power of quizzes and assignments, as well as the HTML capabilities of the resource creation aspects of Moodle. All of these elements can be constructed to create a sophisticated module for learning.

There are a great number of resources about this module on the Moodle site under docs. They can be found at `http://server6.moodle.com/en/Lesson_module`.

This module is also covered in previous Packt books in this series. However, in this example, we are going to create a short lesson to test the students' understanding of some concepts in Product Design. We will design a short lesson, which will test students' understanding of the process of product design by giving them a scenario where they are asked to design a product for a company.

Setting up a lesson in your course

The Lesson module is a core module in Moodle and therefore does not require any setup in terms of an administrator intervention. There are no additional settings at the site level and all of the required settings are carried out by staff at the course level.

The key consideration for this module, implied perhaps in the name, is planning. Just like any lesson that you deliver, there is a need for some detailed planning. What are the objectives of the lesson? What are the learning outcomes expected? What material is required to develop the learner's understanding? Once you have determined these requirements, you can then plan how to incorporate them into the lesson.

Lesson planning overview

As explained before, you need to create a plan for this lesson before you try to implement it. The key points, in terms of matching with the Lesson module's capabilities, are:

- An introduction, including how to use the lesson and what the learner will encounter, that is, quizzes or essays.
- A flow diagram of the steps (or branches) to move through the lesson. In some cases, you may require detailed tangent pages, if the learner gets a wrong answer.

- Testing stages at the end of each branch to check for understanding.
- A concluding page with further instructions or links to other learning resources.

Enabling a lesson in your course

The Lesson module is one of the many activities that are available in Moodle and accessible, as with other modules, by clicking the **Turn editing on** button. Once editing has been enabled, click on the **Add an activity** drop-down menu and choose the **Lesson** option, as shown in the following screenshot:

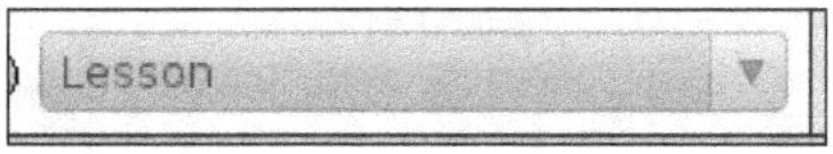

Changing the general settings for the lesson

Once you have enabled the new lesson, you will be presented with the main menu for changing all the options for the lesson. As with other modules, the first task is to choose the name and description for the module, as shown in the following screenshot.

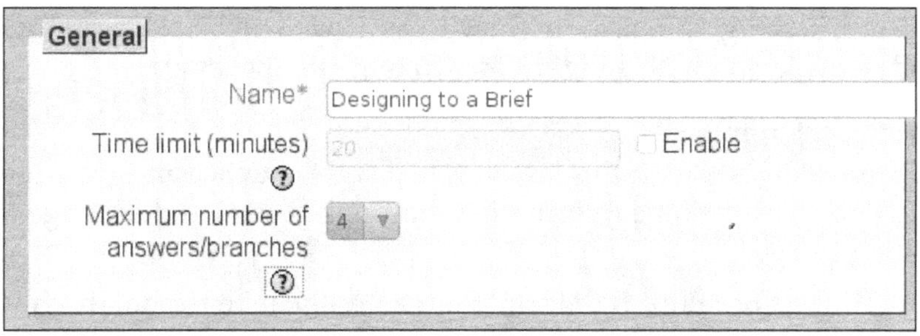

In this example, we are naming the lesson **Designing to a Brief** as that is the nature of the lesson. We'll explain more details to the students in the lesson itself, once we create the actual content a bit later in this section. If you want to test the students' ability to work with very tight time scales, you might enable the time for the lesson. In this example, we are using three key branches, so we have set the **Maximum number of answers/branches** to **4**. Depending on the plan you are working on, this can be adjusted to suit your needs.

Setting grading options for the lesson

The next set of options for the lesson relates to how the lesson will be graded. The options are shown in the following screenshot:

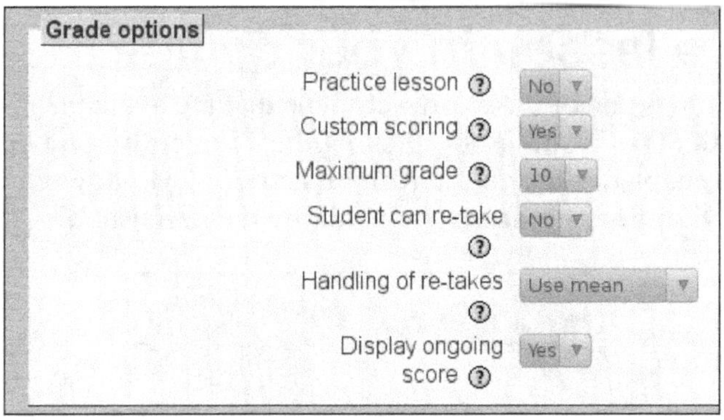

The **Grade options** for this lesson are set as follows:

- **Practice lesson**: In this case, we have set it to **No** as we want the scores to be stored with the lesson. If you do not want to keep the scores and want to use this as a drill exercise, set this to **Yes**.
- **Custom scoring**: We have set this to **Yes** as we will be using an essay at the end of the lesson with a high score to complete the lesson.
- **Maximum grade**: This can be set to 100.
- **Student can re-take**: If this lesson was just for practice and we wanted the students to learn some information thoroughly, we would change this setting to **Yes**.
- **Handling of re-takes**: If the students can re-take the lesson, the system would work out and display their mean. This can be changed to use the maximum score achieved.
- **Display ongoing score**: This gives students an overview of how they are doing, which is a useful motivator (hopefully) for them.

Setting the flow control of your lesson

The way that the lesson flows can be controlled with the set of options is shown in the following screenshot:

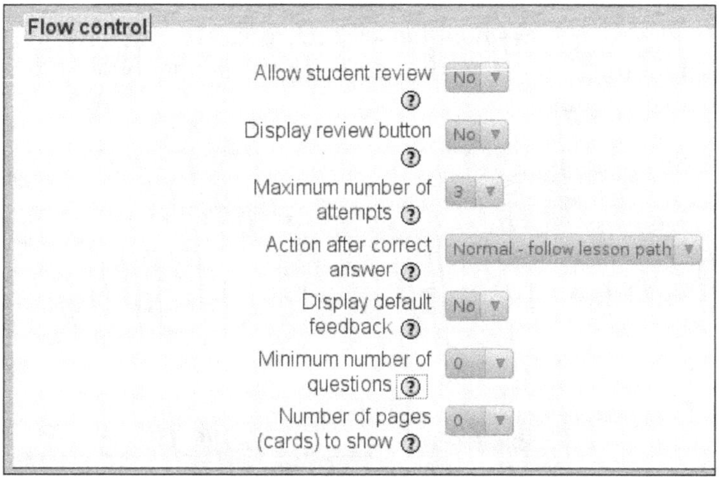

The **Flow control** options for this lesson are set as follows:

- **Allow student review**: This has been set to **No** as we do not require students to go back and change the answers that they got wrong. We are giving them more than one attempt so that they can learn for the next attempt.
- **Display review button**: No review has been allowed, so no button will appear.
- **Maximum number of attempts**: We have set our attempts to **3**, which is enough for this short exercise and enough to reinforce the learning that we desire.
- **Action after correct answer**: The students will be taken to the next page of questions. If we were using a flash-card approach to our lessons, we could allow a random sequence.
- **Display default feedback**: If set to **Yes**, the student will see generic feedback such as "Yes, that is correct". Otherwise, they will just move to the next question.
- **Maximum number of questions**: This setting relates to complex lessons with many branches. If set, students can take sub-sections of the lesson and get the correct grade, rather than getting 100 percent because they answered all the questions on that one section.

We are only using a few questions in this example, so we do not need to set the number of pages or cards to show.

Setting the lesson format for your lesson

The format of the lesson shows how the lesson is presented to the students when they are working through the questions and examples. The following screenshot shows the possible options:

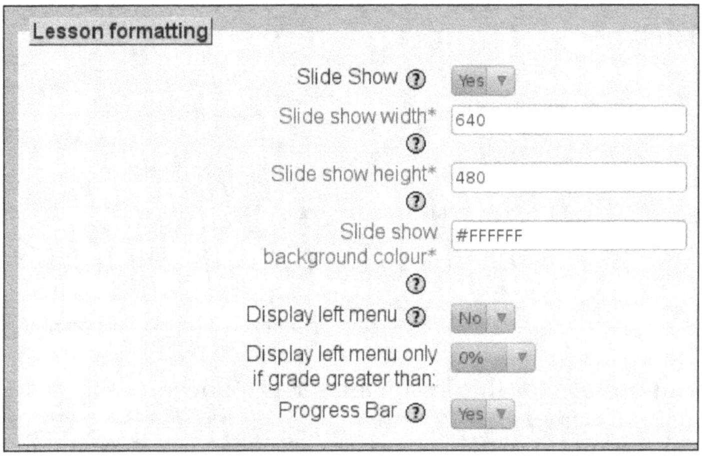

In the example we are creating, we would like to use the lesson as a slideshow, which we have enabled, and therefore, the settings relate to the appearance of this slideshow.

- **Slide show width**: The default here is **640** pixels. It is probably best to use the smallest possible screen width to allow students with older screens to not be disadvantaged.
- **Slide show height**: The default here of **480** has been chosen.
- **Slide show background color**: This is probably best left with the default **#FFFFFF**, which is white.
- **Display left menu**: If you have a very detailed and complex lesson, you might enable a left menu for navigation purposes. You can also specify the grade level for the menu to appear. If you set it to 80 percent, students will need to work through most of the lesson in order to make it appear, which may encourage them to work through the lesson.
- **Progress bar**: This shows a color block of how much the student has attempted and how much is left to do. Depending on your students, this could be motivational or a turn off.

Setting the access control for your lesson

The **Access control** settings for your lesson relate to a situation where you might wish to have more formal control over how and when the lesson is taken. The following screenshot shows the options:

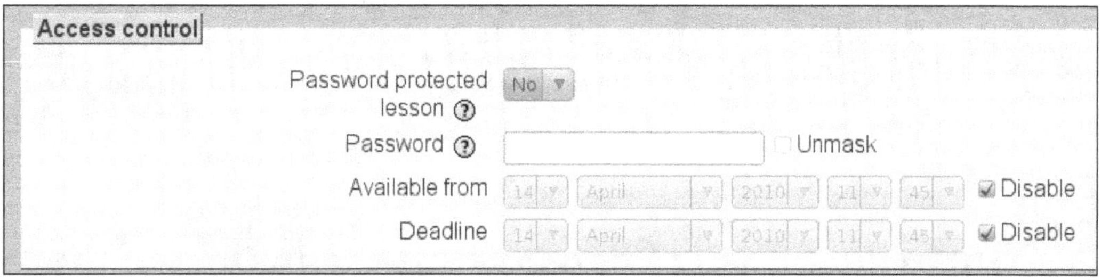

The settings here show that you can set the lesson to only be accessible with a password and also only within a range of dates.

Setting the dependency features of your lesson

The current version of Moodle, version 1.9, does not have built-in activity locking, which means that you cannot make material dependent on the completion of other courses or activities. However, this will be a feature of Moodle 2.0. The Lesson module does allow some level of activity locking by using the **Dependent on** feature, as shown in the following screenshot:

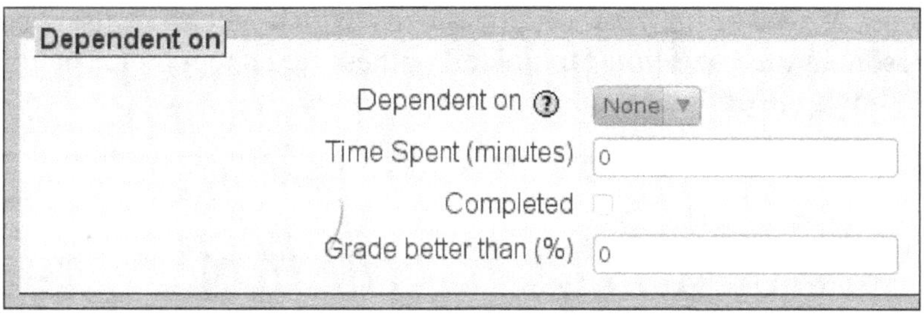

The **Dependent on** choice will relate to another lesson and these lessons will be displayed in the drop-down list. You might have a health and safety lesson, which students need to take before they can embark on their project, for example. The other settings here allow you to set how much time the students have spent on the dependent lesson and even a score they need to achieve. You can also set **Completed** so that the students can only embark on this lesson, once they have fully completed the dependent one.

Using a sample file in your course for instructions

In many cases, especially with visual subjects like Design Technology, it will be necessary to present some images, or video files to students to aide in their understanding. In this next set of options, as shown in the following screenshot, you can allow this material to be displayed to the students before and during the lesson.

This is one of the key features of the Lesson module and allows you to embed some media content into the lesson to enhance the learning experience. For example, you might have a video of someone carrying out some welding and you can then have a series of safety questions relating to the video throughout the lesson itself. Students can refer to the video, if they are unsure. This method will ensure that the students have maximum level of input—visual, audio, and text-based for their learning.

Linking your lesson to other course activities

As with the dependency on other lessons shown previously, you can also link the lesson to other activities in the course. You might have some detailed web pages and web links, as well as information documents, which will assist users before and after the lesson. In this case, you can link all of these items together. The following screenshot shows the options available:

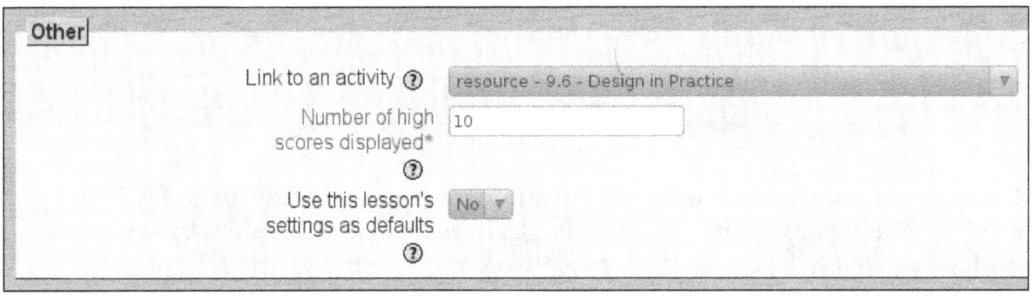

In the example lesson here, we are linking this lesson to an activity in the course, which gives students some more detail about what is required in creating a design. It is hoped that this will help them when they are determining some of the questions in the lesson relating to a design brief from a possible client. We could link it to any other activity in the course such as a quiz or a forum, if required.

Once you save all of these settings, the lesson will be ready to be used in your course.

Creating the lesson structure

In this example lesson, we are creating a quite basic lesson with three main branching questions. A diagram for the lesson will look like the following image:

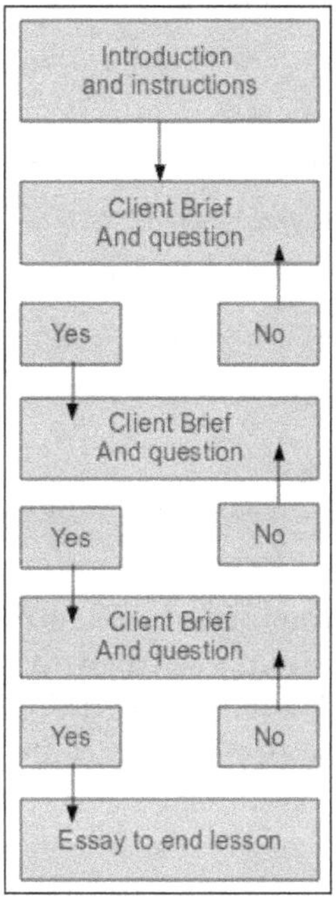

This shows a quite simple linear lesson, but depending on what you are trying to teach, you can have some very complex structures with many branches and sub-branches, much as you would have in a real class-based lesson.

Adding questions and branches to your lesson

Using the previous diagram as a guide, we will need to add a series of questions to our lesson and these can be created as one single branch of questions. If we create a branch for all of the questions, it is easier to organize the content and see the flow of the lesson. Once you click on the lesson to create the content, you will see the main configuration, as shown in the following screenshot:

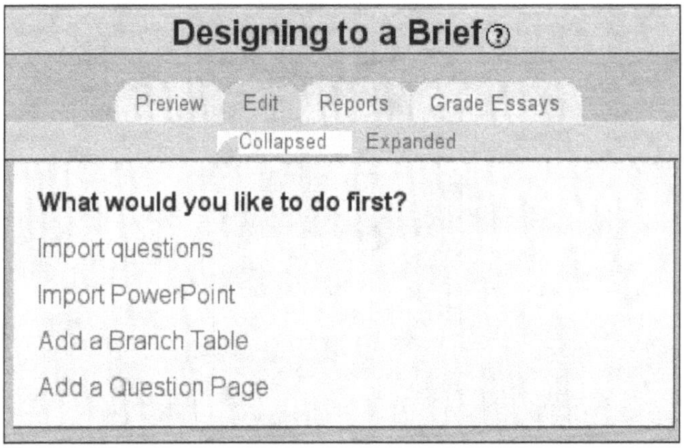

The first two options here allow the import of pre-made materials—either questions from Moodle itself or an other system, or PowerPoint slides, though currently only very simple PowerPoint 2003 slides will work. In our worked example, we are going to create the content and the first operation is to create the structure by adding a branch.

Adding a branch to your lesson

By clicking on the **Add a Branch Table** link, you will be presented with the following menu:

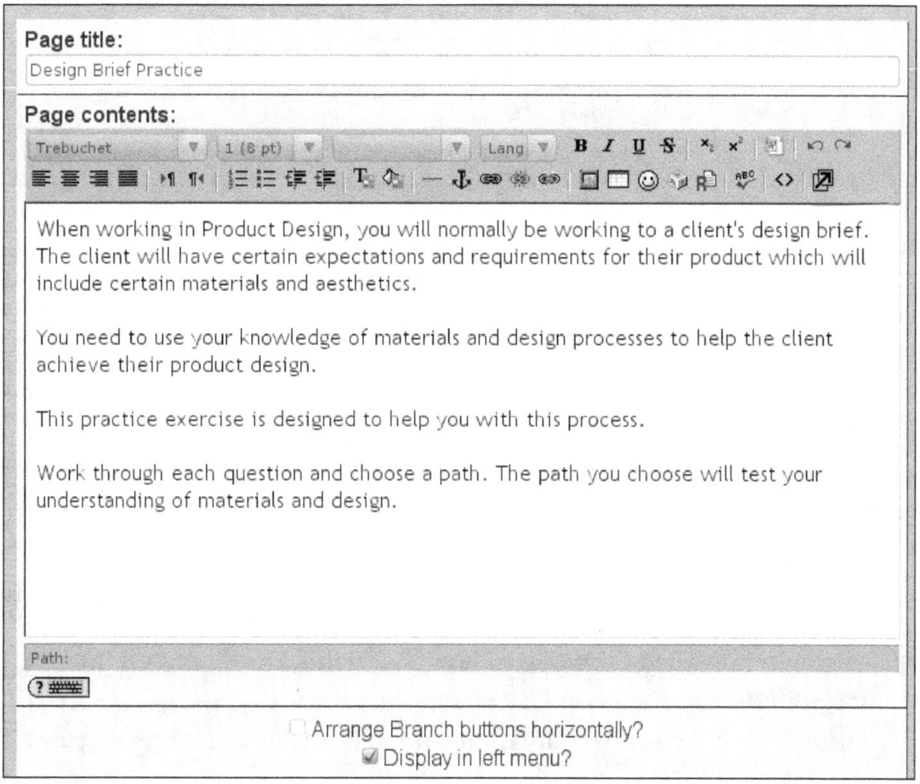

In the example here, and following our plan, we are including an overview of the lesson and some objectives. We are keeping the default option of vertical buttons and allowing any menu items to be displayed on the left. Following the **Page contents** screen, we can then set some basic questions to follow on from this screen. As we have not set the question pages yet, we need to save this page and then add some question pages. We can come back in a moment to work out the flow of questions through the lesson.

Adding question pages to your lesson

When you click on the **Add a Question Page** link from the main menu, you will see that there are several types of question pages that can be added. These are shown in the following screenshot:

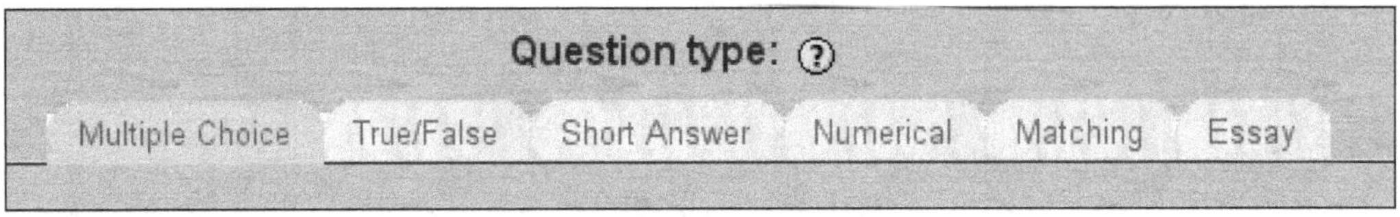

The type of question page you choose will depend on what you are trying to achieve, but the six types here should cover most situations. Each question can have a default, "Correct" or "Incorrect" response, but can also jump to another page. This makes the questions very powerful, as it allows you to reinforce responses with additional learning.

- **Multiple Choice**: Students are presented with a number of choices. There can be one or multiple correct answers, and each answer could jump to another question page or branch of questions.
- **True/False**: Students are presented with two buttons.
- **Short Answer**: This is the most involved and powerful of the response types. It can be used to match expressions and sayings and can be set for case sensitivity. Detailed examples of how to use this type are listed under the help button.
- **Numerical**: Answers here are numbers, so this is useful for testing and understanding something like conversions such as, "How many liters is 6 gallons?".
- **Matching**: You can use this to test students' understanding of for instance tools, that is, "Match the following tools with the job they would be used for". Students would then see a number of tools and jobs and need to match them up.
- **Essay**: The essay gives the students a box to type in and the answer has to be marked by the teacher.

For our example, we are going to have a number of multiple choice questions and then an essay question to complete the lesson.

Adding a multiple choice question page

The multiple choice question page has a field to name the question and a description field to enter the question itself. Following these screens, you are asked to present the possible answers with their corresponding actions. For all of your answers, we will award one mark for a correct response and zero for an incorrect response. The response will also determine where the student goes next. The following screenshot shows the answer boxes:

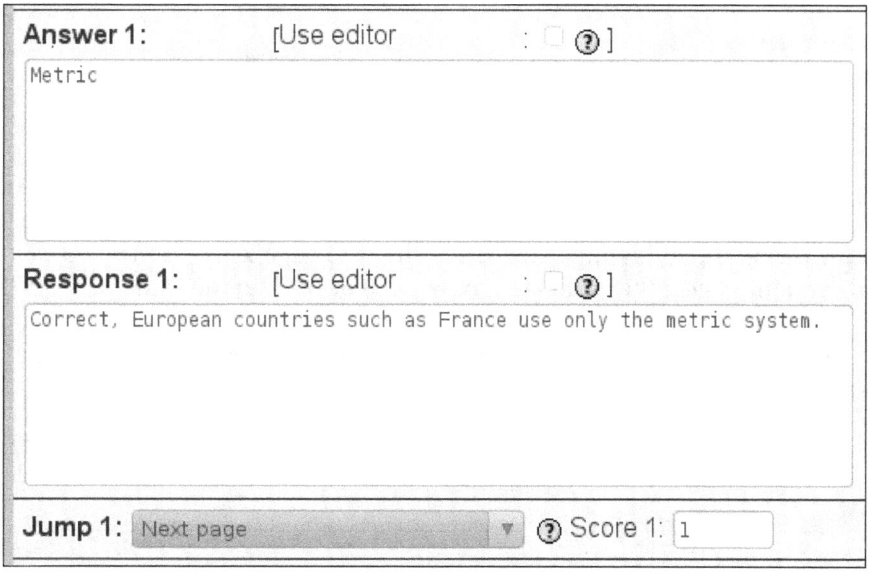

In the example shown here, for a correct response, the student gets one mark and is then taken to the next page after seeing the feedback, **Correct, European countries such as France use only the metric system**. The wrong answer will take them back to the question page until they get it right.

We add our series of question pages, and in the last page that we create, we choose an essay question and ask the students to describe how they will market the product they have been asked to design. For the essay, we will assign a grade of seven, which means that they have three questions with one mark each and one essay worth seven marks for a total of ten. The following screenshot shows the layout of the lesson:

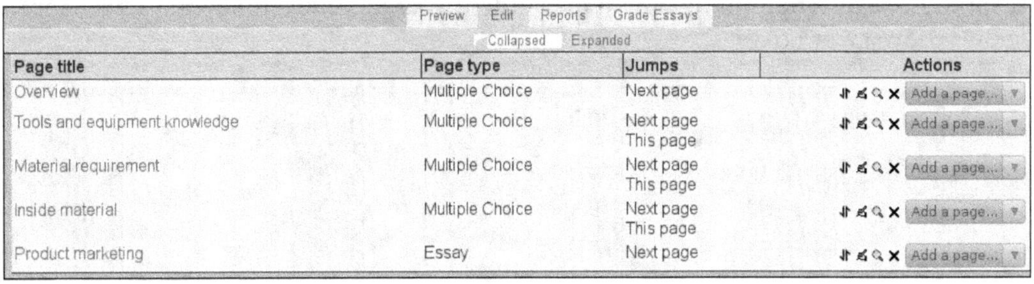

As you can see in the following screenshot, the first page leads to the next page, and each subsequent page either leads to a new page or back to the same page, if the answer is wrong. If you click on the expanded view, you can see that for each page, you can add further pages, branches, or clusters, depending on how much detail is required.

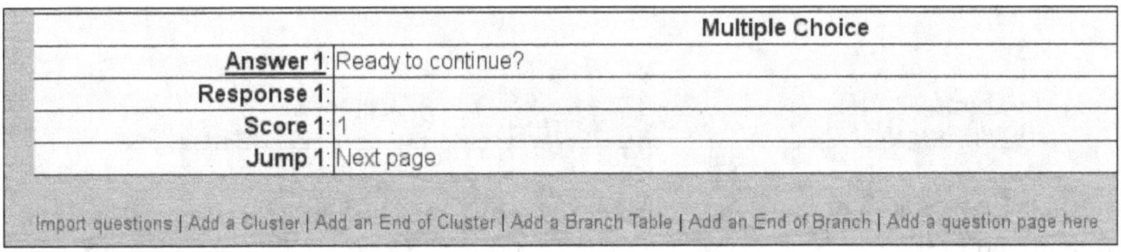

Enabling the editor on questions to add highlights and images

As indicated previously, you can add some additional rich media files to your questions as well as use the HTML editor to highlight and change text size and colors. In order to do this, you need to enable the HTML edit function on each question. This is a simple checkbox, as shown in the following screenshot:

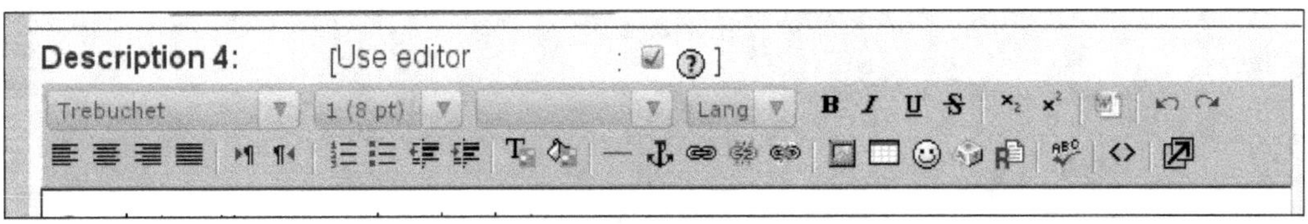

Students' view of the lesson

Once you have created your lesson, it is ready for the students. Once they click on the **Lesson** link, they will see your introductory text, as well as a series of navigation buttons. As we have enabled the progress bar, this will also be visible, as shown in the following screenshot:

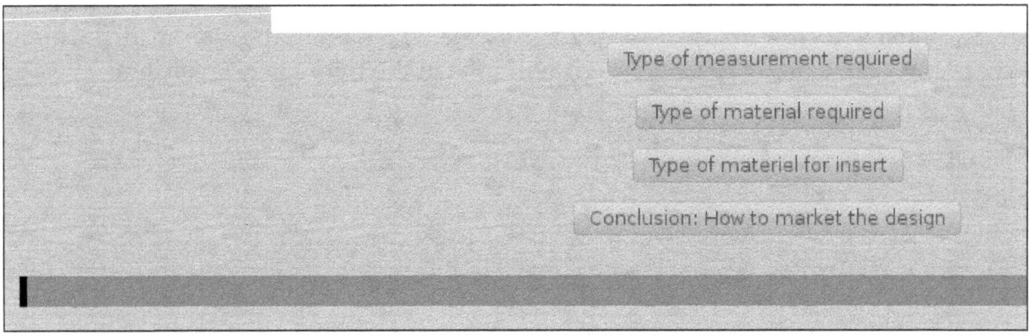

The information above the interactive buttons here tells the students what the lesson is about and asks them to start with the **Type of measurement required** button. The rest of the lesson will follow through in a linear fashion. Each question will give them feedback or direct them to the next question, depending on their answer, and the final question will ask them to write and submit an essay. The students will then be presented with a summary telling them that their final grade will depend on the marks awarded for their essay.

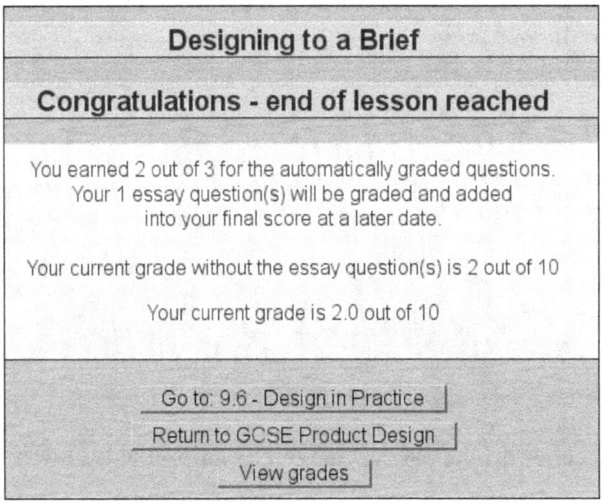

The message also tells the student that this lesson is linked to another activity, which they can now move to, they can return to the course, or check all of their grades in the gradebook.

Marking the essay and giving students feedback

Once the students have completed the lesson, you will need to give marks to their essay. When you click on the lesson, you will see who has completed the lesson and what essays are waiting to be marked, as shown in the following screenshot:

You can click on the link to the essay to mark it and once you have marked it, you can click on **Email graded essays** to let the student know that it has been marked. The marking window will have a basic box to enter your feedback and a drop-down list for the marks awarded.

Checking the reports for the lesson

Once all the students have completed the lesson and submitted their attempts, you can check on the reports section of the Lesson module to see their overall performance and any details relating to each question. The following screenshot shows the report main window:

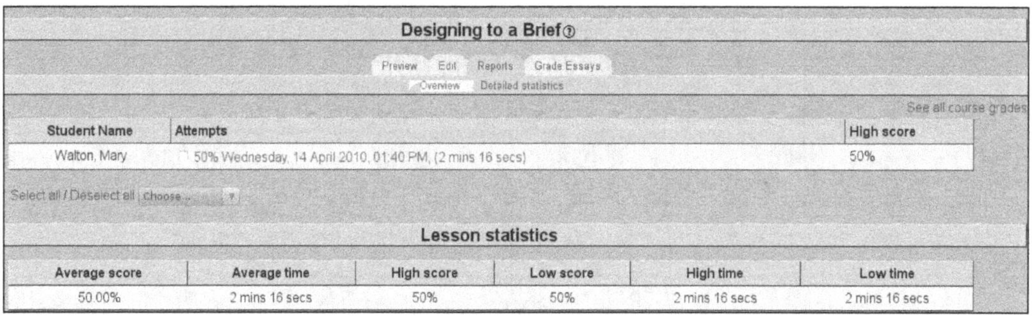

The report shows each student's score as well as some basic statistics and averages of the lesson itself.

Checking the detailed statistic report for a lesson

By clicking on the **Detailed statistics** link for the report, you can see information about each question in the lesson. An example is shown in the following screenshot:

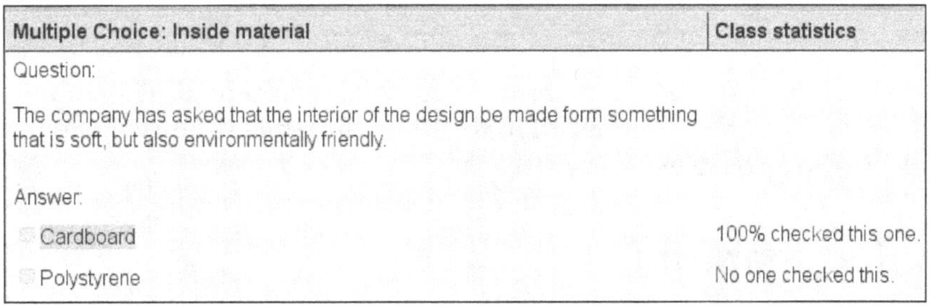

Here we can see what most students have chosen in the lesson. We can use this as a powerful diagnostic tool to test the way we are teaching. If all the students consistently miss a vital piece of information, we need to adjust how we teach this information to make sure that they learn it more effectively.

Distributing interactive materials using the SCORM standard

Most of the interactive materials available for VLEs are developed and distributed as SCORM packages. SCORM is an e-learning material built to specific standards, which means that it can be distributed and therefore, work on a number of platforms such as personal computers or, in our case, a VLE-like Moodle. The packages are usually created as ZIP files, which can be uploaded to your Moodle site and are then worked on interactively by your users. Packages that are SCORM 2004-compliant will also allow students to track their work in detail and return to areas that they were having problems with so that they have the time to reflect.

Adding free resources to your site

For this example, we will use a set of government-based resources. The materials are available from the **National Learning Network** (**NLN**), which is maintained by the UK government and is a repository of e-learning materials that can be used by authorized institutions. Your organization will need to apply for an access key to use the material but it will then allow you to embed these materials into your courses. There is also an add-on for Moodle called Noodle, which will add a link to the site in your resources section. Once this has been enabled, you will see the NLN link appear in the resources section. In order to access this material, you will need to turn editing on.

This will enable the course editing and the NLN link will then appear in the resources, as shown in the following screenshot:

Once you select the NLN learning objects, you will be presented with an interface to search for and add some materials to. In the following screenshots, we are adding some materials to a construction course.

Choosing material

The first task is to search for the materials you require. In order to achieve this, you will need to check the site's resources. This is achieved by clicking on the **Browse the NLN Materials** button, as shown in the following screenshot:

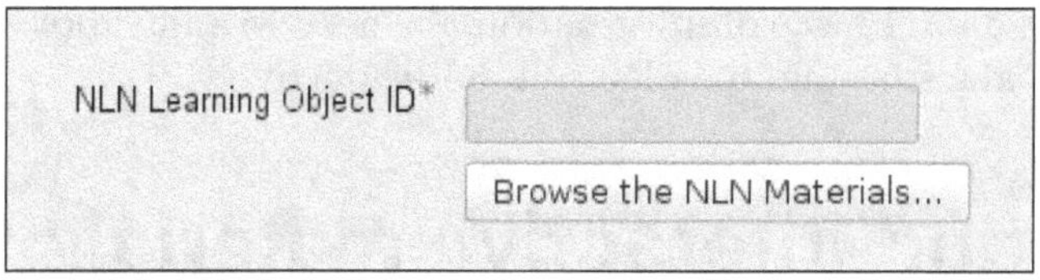

When you click on this button, it will load the NLN interface as a pop-up menu, where you can select the sub-menus that are relevant, as shown in the following screenshot:

From the previous screenshot, we can then check for some vocational items that would be suitable for the course we are teaching. The following screenshot shows some materials related to construction:

The material is available in this case as Level 2 and Level 3 options, which equates in the UK to GCSE A*-C (Level 2) and A Level (Level 3). We are interested in some material on construction for level 2 students, so we select some material, as shown in the following screenshot:

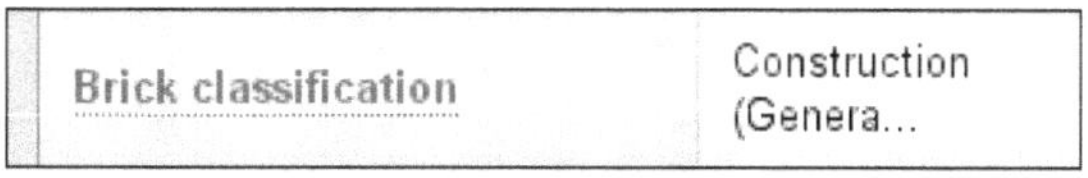

The following screenshot then gives us some more details about the material that we have chosen:

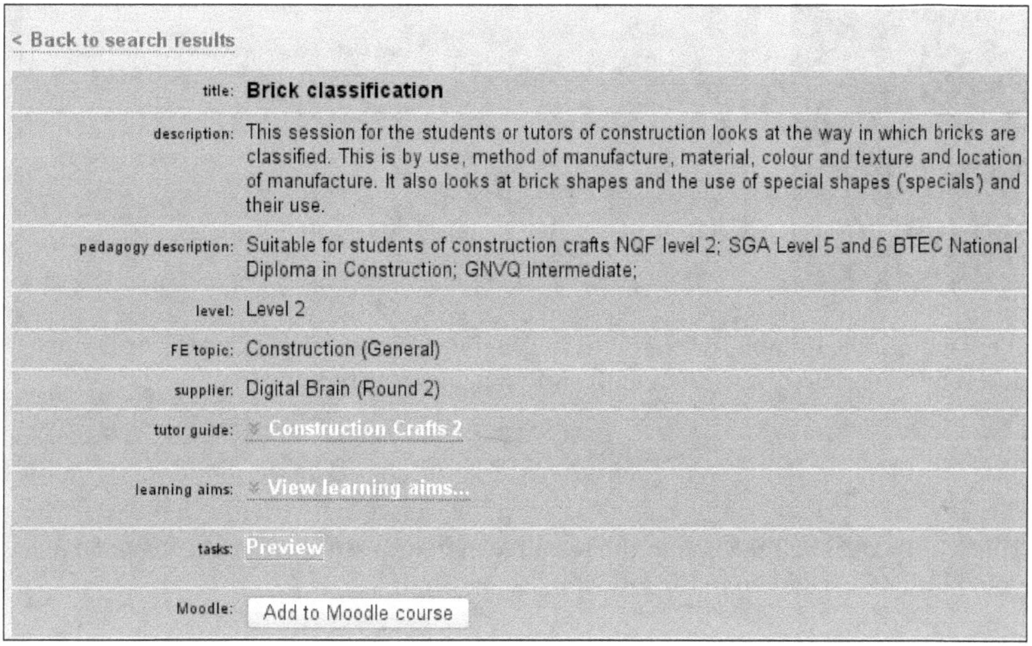

The previous screenshot shows that we can preview this material to check its suitability, as shown in the following screenshot:

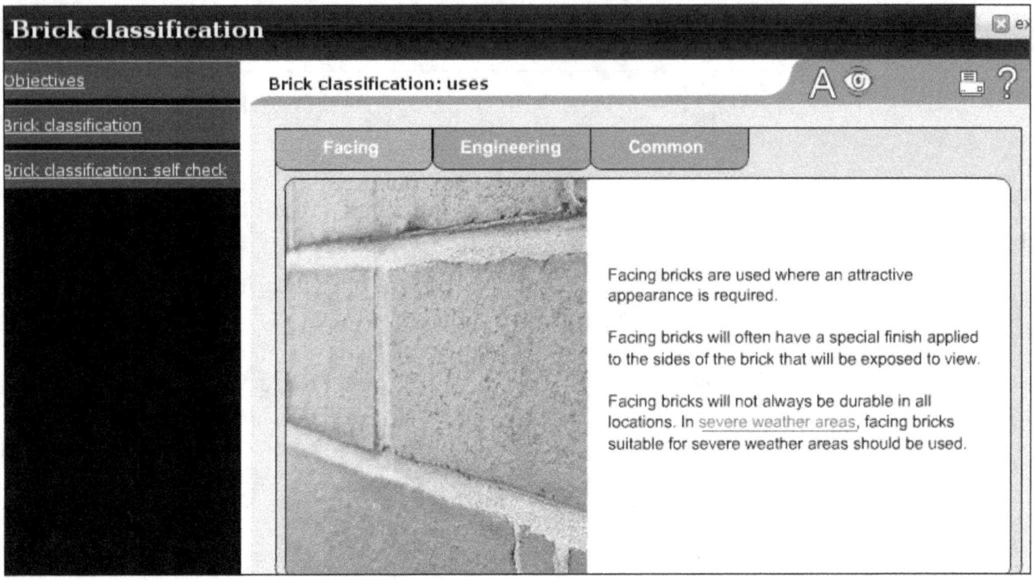

If the material is suitable, once you have previewed it, you can select the option to add it to your course, as shown in the following screenshot:

This will then embed the link to the resource in your course and make it available to your students, as shown in the following screenshot:

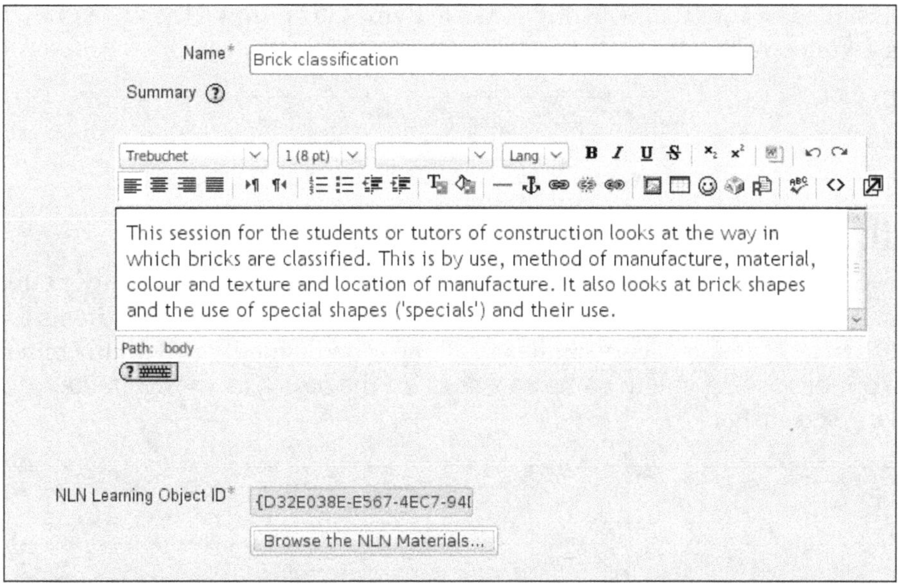

As you can see in the previous screenshot, the **Summary** and the **Name** fields are automatically filled in by the link and the ID is also populated for the course.

International repositories: Adding Ariadne-based resources to your site

The Ariadne project, as quoted in their website `http://www.ariadne-eu.org`, is as follows:

> *A European Association open to the World, for Knowledge Sharing and Reuse. The core of the ARIADNE infrastructure is a distributed network of learning repositories.*

For using their material in your own website, they have provided an add-on tool, similar to the Noodle tool just discussed, called the **Global Learning Objects Brokered Exchange(GLOBE)** add-on. The instructions for installing this tool can be found at:

```
http://www.ariadne-eu.org/index.php?option=com_content&task=view&id=5
0&Itemid=80#
```

Once installed, it adds a new listing to the activities drop-down menu, as shown in the following screenshot:

Adding Ariadne materials to your course

When you click on the drop-down menu and choose the **GLOBE Learning Object** option, it will take you to the menu to configure the object and link the items to your course. The menu is very similar to all the Moodle modules with the initial screen options asking you to name and describe the object, as shown in the following screenshot:

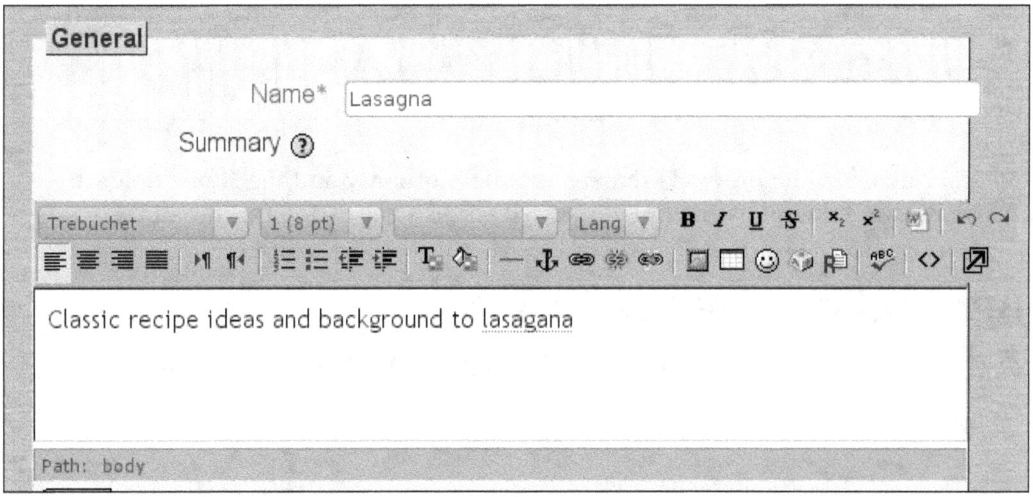

In the previous example, we are adding some links to material that will help students understand the history and relevance of lasagna as a dish. This contextual information will help them to make more authentic dishes and to understand how lasanga fits into a culture.

Adjusting the window size and options

The next set of menu options relates to how the window appears to the user once they click on the link you have created for the repository. Most of the options will be familiar to you by now, such as whether or not to open a new window or use the existing window. Other available options include:

- **Force download**—Whether to make users download the resource rather than opening it immediately.
- **Show navigation**—Whether to use a built-in frame for the resource. This may not work in some custom themes so it may be best to leave the default.
- **Window resizing and scroll bar**—Whether to allow users to resize the object and it if is a big object, to allow scroll bars.
- **Show bars**—Whether or not to show the links or menus associated with the object or other tools. These may be distracting, but could be helpful for navigation in complex objects.
- **Screen size**—Here you can change the default values for the height and width of the displayed screen. The default values are 640 by 480 pixels.

Choosing material for groups or groupings on the course

Once these settings have been decided, the final set of options relates to whether or not the material is going to be used for a group of students or a sub-group (grouping). The following screenshot shows the possible options:

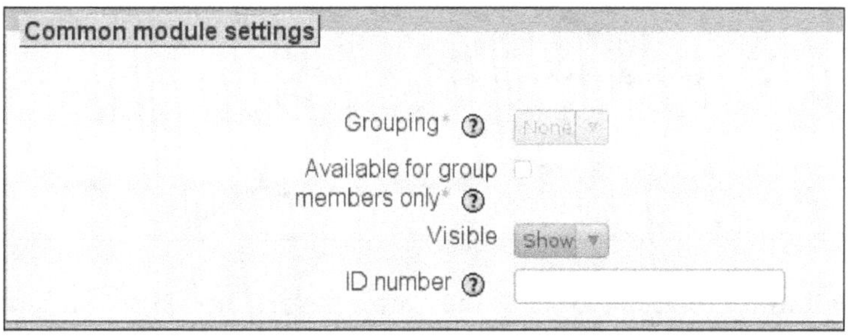

If the groups have been established in this course, then they can be selected from the drop-down list and the additional checkbox can be checked to make it visible only to this group.

Choosing the repository

When all of the settings have been chosen in terms of display and presentation of the repository material, the material itself can now be searched for and added to the course. The initial option window is shown in the following screenshot:

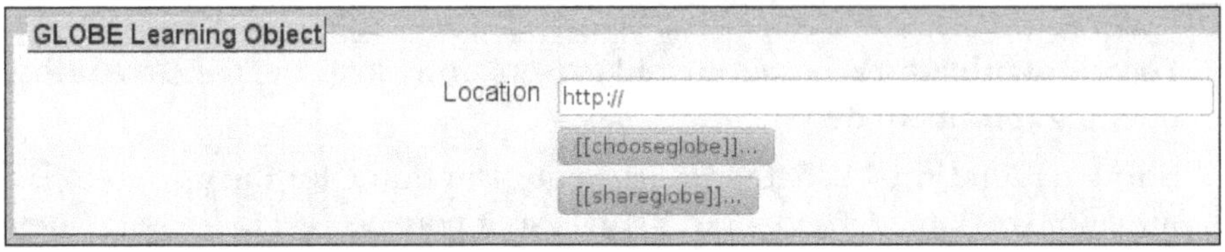

In the previous screenshot, you can see that there is a **[[chooseglobe]]...** button. This will open an additional search screen, as shown in the following screenshot:

In this instance, we are using the GLOBE repositories in order to search for some supporting material. If successful, the search should present some useful results, as shown in the following screenshot.

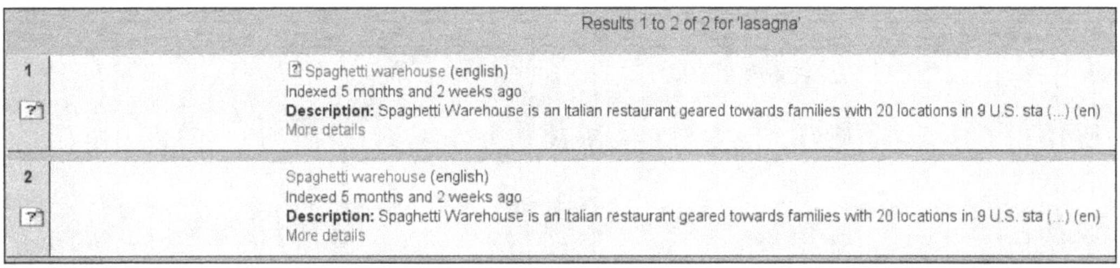

The resources can be checked to see if they are relevant, and if so, added to the course. The following screenshot shows the options available for each resource:

When you hold the mouse over the icons, it will display the available options. The options, from top to bottom, are to view the data, download the data, or as shown here, import the data into your Moodle course.

When you choose to import the data, it will create a link to the repository and display this link in the main menu window option, as shown in the following screenshot:

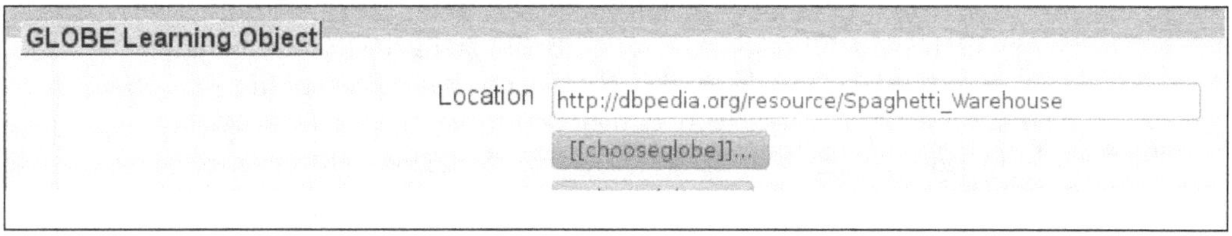

The repository can now be saved and added to the course for students to use.

Viewing the GLOBE repository material

Once the repository has been found and linked to your course, students can access the material and use it for their research and reference. Depending on the type of material chosen, the students will now be able to view or store the data. In this case, the link is to a website discussing the world's largest lasagna.

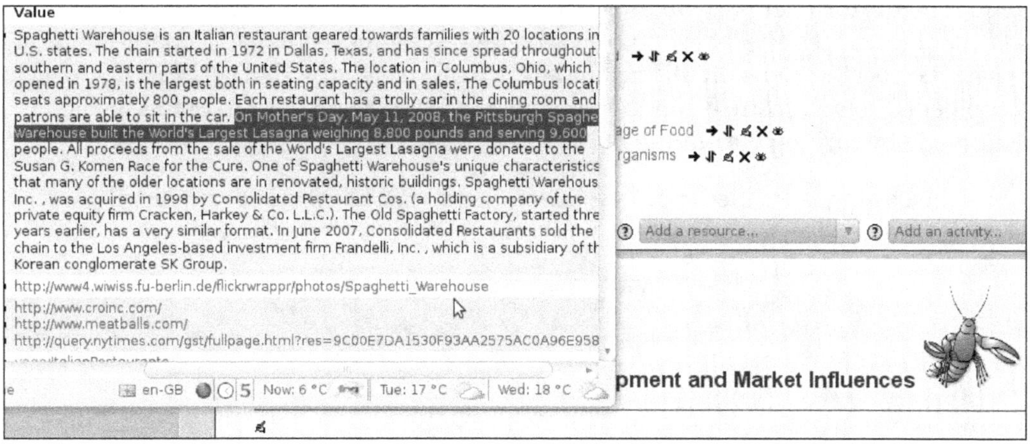

Alternative repositories

If your government does not provide repositories of pre-made SCORM resources, you can organize your own material by creating directories, as discussed in the introductory chapter. There are also other modules that you can add to your site such as MrCute or MrCute Jr, which allow some level of organization.

> The release of Moodle 2.0 (currently scheduled for July 2010) will include the Moodle community hub, which will be a shared repository of Moodle courses that the other members of the community can use. More detailed information about this can be found at `http://docs.moodle.org/en/Community_hub`.
>
> You can also check the following links for information on MrCute and MrCute Jr:
>
> `http://moodle.org/mod/data/view.php?d=13&rid=1237&filter=1`
>
> `http://moodle.org/mod/data/view.php?d=13&rid=2540&filter=1`

Adding proprietary SCORM sources to your site

There are many SCORM resources which are free to use, but they may not meet the requirements for your particular course as they tend to be quite generic. There are also paid resources available and often referenced by the examination bodies that create the specifications. In this instance, the material is provided as a ZIP file, which is uploaded to your course and then linked as a SCORM object. To do this, switch to edit mode by turning the editing on.

Once the editing is enabled, you can then select the SCORM resource from the **Activities** drop-down menu, as shown in the following screenshot:

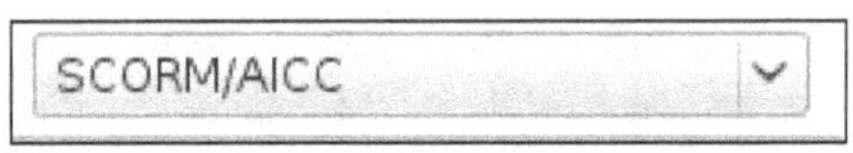

This will open the interface to configure the SCORM module.

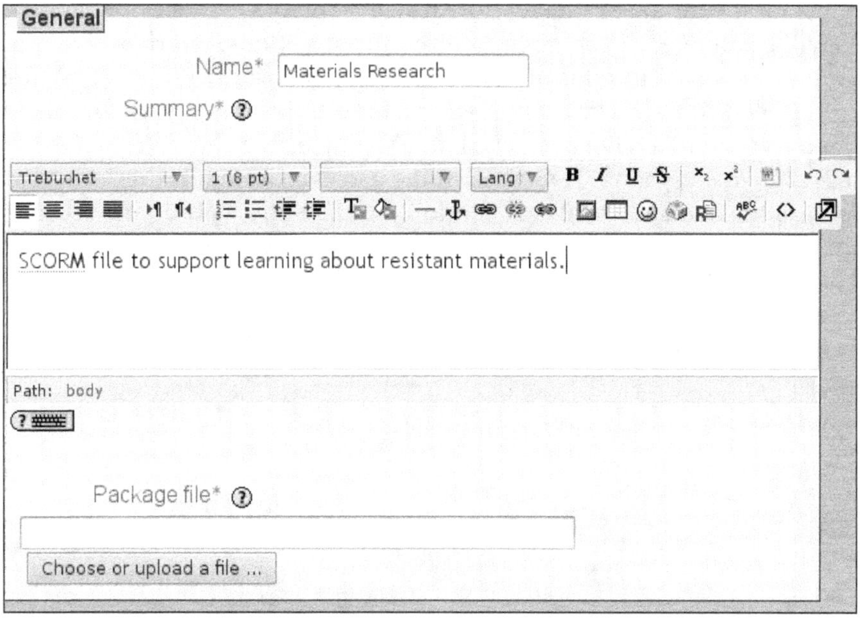

After naming the material and giving a brief summary, you can then upload the SCORM file in order to be able to choose it from the file link window, as shown in the following screenshot:

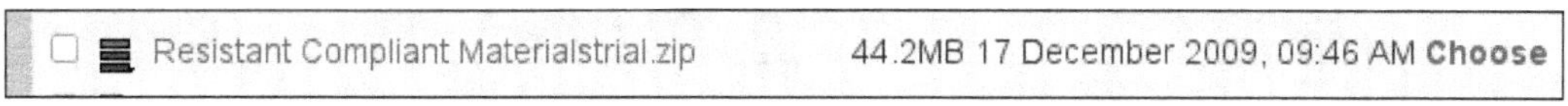

Choosing the correct settings

The settings for the module relate to how it will be displayed and how many attempts will be allowed. There are more advanced options, but these are more than enough for most situations. In the following screenshot, a number of three attempts has been chosen. The default values for grading, saving the highest grade with a maximum of 100, have been chosen. The **Stage size** shown refers to how the resource is displayed when it is viewed in the user's browser. In this case, it will fill 100 percent of the available browser window horizontally, and occupy 800 pixels vertically. The stage size can be adjusted for situations where older monitors might be used and lower resolutions are the default setting.

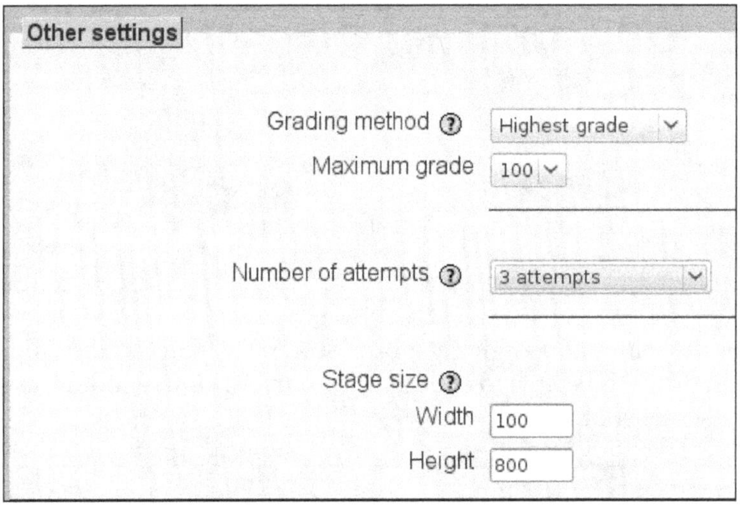

The grading method you choose will depend on how you are using the module in terms of assessment. In most cases, the highest grade, in this example of three attempts, should give a good indication of the learner's understanding.

Grading students' attempts at the SCORM material

As the students work through the SCORM material, they will have an indication of what they have completed and what is still to be done. The following screenshot shows the view a student will have to track their progress:

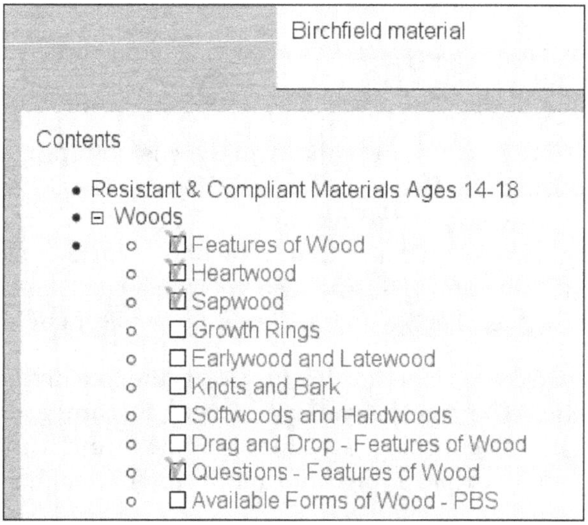

Staff can check the actual marks obtained by the students by clicking on the module itself and looking at the reports of actual users. The report will show a student's progress on each section, as shown in the following screenshot:

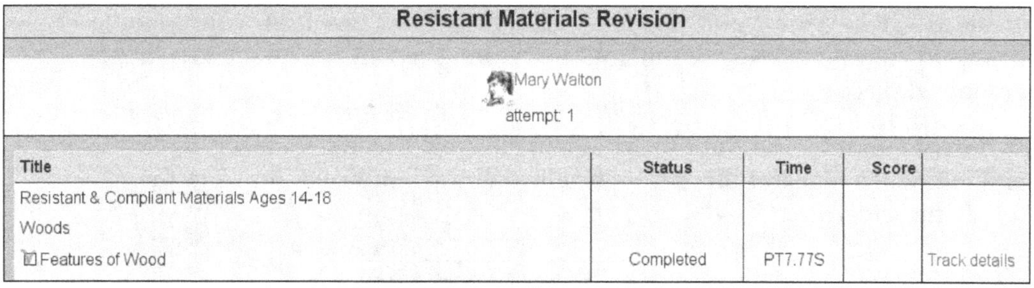

By clicking on the **Track details** link, it is possible to get more details on the student's attempts at each element.

Once the student has completed all the sections, an overall grade will appear in the gradebook. This will be discussed in more detail in *Chapter 9, Tracking Progress with the Gradebook*.

Creating your own learning materials using myUdutu

There are great number of resources on the Internet—both free and paid, which are more than suitable for most requirements. These are:

- `http://www.sharewareconnection.com/education.htm` (Free)
- `http://www.birchfield.co.uk/learning-platform` (Paid for)

However, it may be that in your particular case there is nothing that exactly meets your needs as there are rarely free resources specifically for Design Technology. In this case, the simple answer is to create your own learning materials. The nature of technology as a taught subject dictates that some of the learning elements will be very specific to your locale or region and also you can create some of the material incorporating your own learners, which makes it far more engaging.

One very useful application to use for this process is the free online e-learning creation tool **myUdutu**. The great advantage in using this application, apart from the cost savings, is that it can be incorporated into Moodle through an add-on module, which makes it far more flexible. More information about this tool can be found at:

`http://moodle.org/mod/data/view.php?d=13&rid=888&filter=1`

Creating an account

Once you register on the myUdutu website, you can import the material you create as ZIP files into your Moodle course, or you can link from your Moodle course to your myUdutu account and therefore, keep all your materials in one organized place.

In order to set up an account for yourself, navigate to the site at `www.myudutu.com` and follow the registration process by clicking the button, as shown in the following screenshot:

Follow the set of instructions and create an account for yourself. It is beyond the scope of this book to go into a great deal of detail with this application, but the following exercise will give you a taste of what can be achieved very easily and quickly.

Creating content

For this example, we are going to create a generic health and safety learning module for our construction course. Once you have created your account and logged in, you will see the basic myUdutu interface, as shown in the following screenshot:

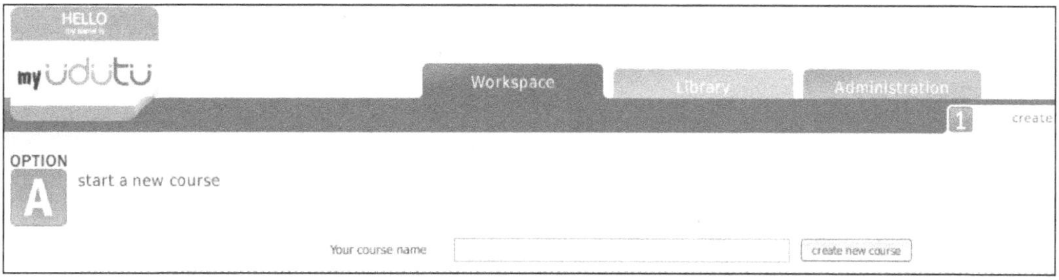

The main tabs here are your current work environment, a library of any materials that you may reuse, such as videos or images, and an administration tab for adding users and modifying your account.

If you have existing material, it will be shown below this section where they can be edited.

Begin the process by clicking on **create new course**, after giving it a working title, as shown in the following screenshot:

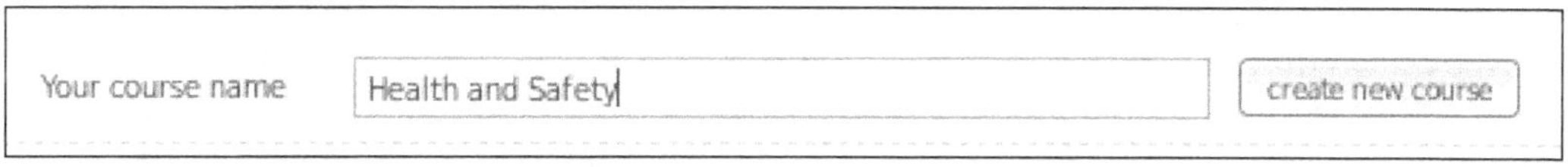

When you are creating the course, it will initiate the editing screens and allow you to build up your course with various elements and interactive pages. The main elements of the design interface are the outline of the course and the edit features.

Course outline

Like all good teaching resources, it pays to map out what your teaching and learning objectives will be before you create your courses. It is assumed here that you have carried out this process and are now transferring your ideas to this medium. The course outline window shows you what type of pages you can add to your learning module and also how you can re-arrange these for sequencing. The following screenshot shows some of these options in progress:

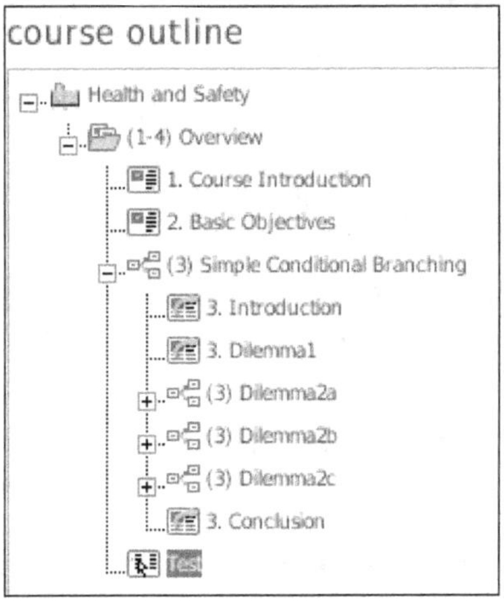

In this example, we have an introduction to the learning module and a set of overall objectives so that the students know what they are studying and why. We then have used a basic scenario which includes a number of dilemmas, each of which leads to a different set of slides to determine what the students have learned and what decisions they make as a result. Each of these slides could have a video sequence showing a person undertaking a task. One of these would comply with the health and safety regulations and the others would not. The following screenshot shows the basic structure used in a bit more detail:

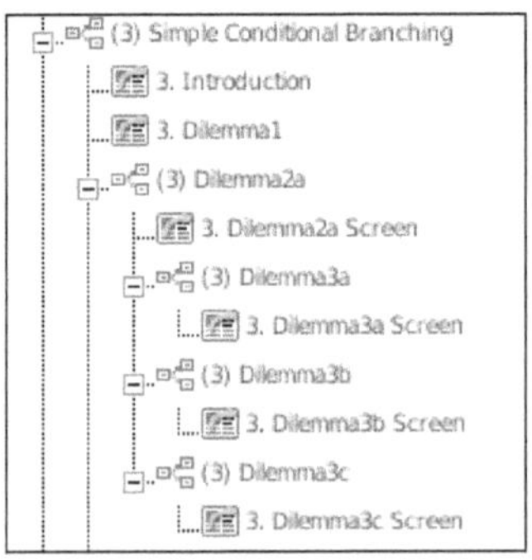

The module would therefore reinforce the correct behavior without threatening the student's own safety in any way. The final slide is a multiple choice quiz to test that they have fully understood the lesson and met the required level set out by the course objectives.

Configuring options

In this example, we have used a preset series of screens based on the choice of a scenario, which is selected from the button, as shown in the following screenshot:

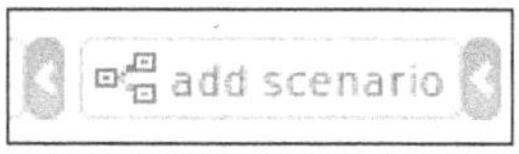

This has a number of preset screen layouts that equate to a number of possible learning outcomes. The options are shown in the following screenshot:

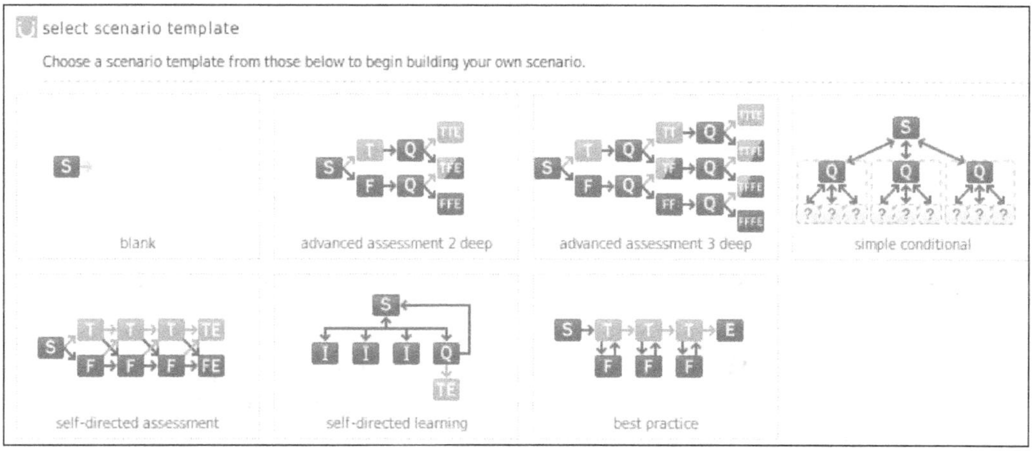

Each scenario has a different method of learning and the one you choose will depend on what your objectives are. For this example, we have chosen the **simple conditional** template as we are looking to find out how students respond in a number of situations that they may come across in the workplace.

Editing your Health and Safety Scenario

Each screen has a similar set of editing options, even though each one will have a slightly different look depending on what style was chosen. The main options relate to what material is used within the slide.

Changing the layout of your course

The layout options relate to how the elements are arranged on the slide, and as the following screenshot shows, you have three core options:

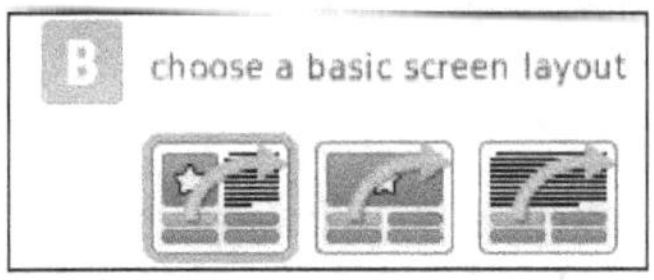

In this example, we are using a scenario slide, which means that an option of one choice from four made by the students will take them to another screen. The option buttons here can be either below some text, an image, or both.

Adding data to the slide

The slide can have some description associated with it and can also be part of the final assessment, if required, as you can see from the following screenshot:

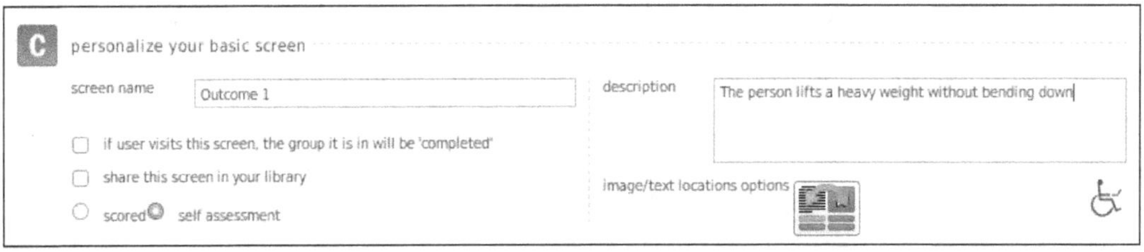

Adding content from your personal library

The content section allows you to add material from your personal library or from your local machine. You can also copy and paste in content, if required. The following screenshot shows a number of options allowed:

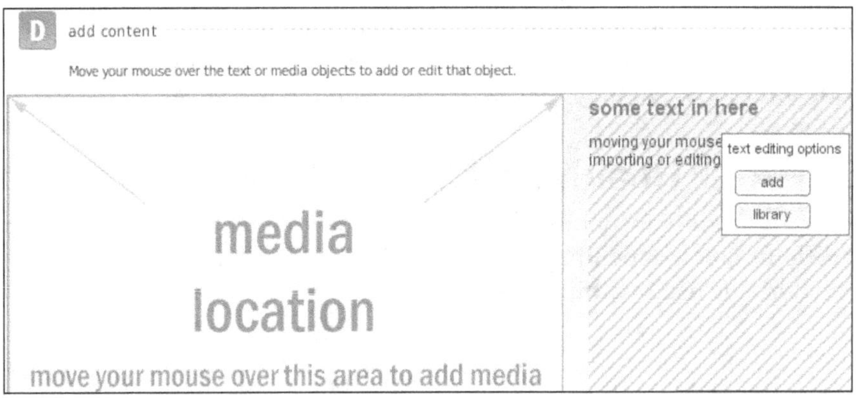

These can always be edited later on if you feel the layout is not clear or if you need to modify any content based on the user's feedback comments.

In this example, there are links to other screens based on options that are part of the design at the base of the page, as shown in the following screenshot:

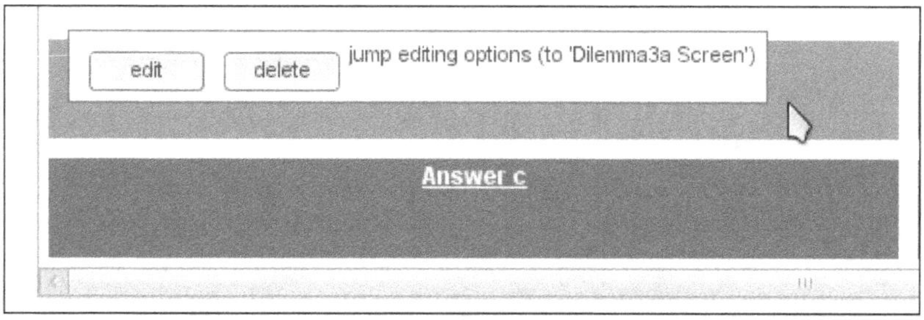

By selecting the edit option, you can change the screen that this **Answer c** points to, as per your plan. The final option allows you to upload and link an audio file for narration. This might be useful to add your own personal set of instructions for students and to personalize the material for your teaching set.

Testing the knowledge learned in the exercise

The final screen, though you can incorporate it into other elements throughout, is likely to be a test screen for assessing what has been learned. This is achieved with an assessment screen. You can add this to your edited module with the following icon:

The assessment screen is quite comprehensive and has an ever-growing number of assessment types to choose from. Each one is roughly explained with a mouse over action, as shown in the following screenshot:

Adding multiple choice questions to a test slide

If you use the basic testing slide, which is the multiple choice one, the screen setup is the same as all other slides, but this one has the option to add the answers and their marking, as shown in the following screenshot:

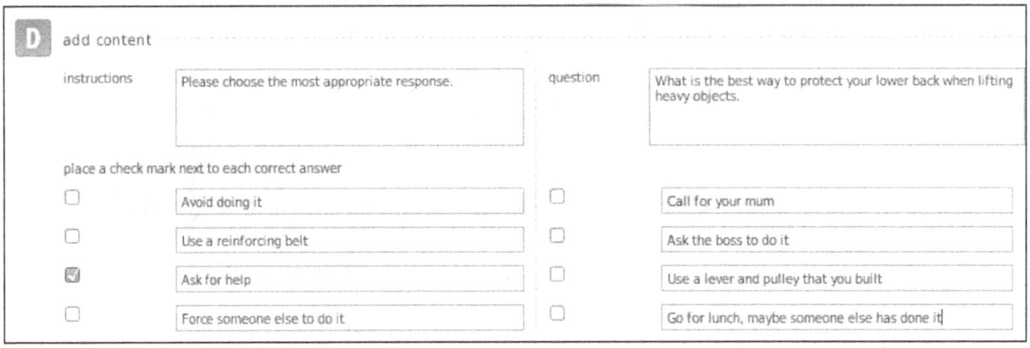

Once you have added the answers and any feedback required, you can check that the assessment is working the way you want by checking the **preview** button. The resulting slide should have all of your elements included. Feedback will pop up with any incorrect or partially correct answers and any correct answers will be marked with a check, as shown in the following screenshot:

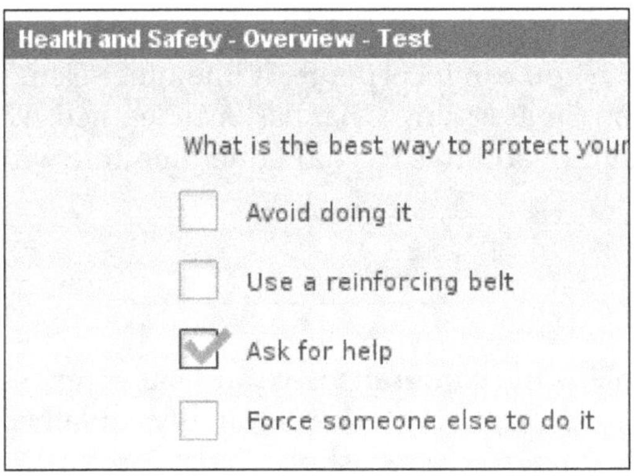

Once completed, you can then publish your work.

Publishing your myUdutu material

You need to click on the **distribute** tab on your workspace. The following screenshot shows the tab:

If you are using myUdutu's service, then you can choose **Option A** to distribute the material. If you choose this option, myUdutu creates a ZIP file in a file area. This file can be downloaded and then added to your Moodle courses as with any other SCORM resource, as discussed earlier in this chapter. Otherwise, if you choose **Option B**, you can save the slides in a repository on your myUdutu account and link to it from your Moodle course through the add-on module. To use the material as a SCORM resource, select the **extract** option, as shown in the following screenshot:

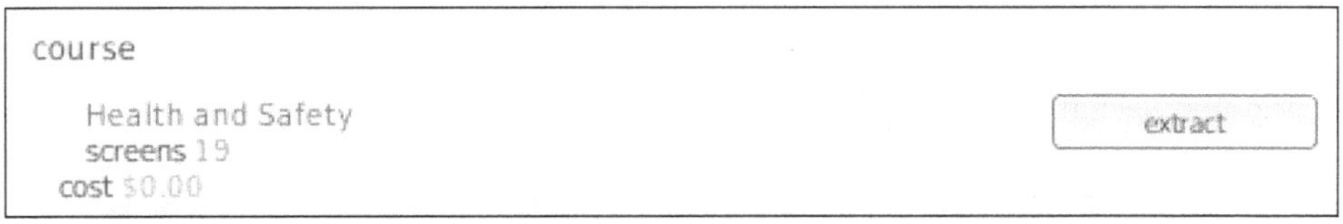

You can see here that there are 19 screens in total as a reference.

You will receive a brief message, as shown in the following screenshot, as your file is prepared as well as when it is done:

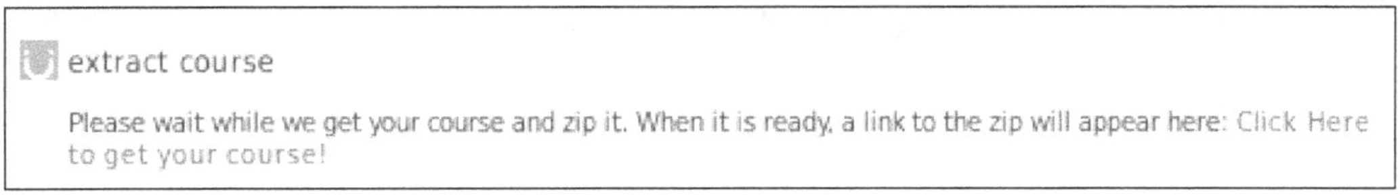

As suggested here, when you will click on the link, it will get you the created course. Depending on your operating system, you will be given the option to open or save the file. In this instance, we will save the file so that we can upload it to our course.

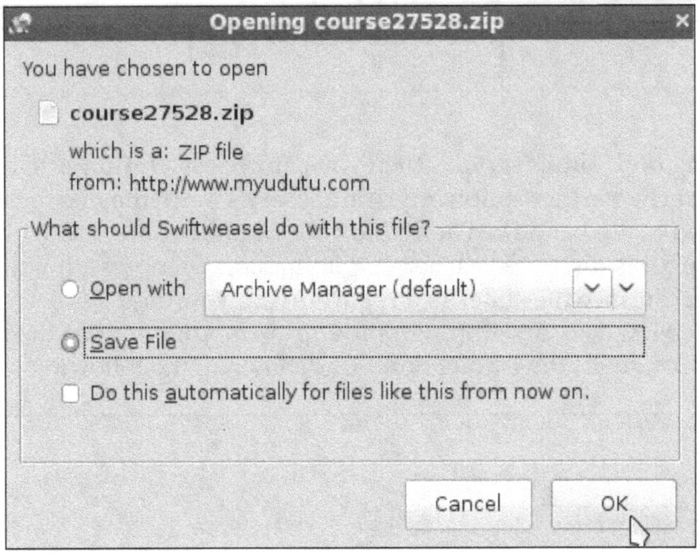

Once saved, the zipped file can be linked as with any other SCORM file under resources. If you have installed the myUdutu module, you can also link it to your own myUdutu course area.

Using the myUdutu module in Moodle

As already mentioned, you do not need to install the myUdutu module in order to use the material that you create on the myUdutu site because it creates standard SCORM material. If you have installed the myUdutu module on your Moodle site, it will appear once you turn editing on in your **Add an activity** drop-down menu, as shown in the following screenshot:

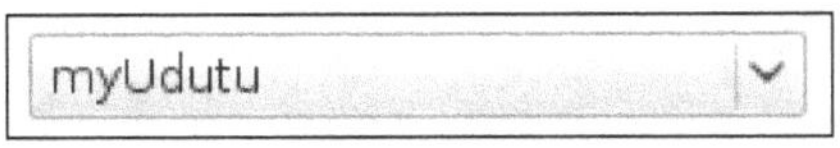

The menu that appears is similar to the SCORM module layout we saw earlier, but there are some notable differences that relate to your myUdutu account. The options can be seen in the following screenshot:

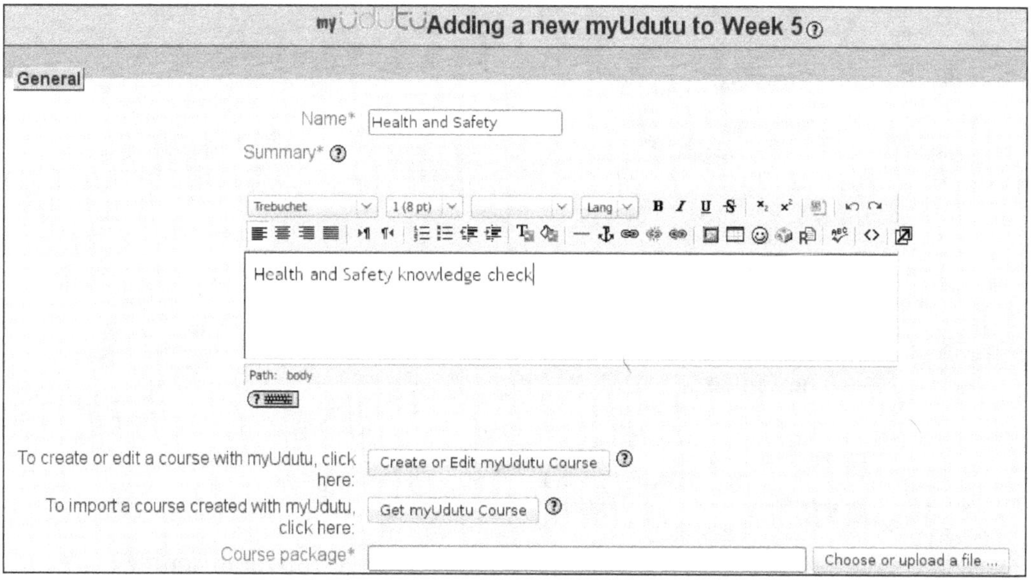

The key difference here is the creation options. If you click on the link to create or edit a course with myUdutu, or get a myUdutu course, you will be taken to the myUdutu login screen, and when you log in, you can use the existing slide sets or create new ones. The following screenshot shows that you can select the course that you just created from your library:

Once you save it, it will be placed into this Moodle course. You can then assign options as you would do with other SCORM materials such as number of attempts and grading level, as shown in the following screenshot:

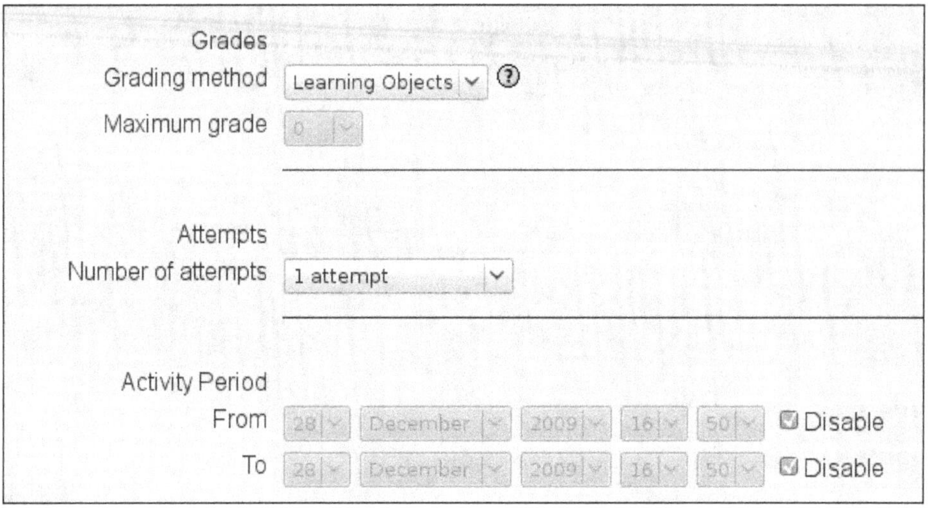

The e-learning course is now a learning module within your overall course design, and in this case, it can test students' understanding of health and safety regarding work issues. The material can incorporate personalized videos and commentary to make sure that it fully engages and challenges the students being taught.

Other options for multimedia creation

There are a great number of applications in the market that carry out similar or more advanced functions, including the excellent open source application eXeLearning (`http://exelearning.org/wiki`) or the commercial application Articulate (`http://www.articulate.com/`), and all of them will generate exciting and engaging e-learning materials for your Moodle site.

It is worth the time and effort to try these, and you can also allow older students to generate material for younger students as a part of their overall assessment. This gives them confidence and experience of instructing others, which is a powerful teaching tool.

Summary

Moodle is fully equipped to handle media-rich content and resources and using these, it can fully engage our students. Moodle has a comprehensive learning module already built in—the Lesson module, which has much of the functionality discussed in this chapter and is well supported by books and Moodle documentation. It can be found at:

`http://docs.moodle.org/en/Lesson#Presentation_Lesson`

The subject matter itself is suited to this type of delivery and the additional tools available for free, such as myUdutu, will allow us to create a library of resources for students to interact with. It can accurately portray the types of working situations the students will encounter as they pursue a career in technology and design.

8

Assessing Student Progress

The final part of setting up a Moodle site to support your Design and Technology lessons is the ability to be able to assess a student's progress. All of the preceding chapters provide various means of delivering content and interacting with the students and thus helping to shape their learning. But an assignment will give us a clear indication of the areas where the students have understood everything or where there is a need for more clarity. This assessment can be formal or informal and Moodle is capable of dealing with both of these instances. The other great advantage of Moodle is that any of the activities you use on the course, including students' **Views** (their digital pages) on something such as Mahara (see *Chapter 4, Exploring Design Portfolios*) or pre-made **Sharable Content Object Reference Model** (**SCORM**) multimedia resources (see *Chapter 7, Adding Multimedia Resources to your Moodle Site*) can be tracked.

In this chapter, we will look at:

- How to create more formal assignments to track student progress and understanding
- Creating a range of assignment types and applications for different assessment requirements

Using the assignments module to gauge student progress

The Moodle assignment module is similar in nature to the Quiz module, but it is more formal and bridges the gap between more formal face-to-face teaching and online learning. Assignments can be created by students as web pages by using an inline assignment type, or they can be a repository where students can upload their work for assessment and feedback, such as the advanced uploading type.

The material that they can upload is just a file, so the assignment can be a word-processed document, an image, or even a video or audio file. This gives a great deal of flexibility for the staff in terms of assessment. For the staff working in the design field, it means that students can upload proprietary files such as design work on software such as Desktop Pro, and as long as the staff has the software on their own desktop, they can open it for analysis and review.

In this chapter, we will look at the different types of assignments that are available and the ways in which they can be used for assessment. As all of the grading and feedback is then applied to the built-in course gradebook, we will also explore how this can be used for monitoring, though we will go into more detail on the Gradebook in *Chapter 9, Tracking Progress with the Gradebook*.

Setting up the assignment module

As with all of the modules in Moodle, there are some basic site-based settings, which can be adjusted with this module. The settings for the **Assignment** module are at **Site Administration | Modules | Activities | Assignment**. This will need to be carried out by someone who is a site administrator, but it is worth knowing what can be done, as it may affect your teaching. The key part of the **Assignment** module is the size allowed for uploading a file. With design technology, it is likely that the nature of any work that is created, for example, images for Resistant Materials, a detailed 3D design file for product design, or a video sequence for a construction course element, could be quite large. The size of files allowed is governed by the server set up and will be reflected in the site settings for the **Assignment** module. The following screenshot shows the settings available for **Assignment** module:

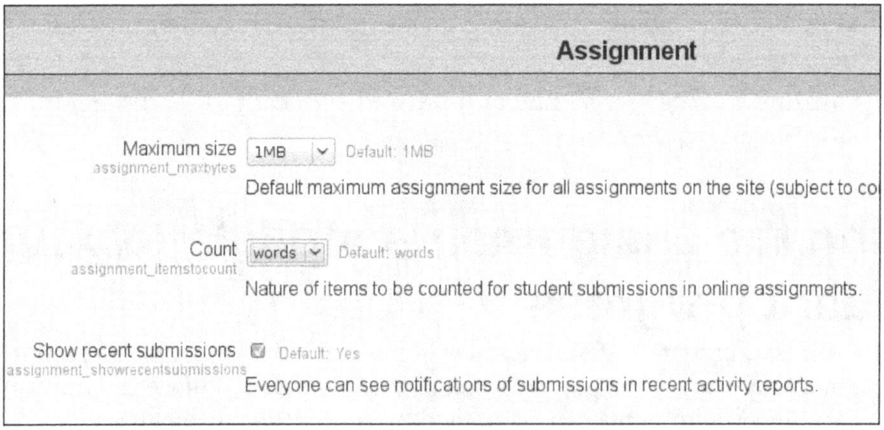

The default maximum upload size for web servers, if running a default installation of Apache, is usually 2 MB. In this instance, the server has been modified and the maximum size has been increased to 128 MB. This needs to be chosen carefully. We need to give students enough head room to be able to upload their work, but we need to monitor how much is used, as a class full of students uploading multiple 100 MB files will soon use up a server's space. The other option here is to have an automatic word count or a count of letters; again, this depends on what you are trying to monitor with students' formative assessment. The default option is to count the words, which is probably more useful perhaps for example, if you have an institution policy that all the assignments have to be over 2000 words.

Creating assignments

The type of assignment you choose will depend on what it is you are trying to assess, as well as what will be the nature of the assessed material. In this section, we will look at the different types of assignments that can be chosen and give some examples of best practices. The types available, in reverse order of complexity, are:

- Offline activity
- Upload a single file
- Online text
- Advanced uploading of files

> If you are using Mahara (see *Chapter 4*), then you will also be able to set e-portfolios as assignments.

Creating offline activity assignments

The offline activity assignment is the most basic assignment type and the one that does not require any activity on Moodle by the students. In some instances, students will be working on material that may be unsuitable for upload and storage. This might be because it is too large or complex to be scanned and uploaded, or it might be because you are working in an institution where the space is not available on the web server to store a large amount of data.

As with all the modules on Moodle, the first step is to **Turn editing on**.

This will enable the **Add an activity** drop-down menu and then you can choose the **Offline activity** assignment from this menu, as shown in the following screenshot:

This option will open the interface for setting up this type of assignment. In this example, we are assuming that the students are creating a design portfolio. The portfolio will consist of many pages with sketches, plans, and essays so it cannot be easily transferred to a web-based resource. However, as we need to track the results formally, we create an assignment in order to store the scores and offer some feedback comments. There will be feedback on the original document, but the feedback on the website can offer the students live links to resources on the Moodle course for supplementary learning support, or web links, which would be hard to put into the paper-based material.

The set up window is quite basic, as it is really just establishing a score. The following screenshot shows the main options that can be applied after naming and describing the assignment. The **Description** field explains that all the detailed feedback will be on the written portfolio.

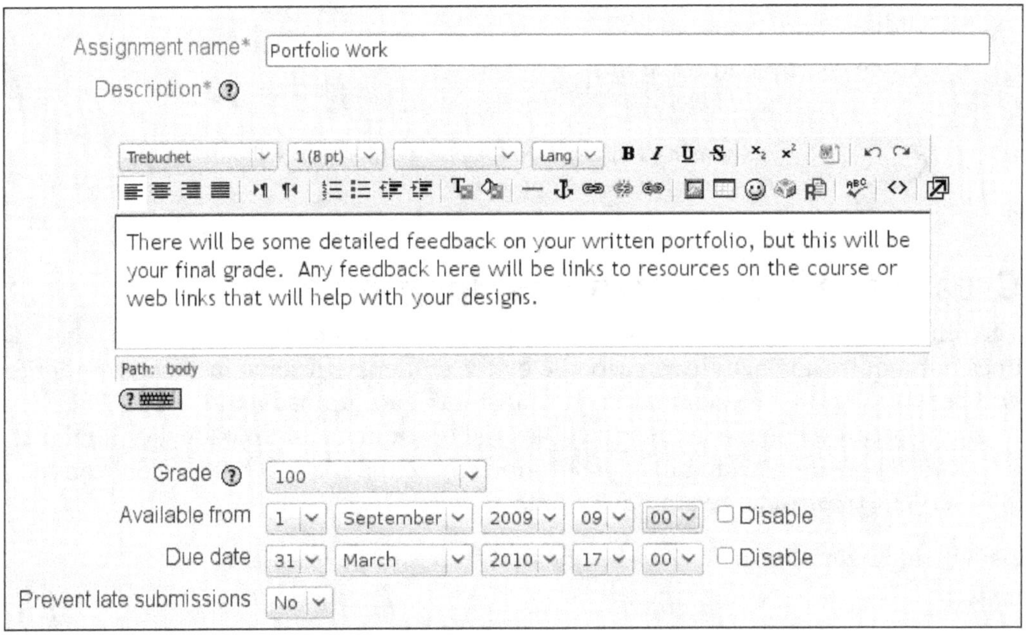

In this instance, we have set a **soft** deadline and have allowed late submissions. This will be the first time it is submitted. We can then change the deadline to be **hard** and prevent any more submissions to track the students' delivery time and date. All of this will be stored against their grades in the gradebook.

If you have enabled outcomes for this course, you could apply the results of the portfolio assignment to course work rather than exam work to give more clarity to your grading. In the following screenshot, we can see this option:

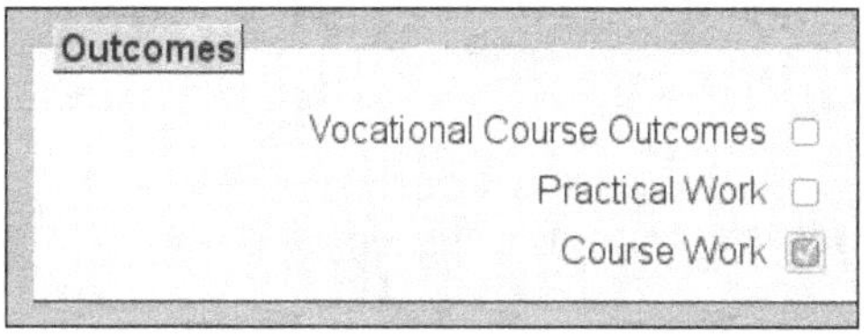

In the example here, this portfolio could be used as 60 percent of the overall grade. By assigning it as a course work outcome, it is easier to organize it in the gradebook and give students a clearer idea of where they are. If you are also using an add-on block, which allows parents to see their own child's work (that is, `http://moodle.org/mod/data/view.php?d=13&rid=2221&filter=1`), then it can prove to be a powerful motivational tool as well.

Once the assignment options have been saved, the new assignment link will appear on the course, as shown in the following screenshot:

Grading offline assignments

Unlike other assignments we will look at presently, this link will only give students some details about what is to be stored. It is only the staff who will be able to fully use the link. When the staff clicks on this link, it shows what has been graded and what is yet to be graded. It will open with the view of all the students on the course, and staff can then have grades and feedback applied, as shown in the following screenshot:

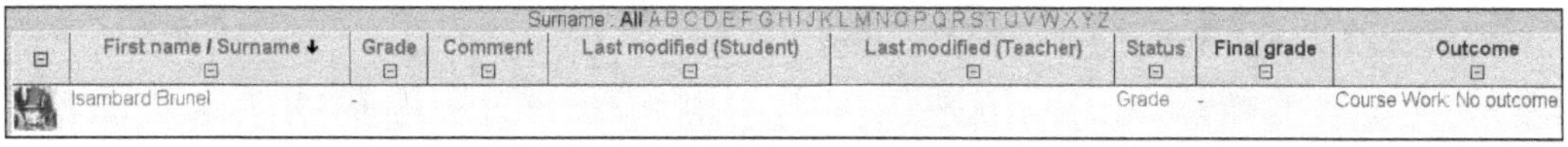

You can now click on the grade link (assuming that your charges have submitted their work on time) and be able to grade their portfolios and give some feedback, as shown in the following screenshot:

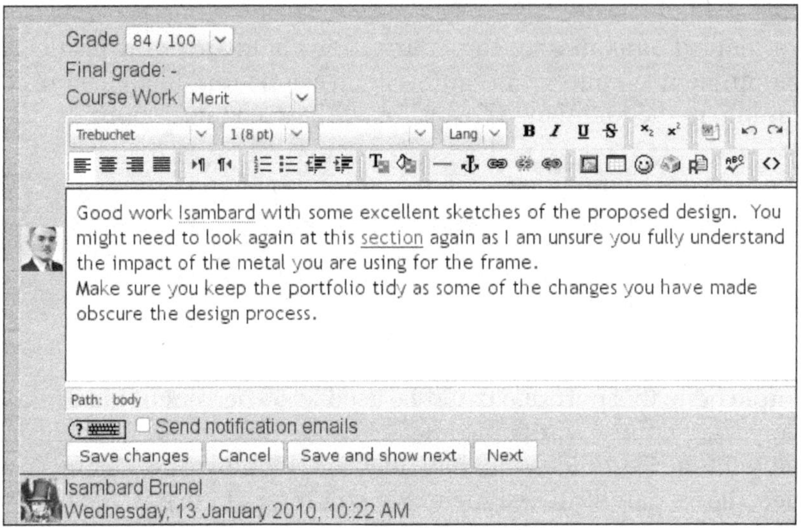

In this image, you can also see the advantage of the HTML editor as the word **section** links to another page on the course, which forces them to re-read your instructions. The students can then view this feedback and see their grades when they log in next time. Their view is shown in the following screenshot:

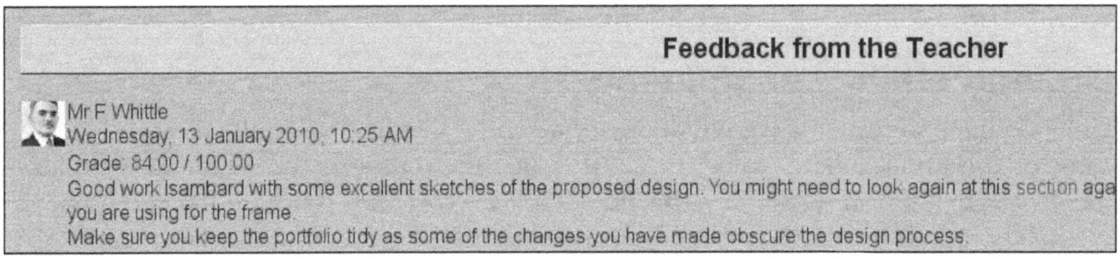

The students can see the grade they have achieved, and in this case, they can go to a useful link to improve their work further.

Creating and uploading a single file assignment

The single file upload facility is exactly the same as the previous assignment, as shown in the following screenshot:

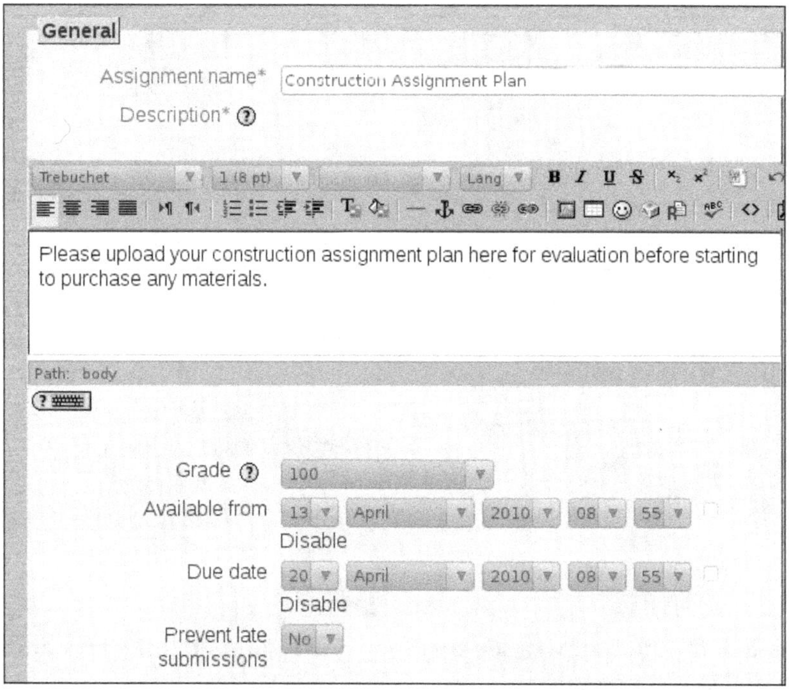

The difference is that this type of assignment involves some Internet activity, and this is reflected in some extra options on the set up window, as shown in the following screenshot:

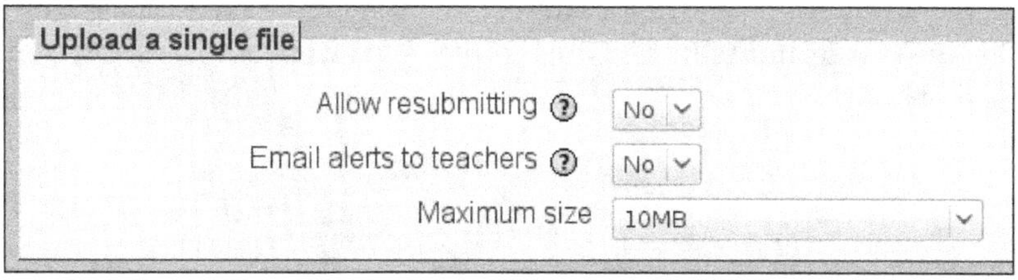

If this is a more formal assignment, then you can prevent re-submission. You can also enable the function so that when a submission is made, any people who are the staff members of the course will be notified through e-mail. This is a useful way to reinforce deadlines with students and also have some evidence of whether or not they meet the deadline as they claim.

Uploading attachments to assignments

Once the students have completed their piece of work, they can click on the icon for the assignment, and they will then be presented with an upload window, as shown in the following screenshot:

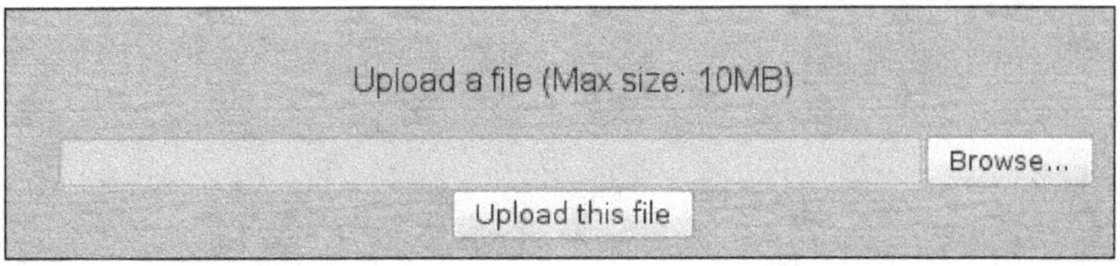

When you click on the **Browse...** button, it will open up your local file manager, so the view will depend on what computer you are sitting at. In the following screenshot, it shows a local computer drive where the student can select the document they wish to upload.

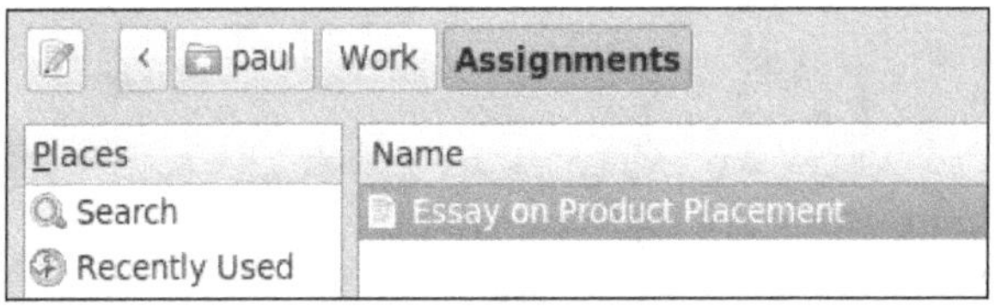

Once uploaded, the student will see that they have completed the task and the staff will be notified of the upload.

Marking assignments

Once the staff has been notified of the assignment upload, they can log in and see which students they have marked and will be advised of how many assignments need to be viewed by them. In their course, once they have created assignments, there will be an **Assignments** link visible in the **Activities** box, as shown in the following screenshot:

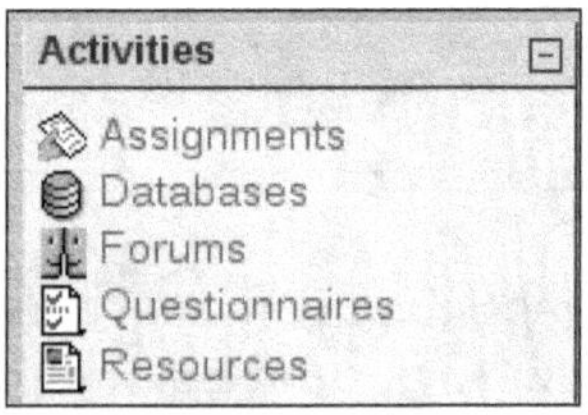

When you click on the **Assignments** link, as shown in the previous screenshot, it will open a list of all assignments on the course and also show how many submissions have been made, as shown in the following screenshot:

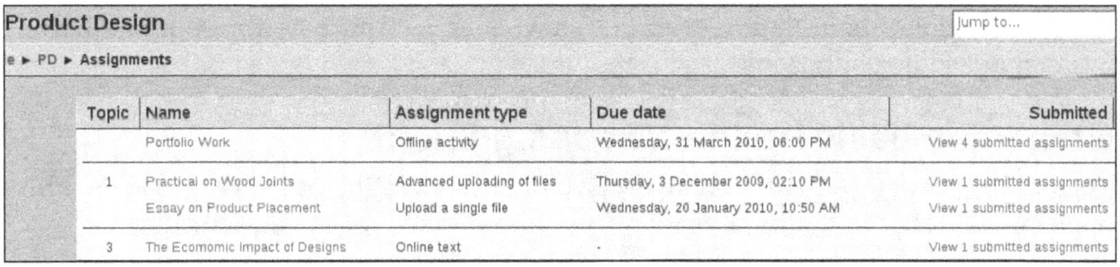

When you click on the **View 1 submitted assignments** links, as shown in the following screenshot, it will show all the uploaded assignments:

When you will click on the link shown in the previous screenshot, it will open the following window and show the assignments that require marking:

The link to the document, depending on your browser, will either prompt to download the file or open the file in the appropriate word processor, if available. However, it cannot be modified in any way, so any feedback required will have to be documented in the feedback box, which is part of the **Grade** link, as shown in the previous screenshot.

Creating an online text assignment

In some cases, it may be useful to have an assignment that allows some comments to be made in the original file. In the upload assignment files, staff can only read the proprietary file, like a word-processed document, but cannot modify the file at all, as it exists in the database. The advanced upload that we will look at next allows multiple uploads, so it allows the students to add revisions and the staff to attach modified files for feedback.

With the online text style of assignment, students can submit an assignment with the HTML editor, which means that the students' work can be edited as it is on the site. However, unlike an offline assignment, this will require some storage space on the server. This is a very useful assignment type if you wish to give students some clear instructions about their work, such as when it is important for them to fully understand some definitions.

Creating a basic online text assignment

The online text assignment is created in a similar way as the other assignments with one key difference in the options menu, as shown in the following screenshot:

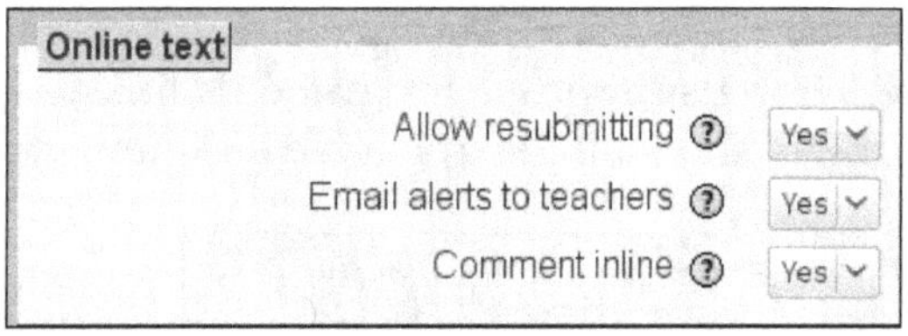

The key difference here is that it allows you to enable the **Comment inline** option. This option means that when you click on the assignment to mark it and give some feedback, Moodle copies the entire contents of the assignment into the feedback window so that the staff can highlight text with color, score through wrong words, or even link words to websites such as Wikipedia. This allows for a very detailed level of feedback, which will greatly benefit a student's understanding.

Students can create the assignment by clicking on the **Edit my submission** button, as shown in the following screenshot, which will open the basic HTML editor window for them.

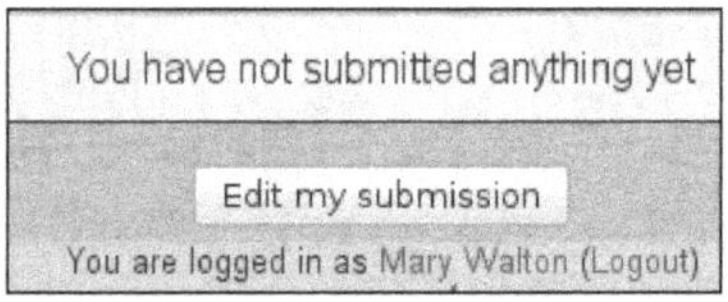

A student is presented with the usual HTML editor window that allows them to insert web links, as well as highlight text, as shown in the following screenshot:

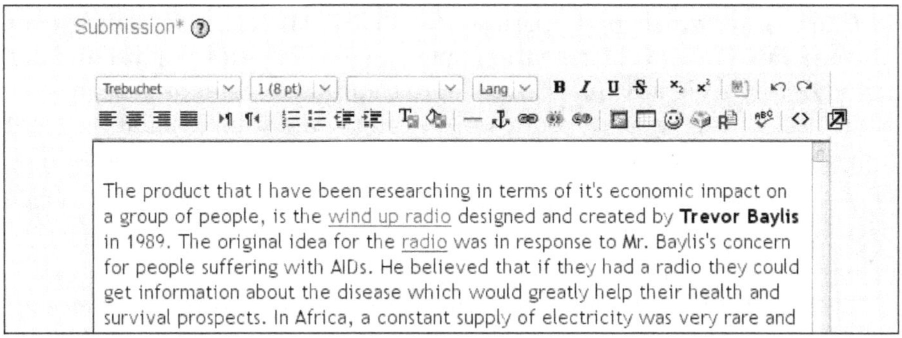

In the previous screenshot, you can see that there is a hyperlink to an article on Wikipedia referencing the item under analysis as well as a link to the image itself called **radio**. The student has also highlighted the name of the developer of the product in bold.

Marking the work

As mentioned earlier, once the staff clicks on this assignment to mark it, because the inline marking was enabled, the entire text will be pasted into the grading feedback window. This is shown in the following screenshot:

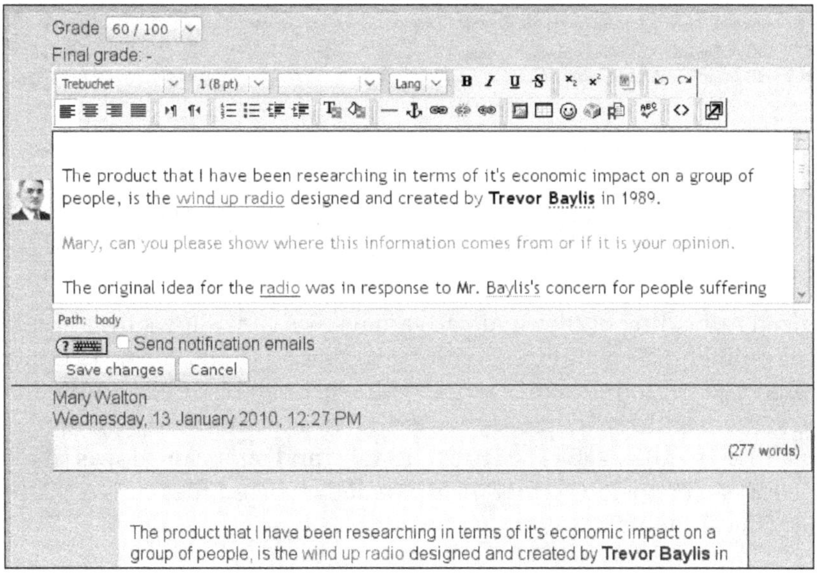

In the previous screenshot, the inline comments have been made in a different color so that they stand out. You could also highlight some of the work with a background color or strike through incorrect words, much as you would do in a traditional paper-written essay, which gives it greater flexibility. You can also highlight a word or phrase and link it to a website in the same way that the students did initially, which is obviously a big advantage over more traditional methods. The previous screenshot also shows the word count so you can tell the students that they still need to write in more detail as the assignment needed at least 1000 words.

The student's view

When the student logs in the next time, they can see all of the staff feedback and click on any hyperlinks that have been embedded to help them with the assignment. Once they have done this, they can re-edit their assignment and submit it for further marking and comments. The screenshot they see is shown as follows:

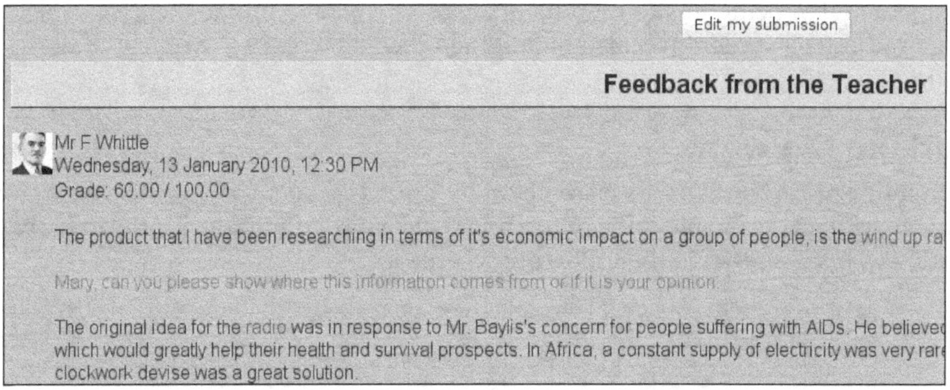

The student can click on **Edit my submission** to make the required changes.

Creating an Advanced uploading of files assignment

The advanced uploading of files main advantage is that it allows the student's work to be commented on and re-submitted so that all drafts can be commented on and stored against the student's name. The work can be directly edited with some software add-ons (`http://www.educationlabs.com/projects/officeaddinformoodle/Pages/default.aspx`), and staff can allow some notes to be made for each revision so that the uploaded changed files can be properly corrected by the students.

Setting up the assignment

The basic setup of this assignment follows the same pattern as all the previous assignments. The key difference, as with the other assignment types, is in the options available, as shown in the following screenshot:

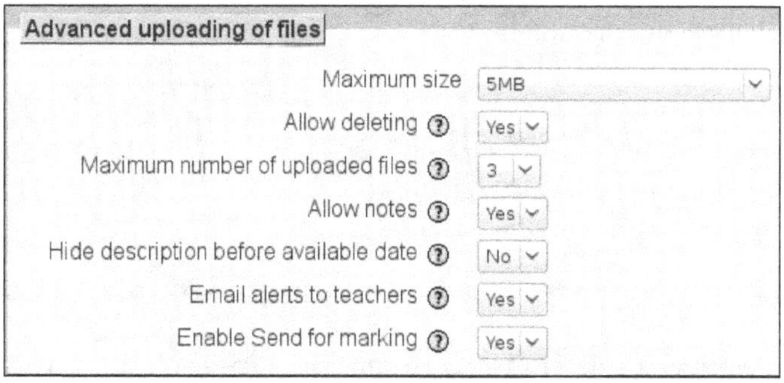

The options are quite clearly described in their associated help file, but in brief:

- **Maximum size**—allows you to restrict, if necessary, the size of the files submitted.
- **Allow deleting**—allows files to be deleted to give students a chance to fix their own mistakes. They might upload a file by mistake and if you only allow two uploads then they are stuck. Allowing them to delete the files permits them to correct their own mistakes that can happen.
- **Maximum number of uploaded files**—is the number that can be associated with this type of assignment and can be set up to 20. If this is an assignment related to product design, or even a design portfolio, students can upload multiple files. These could be a combination of research texts, PDFs, video and audio files, as well as proprietary files such as Desktop Pro design files. Each one of these can be commented on, and a complete picture of their learning can be viewed.
- **Allow notes**—This option allows students to add notes to their uploads such as comments about why the assignment does not contain a video as requested.
- **Enable Send for marking**—allows students to decide when they have a final version. Once they click on this option themselves, the assignment is closed for them and no further uploads are allowed.

Once these settings have been made, the assignment can be set and will be available for the students.

Allowing students to upload assignments

Once the options have been set for the assignment, the link will appear on the course, and the students can then upload. The **browse** and **upload** button will appear as long as they have the right number of options. Once they have uploaded their files, they will be displayed with the assignment description (so that they can check them), as shown in the following screenshot:

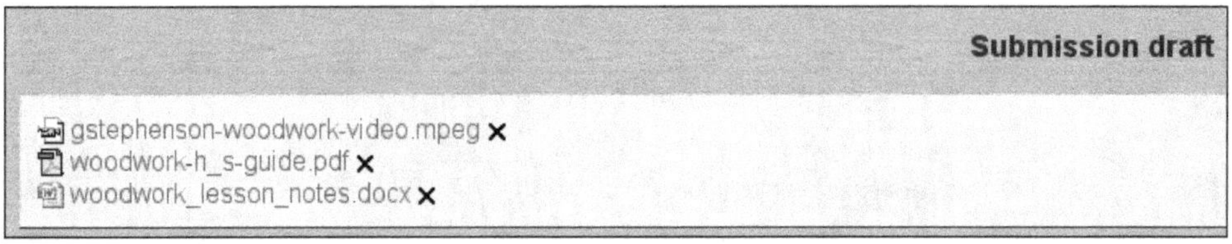

In this instance, there is a selection of different file types relating to a woodwork project. As we have also enabled the notes for this assignment, the students can add some of their own comments to explain what their work is and any problems they might have had, which would affect the marking applied. The **Notes** window, as shown in the following screenshot, appears with the uploads:

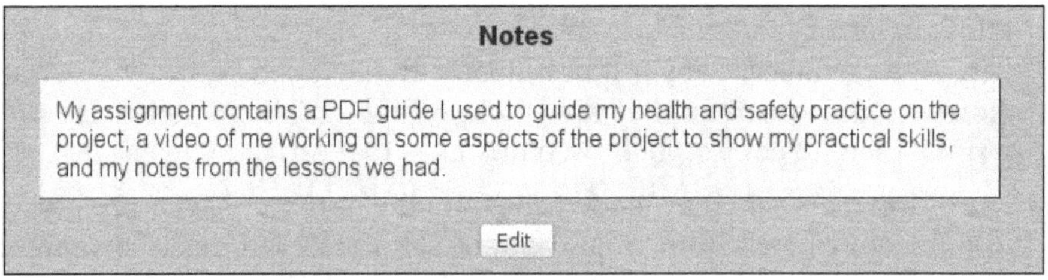

As mentioned earlier, once the students are happy with all of their work and have had the requisite feedback, they can click on the **Send for marking** button, as shown in the following screenshot, to close their uploads for final submission:

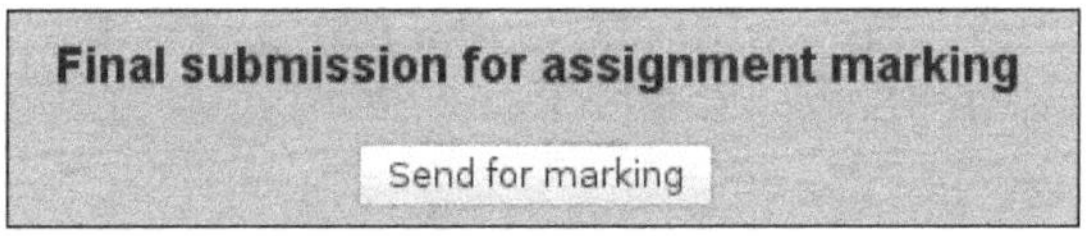

The students are given one more chance, just in case they make a mistake. The screenshot can be shown as follows:

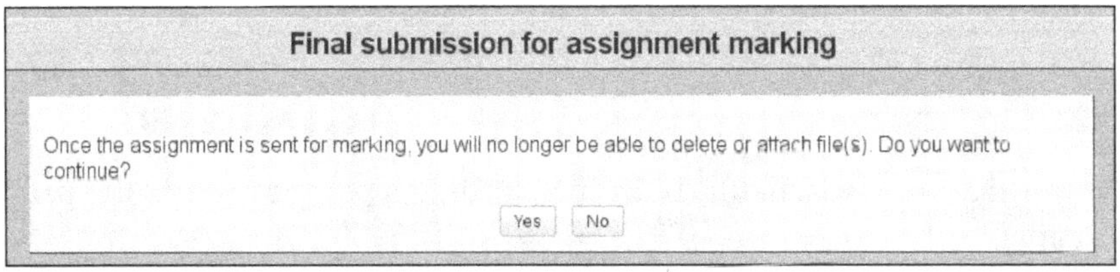

Marking the assignments

Once students have submitted their assignments, they can be accessed by the staff for marking. There are a few extra options for staff with this type of assignment, as shown in the following screenshot:

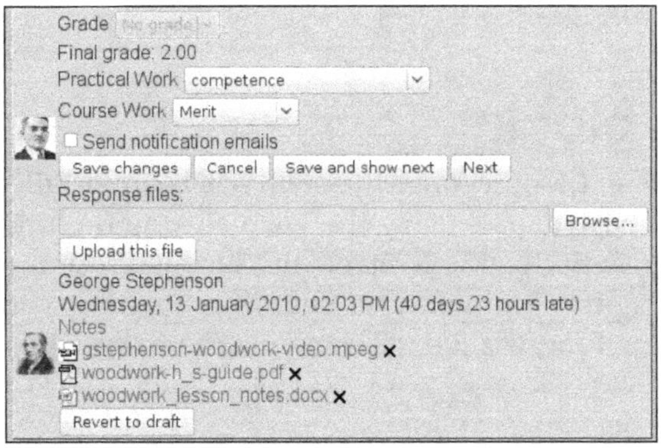

The students can receive an e-mail once their work has been marked using the **Send notification emails** checkbox, as shown in the previous screenshot. If there is a detailed report of their project, staff can upload a word-processed document with the response files option. If the staff has enabled the tracking feature on this document, the students can see exactly what has changed and can therefore learn from the interaction. If the staff is not convinced that the work is of a good standard and have detailed feedback, they can click the button to **Revert to draft**, which will allow the students to upload their work again.

Creating a summary for assignments

There are various means and methods for creating opportunities for assessing students' work and various ways for them to send that work to the staff. In all cases, the students' work can be formally assessed and a record can be maintained of their work and progress. For a better overview, the staff can then use the gradebook facility of Moodle, which we will explore in detail in the next chapter.

In addition to the standard Moodle modules for assessment, there are also a number of useful add-ons that help with more specialized qualifications such as Vocational qualifications. These will be explored briefly here.

Creating a progress bar summary

One very useful add-on, particularly from a student's perspective, is the progress bar. It is available at:

`http://moodle.org/mod/data/view.php?d=13&rid=2524&filter=1`

This block can be set up by the staff to give students an instant view of what work they have completed and what has yet to be done. These events are color-coded so that a quick impression can be gained and a decision can be made. If used as a part of a tutoring program, it can be very powerful, especially with time-dependent courses with deadlines that are rigid.

Adding the block

As with all the blocks in Moodle, once this item has been installed by a site administrator, it will be available using the **Turn editing on** function on a course. When you turn on the editing, it will enable the **Blocks** drop-down menu to appear at the bottom of the right column on your course. From here, you can select the block to add, in this case, the **Progress Bar**, as shown in the following screenshot:

This will then place the **Progress Bar** block onto the course on the right-hand side. You can move this block with the edit arrows if you wish to place it somewhere else, or by dragging-and-dropping, if Ajax is enabled. The block will initially be un-configured, and a message will inform you of this fact, as shown in the following screenshot:

When you click on the configuration icon shown in the previous screenshot, you will be taken to a screen that lists all of the elements of your course where you can select the items that will be used to track your students' progress. This configuration screen is shown in the following screenshot:

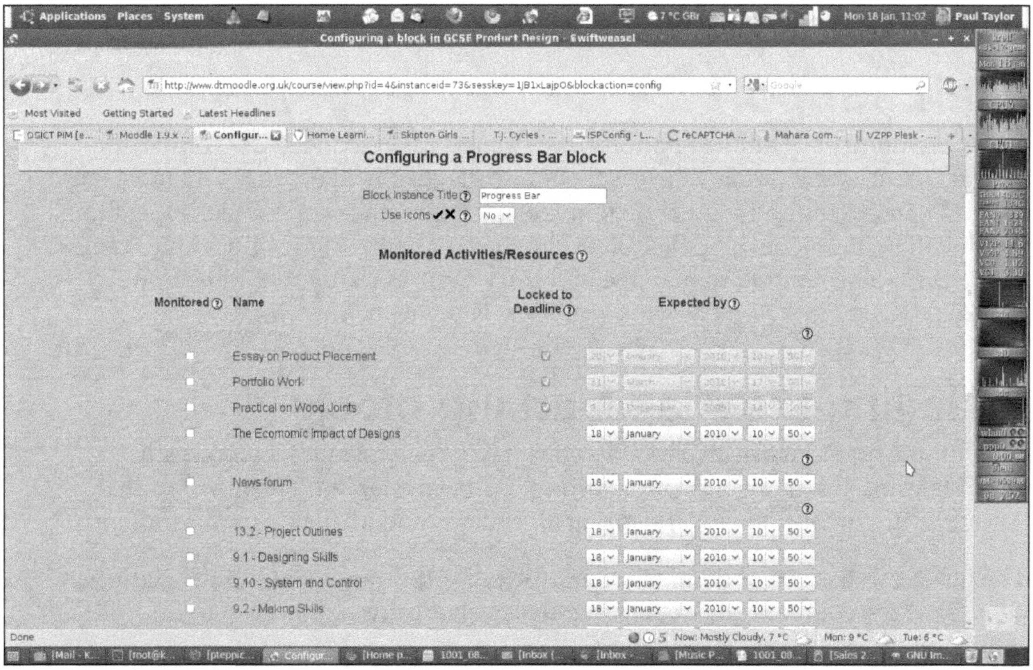

In this example, we only really want to track formal assignments, so we will only choose the top four items. The items are shown in their respective grouping, so you could choose forums or glossaries, if they were part of the tracking process for your institution.

Once selected, the block will show the students where they are in terms of the work being tracked, as shown in the following screenshot:

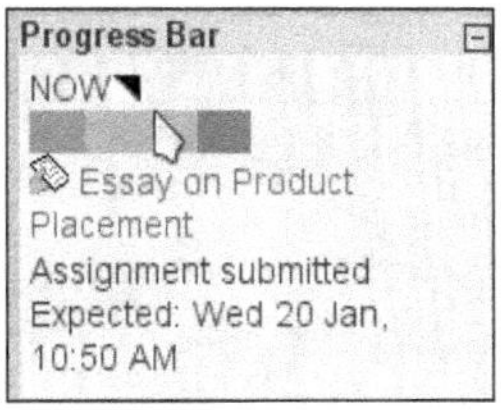

In case of the student in this example, the progress bar is color-coordinated to show which assignments are overdue and which ones are becoming deadlines soon. When you hold the mouse over the colored blocks, it gives some extra detail about the assignments. In this example, the middle bar (green) shows that the assignment has been completed and marked.

Staff support

There are number of add-on options that can help you to organize your work load better. If you work at a large school or college, it is likely that you have large cohorts of students and a great deal of work to keep track of. As with most things in education, these marking blocks tend to be compressed into short time frames. Therefore, some method to manage and track your marking would be quite beneficial. One block, which helps with this, is the **Ajax Marking** block.

Installing the Ajax Marking block

As with the other blocks on Moodle, once it has been installed by your site administrator, it is available, once editing has been enabled. The now familiar **Turn editing on** button is at the top of all courses and available to the staff.

The block can then be added from the **Blocks** drop-down menu on the right-hand column of the course. They are arranged alphabetically so it is easy to find, as shown in the following screenshot:

The resulting block will run some code to search the course database to find the status of the assignments, in terms of marking, and present this to the user. In this case, it is only visible to staff-based users. The following screenshot shows the view of a member of the staff.

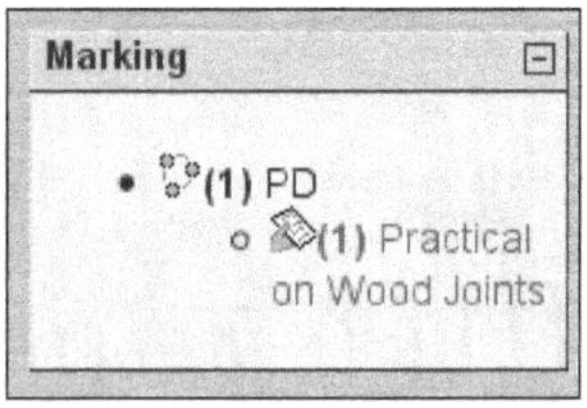

In this example, the staff can see that they have one assignment still to mark on this course. By clicking on the link, the block will display more details as it will go directly to this assignment to show submissions and feedback. If the block is placed on the front page of a site, it will pick up all the assignments still to be marked by the member of staff logged on. If the staff is teaching on several Design and Technology courses, their marking will be shown across the whole site.

> There are other add-on blocks that track your marking and all of these can be found on the `http://moodle.org/` website in **Modules and plugins** under the **Downloads** section, as shown:
>
> `http://moodle.org/mod/data/view.php?id=6009`

Summary

Moodle has a range of assignment types to cover most requirements in Design and Technology courses and gives enough flexibility to allow staff to track all aspects of their students' learning. The range covers the ability to track work that is not submitted electronically, as with offline types, right through to complex multiple file assignment uploads that can be used for project work involving text documents and videos. In addition to the assignment types addressed in this chapter, including the ones linked in to internal/external e-portfolios, staff have various blocks and modules to help them manage their workload such as Progress tracking bars. All of these make Moodle ideal for formative assessment of vocational-based and examination-based work and also create a structured area to store and give feedback on all of the students' learning. Once this material has been organized in this fashion, it can be properly graded and analyzed. This grading and analysis is carried out by the Gradebook, which is the final module we will turn to in the next chapter.

9

Tracking Progress with the Gradebook

By this stage, you should have a well organized and comprehensive set of resources on your courses and various activities to stretch and challenge your students. The previous chapter explained the tools with which you were able to set assignments and formative assessments for your students. All this data will be tracked and stored against the student's ID, which means that we are now in a position to analyze the results that students create. This is possible through the comprehensive gradebook that is built into Moodle.

The Moodle gradebook can cater to many complex situations that an organization might encounter, but it is also intuitive and easy to use. If all you require is a simple view of what students have achieved in a few quizzes, then the gradebook will display this for you. For example, you might wish to have a basic course for Food Technology that introduces students to the basic ingredients in cooking. After each session, you can set a short quiz to test their understanding and view this in the gradebook. If you require more complex views based on a number of varied criteria, then the gradebook can also help you with this.

In our on-going example with Design and Technology, we are veering somewhere in the middle of these two requirements. In the worked example, we are assuming that students are required to meet a mixture of formal and informal criteria and that the work they carry out, given the nature of technology as a subject, is both externally assessed material such as examinations and internally assessed vocational and practical work. As such, the sample gradebook will have the ability to monitor these two requirements and give both staff and students the overall ability to see where they are in terms of grades, and importantly, where there are areas of weakness that must be addressed.

In this chapter, we are going to look at configuring the gradebook to track both our coursework components of Design Technology, as well as the public examinations that take place as part of any course. This process will require us to:

- Configure some overall settings for the gradebook
- Create some categories for the grades such as coursework and examinations
- Establish some scales for the courses
- Set up and use outcomes to track practical skills and competencies, for example, woodworking competence
- Configure and examine the reporting options

Configuring the gradebook for your site

The gradebook itself is an integral part of all Moodle courses, as you might expect, and is also highly configurable at the site level and at the course level. In the UK at least, technology-based courses usually comprise a split of 60 percent coursework or practical school-based grades, and 40 percent external examinations. The gradebook can be configured for this type of structure and the worked example in this book will be based on this division. In addition to this, it is configurable to some extent by the students themselves, at least in terms of the view they have. This level of flexibility requires the site admin to adjust a number of settings that can then be modified by other users, though within certain boundaries.

Setting the site options

At the site level, the gradebook, and more generally, the grades, appear under their own section of the administration panel, and as you can see in the following screenshot, there are a number of options:

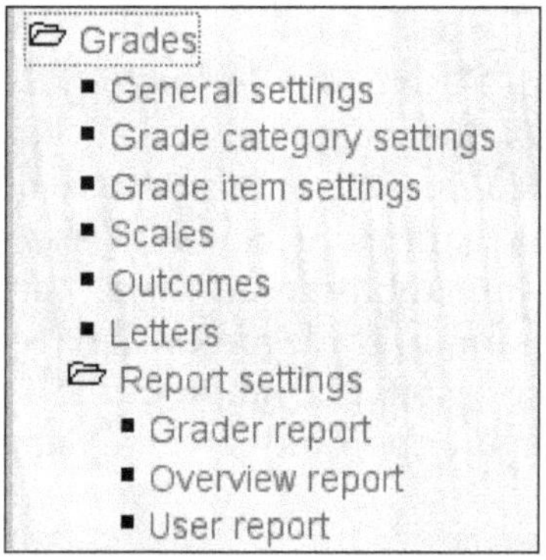

Configuring general settings for the gradebook

The general settings for the gradebook relate primarily to the way that the gradebook will be used. For example, will students only be graded, or will there be courses for non-editing teachers such as classroom assistants. In many design subjects in UK schools there are full-time technicians who help with practical demonstrations. The technicians can be used as non-editing teachers to add marks to students' gradebooks, as the main teachers are not always around to observe the practical work that students carry out or the level of competence they are achieving. A similar consideration would be 'will outcomes be used in courses to create custom grading scales of competencies, rather than the usual 0-100 grades'? Most of the options here can be left at their default setting, and there are detailed explanations associated with each one to help in the decision to change them or not. One or two recommendations from experience and relating to the examples here would be:

- Setting outcomes to **Yes**—the default is **No**.

With outcomes enabled, as we will see later in this chapter, it is possible to create a competence outcome for a course such as knife skills in Food Technology or CAD/CAM competence in Product Design.

- Changing the default navigation method from **Dropdown** to **Tabs and dropdown** because it is generally easier to navigate the gradebook.

The tabs menu will list all of the options, (such as grades, letters, views, and so on) in the tabs at the top of the gradebook view. Adding **Tabs and dropdowns** will allow a drop-down list of options to appear in the top-left corner of the gradebook.

- Another useful consideration would be the ability to publish the grades as a web link. The default is **No**, but if enabled, as shown in the following screenshot, you can create a link to the grades and have it restricted to certain IP addresses:

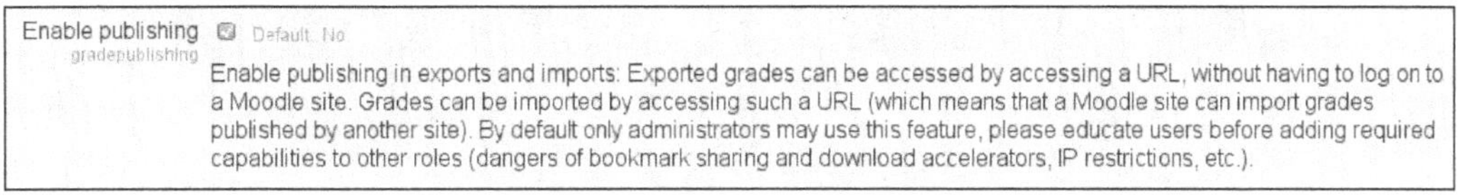

This export is very useful where you have external moderation of your results. You can send the URL to the examiner and they can then check the grades for themselves without requiring a login. The link will prompt them to download the results into a local spreadsheet such as Open Office Calc. Obviously this needs to be used with caution, as you don't want the link to be published publicly. The following screenshot shows the view an examiner would be presented with:

Configuring grade category settings

The settings here relate to the way that the grades are calculated and whether or not you require specific grading ranges to be available. In most cases, you will not need to change the default settings unless you have specialized grading across your entire institution. These are the default values, but they can be changed by course tutors, if required. For example, a diploma course may be based on a specific skill that would be graded by the tutor, such as measuring competence in building. In this instance, you could change the default setting to include outcomes, which are no, to yes. In this way, the gradebook will aggregate a student's competencies. Most DT courses will be based more on competencies, as they are inherently more practical and hands-on subjects.

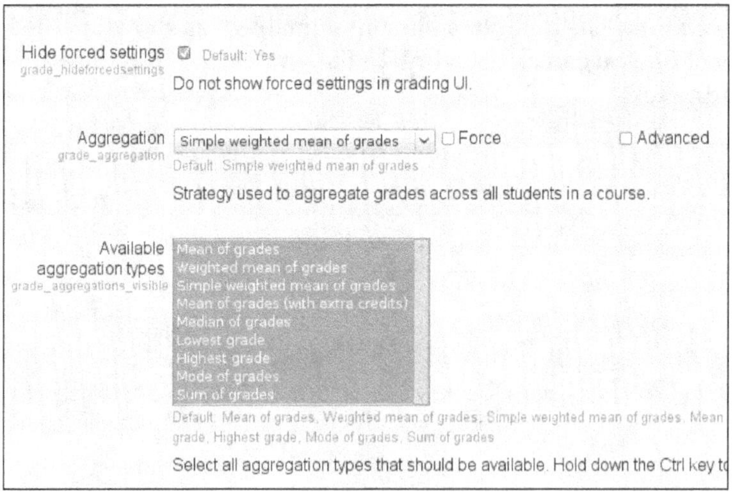

The options, as shown in the previous screenshot, are all similar in that if you select to **Force** an option, it will disable all other choices for staff. Equally, if you enable **Advanced**, the staff will be able to select an advanced view and add extra choices to their settings. It may be worth deselecting everything initially and introducing things slowly as staff become used to them. One problem with most technologies is scaring staff away with complexity, so here is a chance to make the transition slightly easier.

Configuring grade item settings

This option allows you to modify the default way that the grades are calculated and displayed. The main setting is what type of grade is displayed, which will depend on how your organization works. The three main types are:

- **Real**: Grade from minimum to maximum range indicating total points received. Default value ranges from 0 to 100 but may be arbitrary.
- **Percentage**: Grade from 0 to 100 percent indicating the total points received divided by the maximum possible amount, multiplied by 100.
- **Letter**: Grade in the form of a letter representing a range of percentages.

These three standard types can then be mixed, for example, if you want students to see their real raw score for reference, but also what this means in terms of a letter grade, you can select this choice. For example, a student may have a raw score of 50 percent in Resistant Materials, but due to the complexity of the subject, this might equate to a B grade. With just the raw score, the student may feel that they have achieved a low letter grade so they will be demotivated, but with the letter grade they can see that their work is on target.

As you can see in the following screenshot, you can also decide which advanced options staff are allowed to see and adjust:

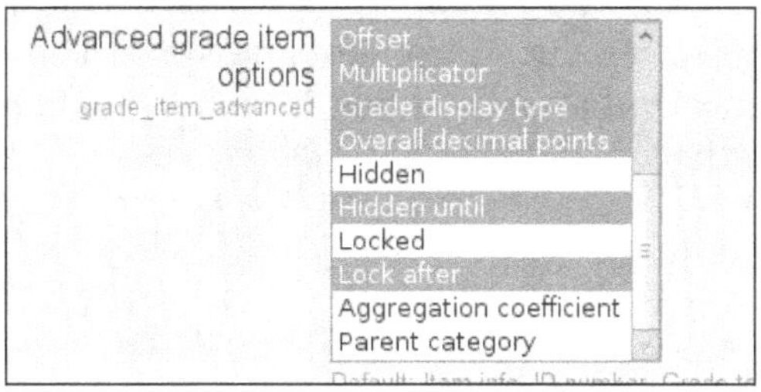

As with the previous option, and all options, it might be best to go for minimalism so as not to put off staff who are nervous of technology and change (yes, they do exist!).

Configuring scales

This option is likely to be used quite a lot in Design and Technology, as it does involve more aesthetic and practical skills, which might not be easily quantifiable in terms of a numbering system. The use of scales here makes it slightly easier as it allows some custom-made classifications to be used that can then be translated to quantitative data, if required. For example, you might be focusing on making sea-based products because your institution is located near the sea and most employers are involved in this type of manufacturing. In this instance, you could use nautical terms of reference to lighten up the practical work such as walk the plank, keel haul 'im, shiver me timbers, extra grog, pieces of eight, and so on. These would then be calculated by the system as multiples of 0 to n, where n is the total number of scale options, so students would get 4/5 for **extra grog**. These scales should be used for non-formative assessment, as the calculations will not always be precise. However, for vocational aspects of the course, it is a good way for students to appreciate where they are. In the following screenshot, a scale has been created for practical assignments and has a choice of competence levels, from no competence to advanced competence:

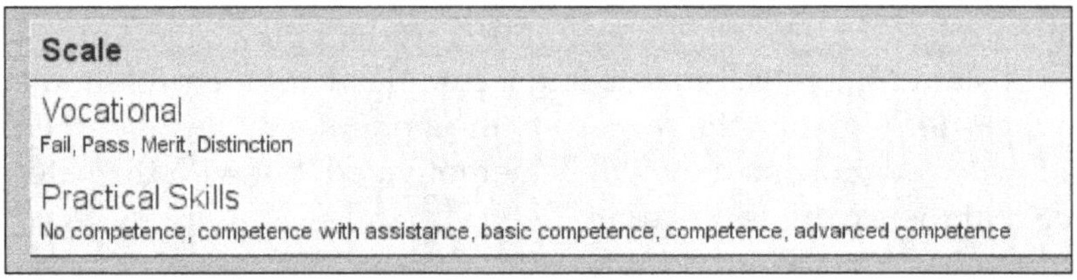

In the previous screenshot, there is also a basic scale for vocational subjects that involves **Fail**, **Pass**, **Merit**, and **Distinction** grades, as well as a practical scale rating a student's competence with equipment and skills. These can be used for all assignments and activities and then modified in terms of whether they are for formal assessment or extra credit.

> When creating your own scale, you need to enter it in reverse order in the editor. Therefore, A, B, C, and D would be entered D, C, B, and A, as shown in the following screenshot:

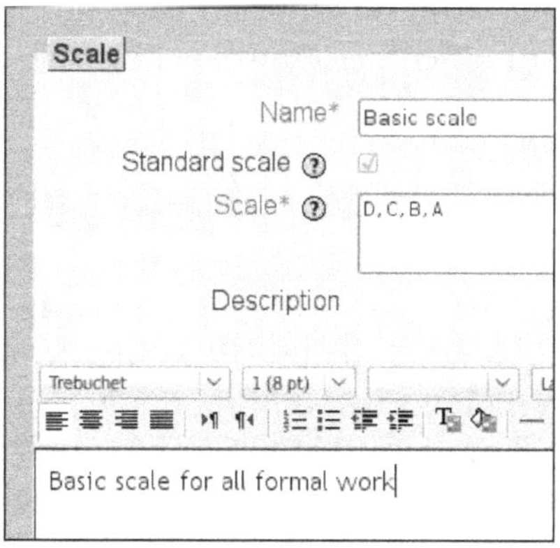

Enabling outcomes for courses

Under the general settings above, we mentioned that there is an option to **Enable outcomes**, as shown in the following screenshot:

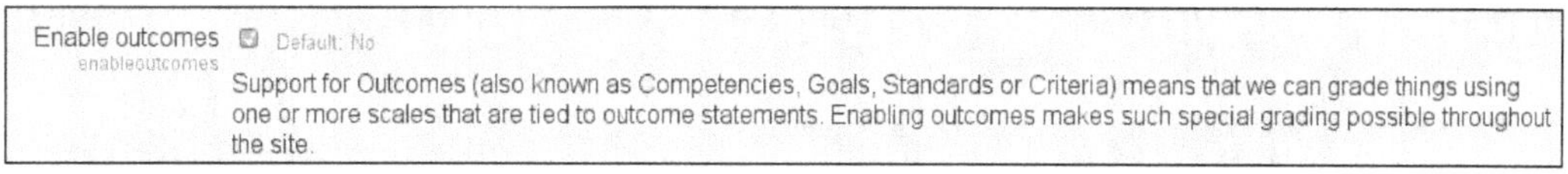

In the current version of Moodle (1.9), these outcomes can be attached to elements within a course, such as assignments, forums, and blogs, in order to give a clearer idea to students of their achievements against more formal targets. The outcomes are goals or types of competence. There can be outcomes set across the whole site, as well as within a specific course. All of this gives a huge amount of flexibility to the types of assessment carried out. If you have enabled the Mahara plugin, you can also use views in Mahara to meet specified outcomes. For example, if the students are set a research task to explain the use of plastics in industry, they can build a digital portfolio of images, video sequences, blogs, and web links into Mahara, and these can be linked as their assignment. If the outcome is set to **Competence**, the staff can attach a grade that students can use effectively to explain the key concepts in design and the use of materials such as plastics.

Meeting key skills requirements using outcomes

One possible use for outcomes might be to meet the requirements that are not a part of the formative grade, but are still required. In many cases, students will be expected to have a certain level of literacy, numeracy, or IT skills. These would not be formally assessed in your subject, as they may well be taking these subjects separately. However, you may still be expected to have some way of tracking their performance here. The use of outcomes would enable this and will be discussed in detail later in this chapter.

Translating numerical grades to letter grades

The letters option allows you to set a site-wide system for translating numerical grades and boundaries into letter grades. The defaults can be modified for your institution, for example, you might only use Pass, Merit, and Distinction grades for vocational courses with their corresponding grade boundaries or the more traditional (in the UK) GCSE grades of A* to G. These will then be displayed in the gradebook. The defaults are shown here with the corresponding drop-down lists. Once modifications are made, you need to save the changes. You can be very precise here and match to the exam board's published grade boundaries, so that the students have an exact idea of where they are in terms of their course grades.

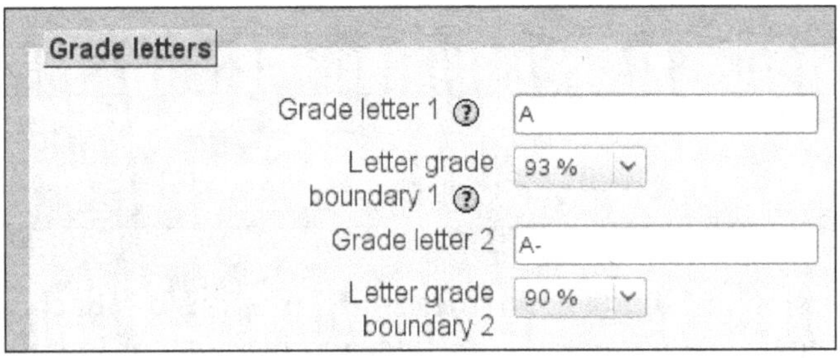

Configuring the grader report

The settings here relate to how the actual gradebook is presented and what options are available to users:

- If you have some feedback comments that go out to all students in a class at once, such as **good overall effort**, you can enable the quick feedback option.
- You can also select to hide the calculations for each grade, as these may be distracting and unnecessary.
- If you have a large amount of activities, you might want to enable the static student column, which will allow you to scroll across grades while still viewing the student names.

> If the site admin has already enabled scrolling columns, you will not be able to adjust it.

In most cases, the default settings will be most suitable and as with all things in the gradebook, they can be adjusted by the staff, if inappropriate.

Displaying a student's rank

The main choice for both of these options, which is not enabled by default, is the rank option. In most cases, you would probably not like your students to see their rank in relation to their class, as it may be demotivating, but you might want it for the staff so that they can write reports to parents or guardians. With ranking enabled, you can see how each student compares to their classmates on each assignment. The following screenshot shows the output for one student in the gradebook showing that she is at the top of her group. This could be useful for parent evenings or tutorial sessions.

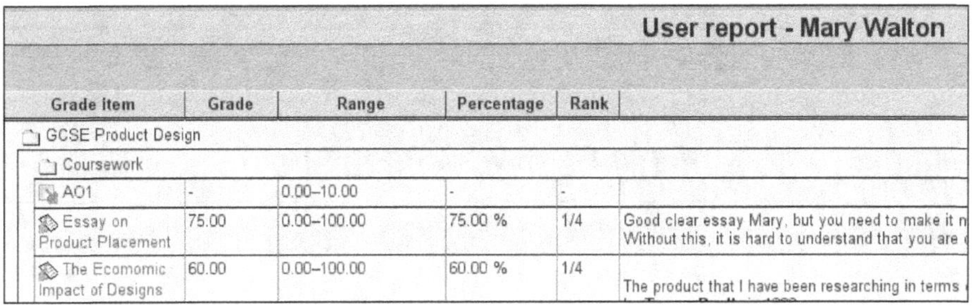

Assessing and using the gradebook

Once you have set your overall options for the gradebook, you can then begin to use the gradebook to track your students' progress and give them some feedback on their work. It also gives a snapshot of student output so that you can modify your course if there are identified areas of weakness.

To access the gradebook, you will need to click on the icon on the admin panel of your course. This icon will be the same for staff and students, but staff will obviously have a view of all students whereas students will only see their own grades. The link is shown in the following screenshot for reference:

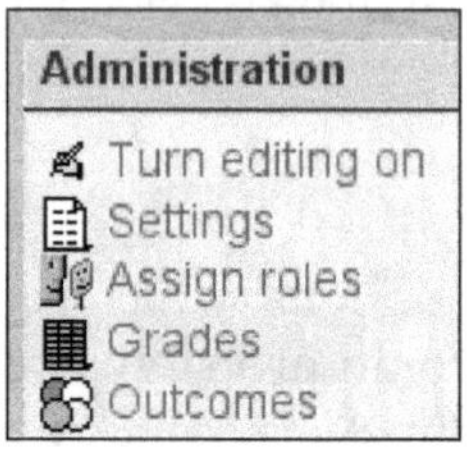

The link will open the gradebook, as shown in the following screenshot:

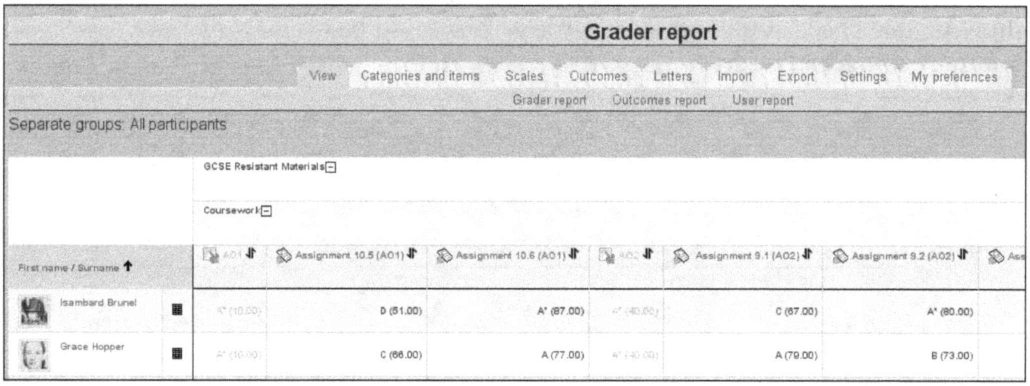

Categories and items

The view that you will be presented with as a member of the staff if you click on the grade will be the **Grader report**, as shown in the previous screenshot with our sample students.

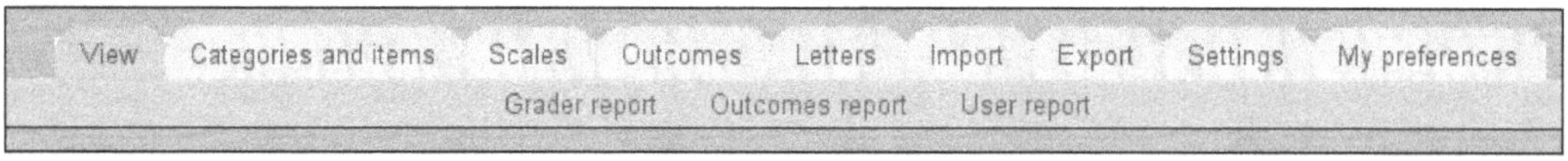

The tab view, shown in the previous screenshot, is the default view. The first thing we need to set is the **Categories and items**. This will allow us to divide our assignments and activities into the coursework-based material and examinations. We do this by selecting the **Categories and items** tab.

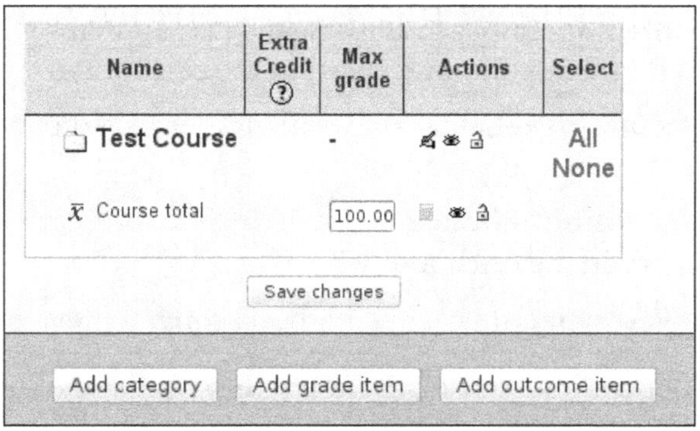

The **Categories and items** tab has the option of simple or full view. For now, we only need the simple view. In a course where no assignments have yet been set, the view will be very basic, as shown in the previous screenshot.

For our worked example of a Resistant Materials class, we need to have two categories—Coursework and Examinations. To do this, we need to select the **Add category** button shown in the previous screenshot.

The view shown will be dependent on what items we choose at the site level, as discussed earlier in this chapter. If we selected the advanced option, then the advanced button will also be shown for extra options. The category needs to be named and if there are any advanced options that are relevant, they need to be included. The main one, as shown here, is whether we want to include outcomes in the score aggregation. In most cases, we will probably use this for extra credit, unless it is a required component of a course such as key skills in the UK.

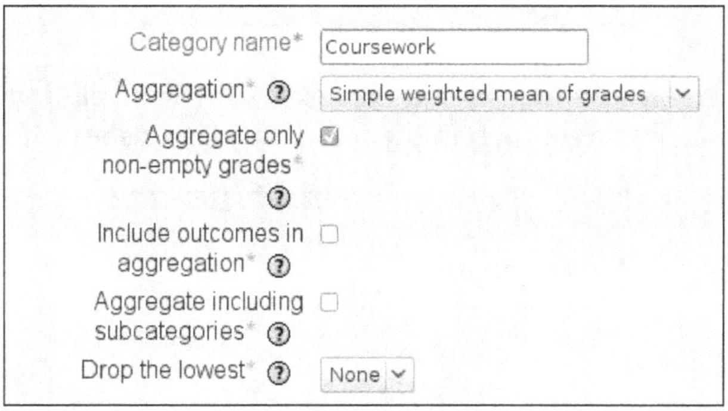

In this view, we are sticking with the default options:

- **Simple weighted mean of grades** for the aggregation method that will add up all the scores and divide by the number of grades and then multiply by 100 to give a percentage score
- **Aggregate only non-empty grades** means that all items with no grade associated with them will not be used in the calculation
- **Include outcomes in aggregation** would add selected outcomes to the marking and aggregation available
- **Aggregate including subcategories** will include one category below this chosen category in the calculation
- **Drop the lowest** will only use the highest scores achieved

Other options will depend on your institution policy on these options.

The grade item, in this case, allows us to set the weight for this category. In our worked example, coursework represents 60 percent of the overall grade, so we set this as the maximum. Any elements inside this category will automatically be adjusted to represent 60 percent of the total. The settings are shown in the following screenshot:

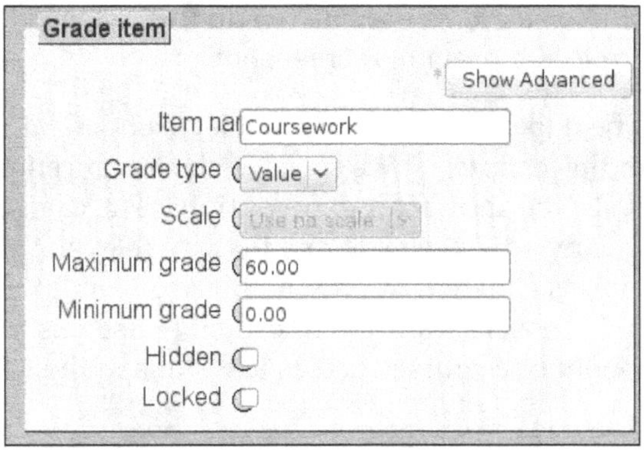

You then need to create another category for examinations, and in this case, we set it to a weight of 40 percent, as shown in the following screenshot:

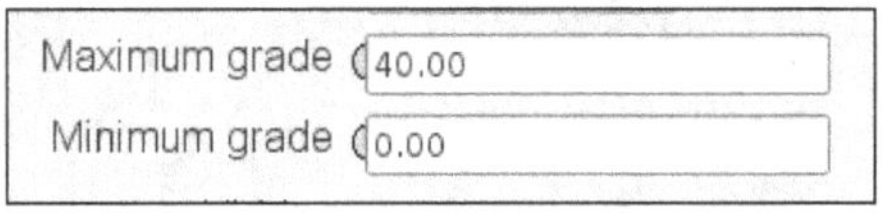

In this example, both of these categories are part of the overall course, which is the parent, as shown in the following screenshot:

You can create a number of sub-categories and divide up the Gradebook as much as required to track your students' learning. For example, you might have the individual elements of each main category created, and therefore, the coursework or examinations categories will become the parent.

Suggested areas of study

If you are working with something like the Diploma in Manufacturing and Product Design, you might use the six specified areas of study for your categories:

- Principle learning
- Additional and specialist learning
- Functional skills
- Personal, learning, and thinking skills
- Work experience
- Student project

Within these main categories, you could then add sub-categories such as English, Math, and ICT as part of the functional skills.

You should end up with a basic gradebook that represents the different elements that make up the entire course grade, as shown in the following screenshot:

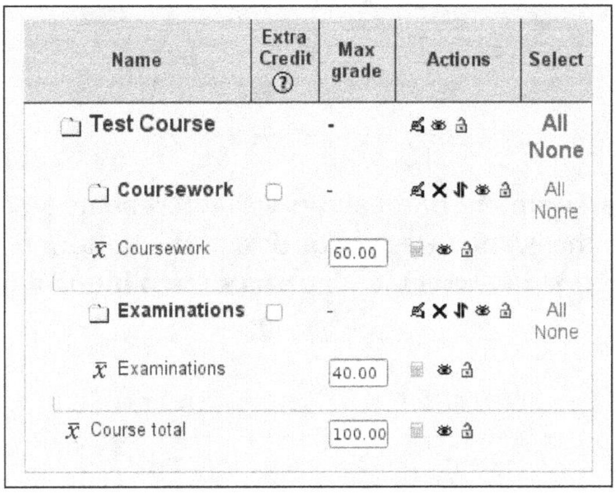

Now that this structure has been established, you can start adding assignments or other graded activities to this structure to construct the gradeboook and the assessment that is possible.

Adding items for grading

Now that the gradebook has some structure, you can begin adding assignments to the book and into the organized categories. As you make activities, such as quizzes or assignments, there is an option to associate them with a category in the gradebook. The graded items can also be moved using editing functions in the gradebook itself. In the previous screenshot, you can see that there are icons to move elements.

Clicking on the move icon will open a new window showing empty fields, as shown in the following screenshot. Clicking in the empty field will place the item to be moved there.

> Please note that if the site administrator has enabled the Ajax function under **Site Administration** | **Appearance** | **AJAX and JavaScript**, the elements can be dragged and dropped.

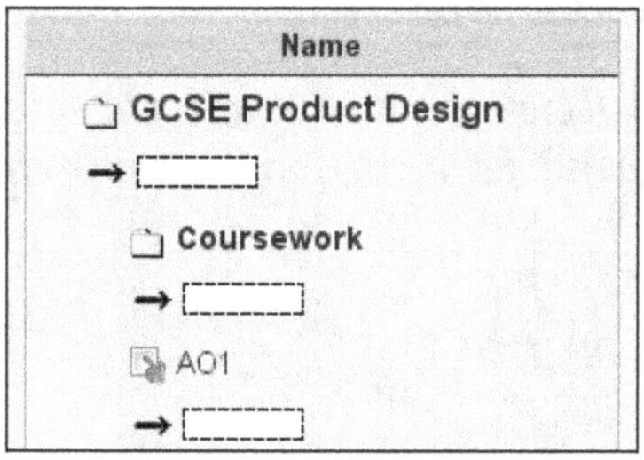

When you create an assignment or an activity that has some assessment associated with it, you will have the grade category option at the bottom of the setup window to add it to the gradebook in a specific place, as shown in the following screenshot:

In the **Grade category**, you will have a drop-down list that will have a listing of all the categories you established earlier. It also has the option to add a new one if you come up with perhaps a one-off exercise.

You can create as many grade items as you require. If you wish to sub-divide the gradebook into manageable elements, this is also possible. In the following screenshot, you can see how the coursework has been divided into elements that carry their own weighting for the overall grade:

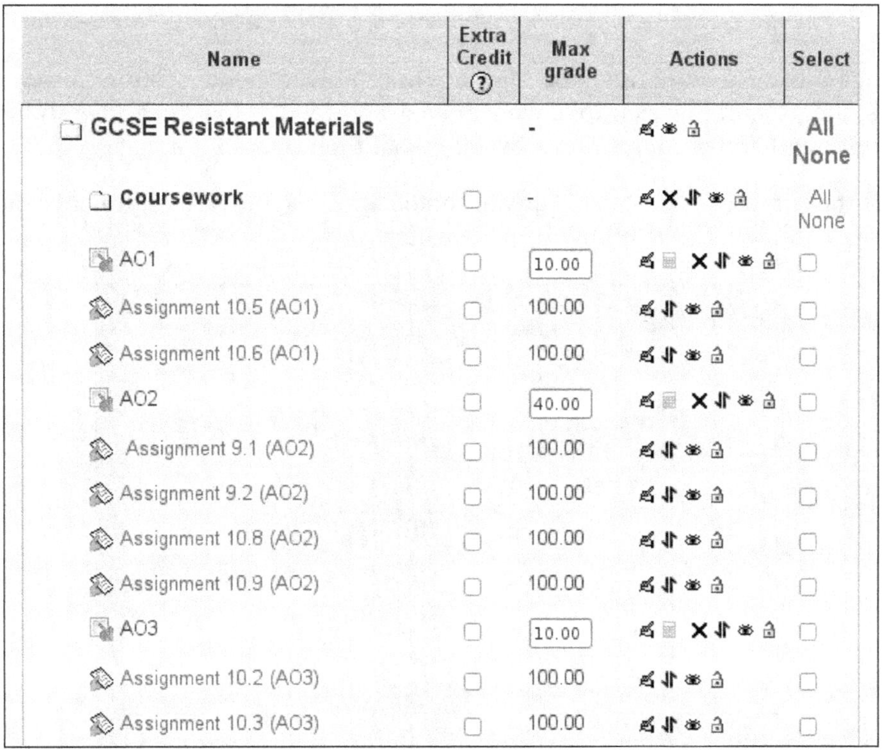

As you can see here, there are four elements that make up the coursework grade in this specification, and these are broken into three sub-categories that carry 10 percent, 40 percent, and 10 percent of the marks respectively. The assignments associated with each of the elements will be calculated to equal the overall weight, such as 10 percent, and the overall marks will be aggregated to the 60 percent weight of the coursework category. It can be as detailed as you require it to be.

Creating custom calculations for categories

In many cases, it will be useful to tell the gradebook exactly which elements or assignments will be required to make up the grand total. In the previous screenshot, you can see that there are icons that show a calculator, as shown in the following screenshot:

Clicking on this icon will open the interface to be able to create custom calculations for this category. In this example, we want a grand total of the categories and work so that the staff and students know exactly what their overall grade is.

The first task in the interface is to create some identities for the assignments and activities, as shown in the following screenshot:

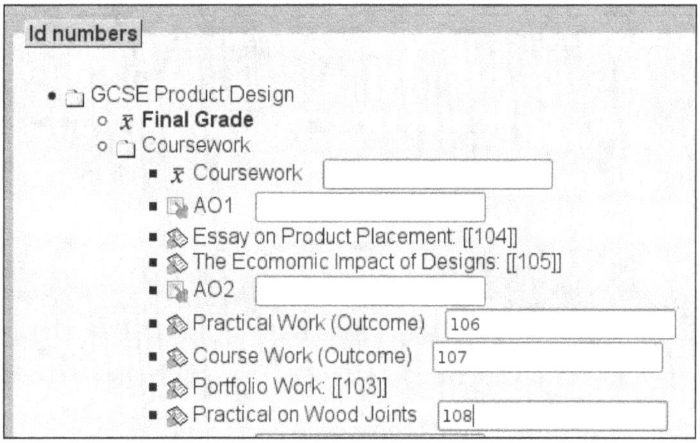

The new assignments have been assigned an ID, but some already have one assigned and can be identified by the square brackets such as **[[104]]**. All of these IDs need to be saved so that they can be used in the formula. There are a number of calculations that can be made such as sum, average, and mean. For our example, we just want the sum of all the material. The formula is shown in the following screenshot:

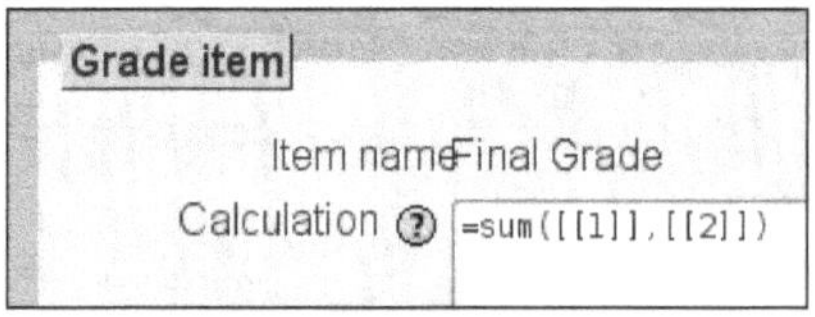

In this example for our course, the IDs are for coursework and examinations that just gives us an overall grade for all of the work undertaken. The result, for our example students, is shown as follows:

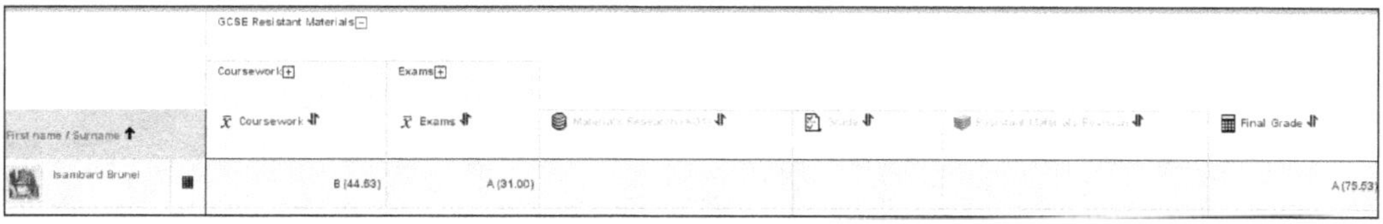

In this example, we have collapsed the full view of assignments for coursework and examinations, but we can see that they have been sub-totaled for Brunel to 44.53 percent and 31 percent for a final grade of 75.53 percent, which, in this case, is equal to an A grade. Well done Isambard!

Tracking and monitoring competencies

Outcomes is a relatively new feature in Moodle and was introduced in version 1.9 of Moodle. The main usage of this feature is the tracking and monitoring of competencies or abilities. These competencies might not necessarily comprise the core of an accredited course, but do give more depth and clarity to the final award. For example, in the UK, all courses have a requirement that the course is taught with the opportunity for students to gain key skills. For most Design Technology courses, these key skills will include: communication, application of number, IT (or Information and Communication Technology - ICT in the UK), working with others, improving own learning and performance, and problem solving. The assumption is that these competencies will be gained through the guided learning taking place and some of the practical exercises undertaken.

Enabling outcomes at the site level

Outcomes can be enabled at the site level by your site administrator so that all staff can use them in their courses. This will be made possible by a checkbox, which can be found under **Site Administration | Grades | General Settings**. Here you will find the button to enable outcomes for your site, as shown in the following screenshot:

This may be a generic set of competencies such as grammar or spelling, as shown in the following screenshot:

However, for our worked example, we are applying outcomes that are specific to our particular course, which is Resistant Materials.

Enabling outcomes for Resistant Materials

For this example, we will consider the key skill of IT (Information Technology). In most cases, IT competence would not be formally assessed other than the overall grade attained. In Resistant Materials, one of the main tasks of students is to gather data to explain their project briefly. This particular module is called **Designing and Making**, and the sub-topic is **Developing and Writing a Design Brief**. Students are required to gather and display a range of source materials such as pictures, text, graphs, and so on to support their overall design idea. They can store and comment on this material as they prefer, but the recommendation from the exam board specification is that they use a database. Using a database does not affect the quality of the data directly, as they could produce a quality piece of work in paper, but it would aid in presentation and they would also develop a key skill in the process by using a computer. We could equally look at the finished design itself. In many instances, this will be made on some form of **Computer-Aided Design/ Computer-Aided Manufacture** (**CAD/CAM**) package or piece of equipment, which assumes a high level of competence in specialized software and hardware. Therefore, by using the outcomes feature, we are able to track their competence in IT and award a mark based on a scale.

Using course-based outcomes to track competence

On each course, once outcomes have been enabled, staff will see an icon showing a link to **Outcomes** for the course, as shown in the following screenshot:

Outcomes can also be reached through the gradebook; the end result will be the same editing screen, as shown here:

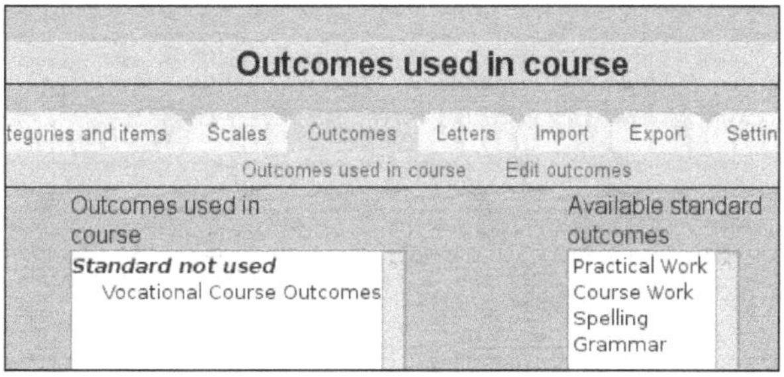

In the previous screenshot, the site already has a number of outcomes that have been set for all courses, which includes **Practical Work** and competencies such as **Grammar** and **Spelling**. In this instance, we need to set an outcome for our Resistant Materials course based on IT competencies. To do this, we need to choose the tab to **Edit outcomes**.

Creating an IT outcome for Resistant Materials

Choosing the **Edit outcomes** tab will enable the editing interface that will show any existing outcomes for the site and also show if they have been applied to any courses. Select the **Add a new outcome** button, as shown in the following screenshot, to create a new outcome:

You will be presented with the basic interface for creating your new outcome, and you can then create some of the detail, as shown in the following screenshot:

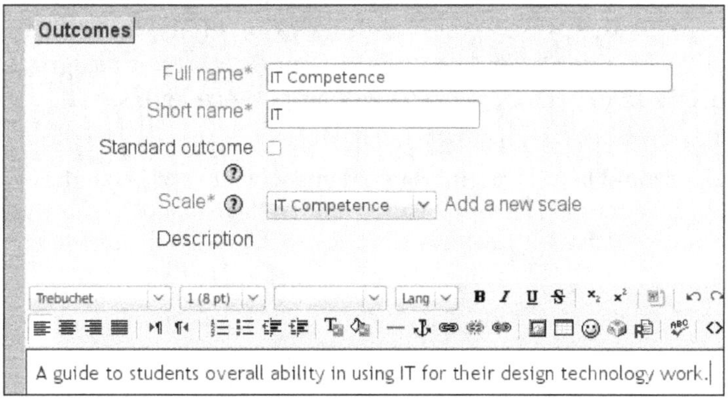

For the scale to be used, you can select an existing scale if you have already created one. Otherwise, you can click on the **Add a new scale** link in the previous screenshot and create one for this competence, as shown in the following screenshot:

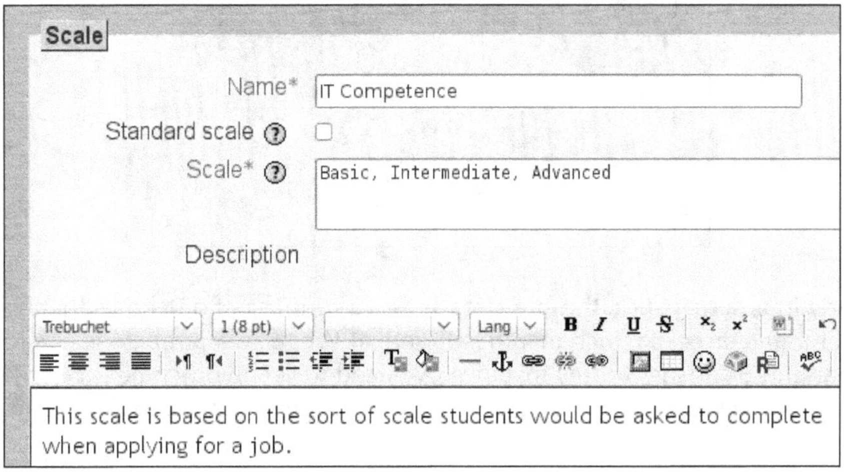

If you are a site administrator, you may wish to check the box for **Standard scale** so that other staff can use this scale in their own courses.

Once the new outcome has been saved, it will be available to add to elements within the course, such as forums or assignments. In this example, we are going to apply it to our assignment relating to designing and making, as discussed at the beginning of this section.

Applying the outcome to an assignment

Now that we have an outcome, we can use it to track the competence of our students in areas of their work. In this instance, we will create an assignment for the student's design brief. As already discussed, the expectation is for students to use a database to store and organize their research, though they don't have to. With an IT outcome now enabled, we can give students some extra marks on their assignment to show that they have also achieved some IT-based competence levels.

> This would be very useful for students who are not given the opportunity to gain a formal IT-based qualification in their school to show potential employers that they have reached a specific level of competency.

We have already discussed creating assignments in *Chapter 8, Assessing Student Progress*. However, now when we create our assignment for this module, we will see an extra set of options for outcomes, as shown in the following screenshot:

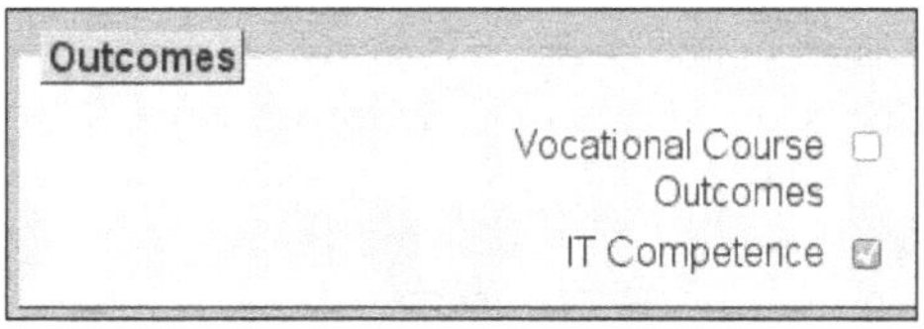

We now have the option to select an **IT Competence** outcome as part of this assignment. When we go to this piece of work to mark it, we can see that we have the additional option to apply our new scale to the IT aspect of their work, as shown in the following screenshot:

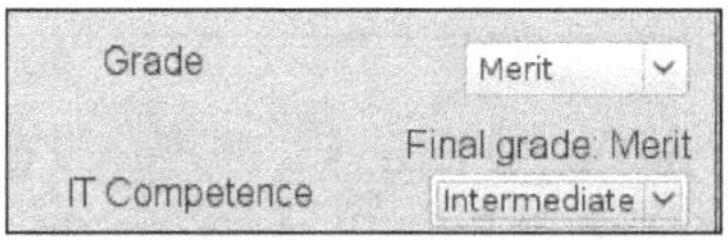

For this student, they now know that they have achieved a **Merit** grade with their assignment, but also that they have reached an Intermediate level of IT competence, based on their knowledge and application of database skills. As the hunt for jobs becomes more competitive, it becomes more important for students to be able to show not only that they can achieve their academic goals, but also that they are competent in IT, working with others, literacy and numeracy, and so on.

Implementing letter grades for Resistant Materials

In many educational environments, the most familiar form of grading will be a letter-based grading system. In the UK, for the 14-16 year old students, this is the A*-G scale used in GCSEs; or for 16-18 year olds, the A-E scale of A Levels. Moodle has a default letter system based on some preset percentages that will be applied to all assessed material. For example, with the default settings, a percentage of 84 percent will be awarded a B. However, many courses work on sliding scales and their own percentages, so this may require some modification. In our worked example of Resistant Materials, a percentage of 84% would have achieved an A or a B, depending on what the overall marks were for the subject. For our course, we need to change the letters to reflect what we will be awarding.

Grading with custom letters

The standard scale in Moodle runs from A to F, with gradations of + and –, as shown in the following screenshot:

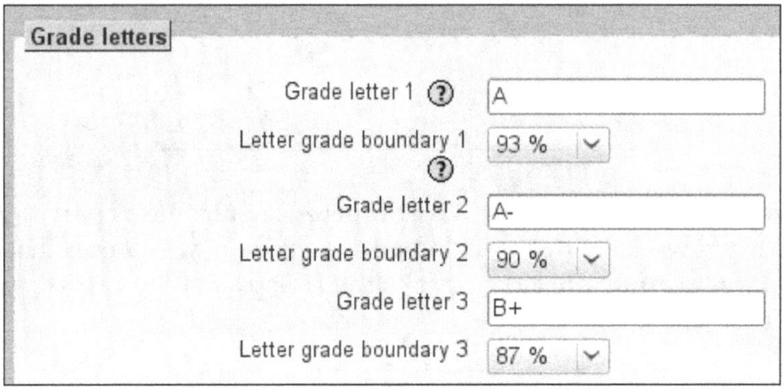

To change this, we merely type in the letters we require and select the percentage for the boundary from the drop-down menu. Once completed, we can save our new letter scale and can view it in the gradebook under the **Letter** tab, as shown in the following screenshot:

View Edit

Highest	Lowest	Letter
100.00 %	80.00 %	A*
79.99 %	75.00 %	A
74.99 %	69.00 %	B
68.99 %	66.00 %	C
65.99 %	55.00 %	E
54.99 %	49.00 %	D
48.99 %	44.00 %	F
43.99 %	33.00 %	G
32.99 %	30.00 %	Fail

We now have a scale of letters and corresponding percentages that accurately represent our own specific Resistant Materials course. The grades that we apply will now give students and ourselves an accurate picture of where students are in terms of their final award.

Importing and exporting Moodle grades

In the majority of cases, Moodle will hopefully be used for all grading of work, and therefore, there will be little need for importing grades to the system, though you might prefer to work on your own spreadsheet for convenience. In this case, you can import the grades into Moodle for consistency. The more likely case is that you have already exported grades from Moodle for detailed analysis or modification and wish to import them back for update purposes. The export facility is useful as the grades can be further analyzed with the extra analytical functions of a spreadsheet. In addition, you can create an export link for external examiners to review the grades.

The export facility will allow you to export any aspect of your gradebook and then subsequently download this into a number of formats, such as OpenOffice Calc or Excel spreadsheets, as shown in the following screenshot:

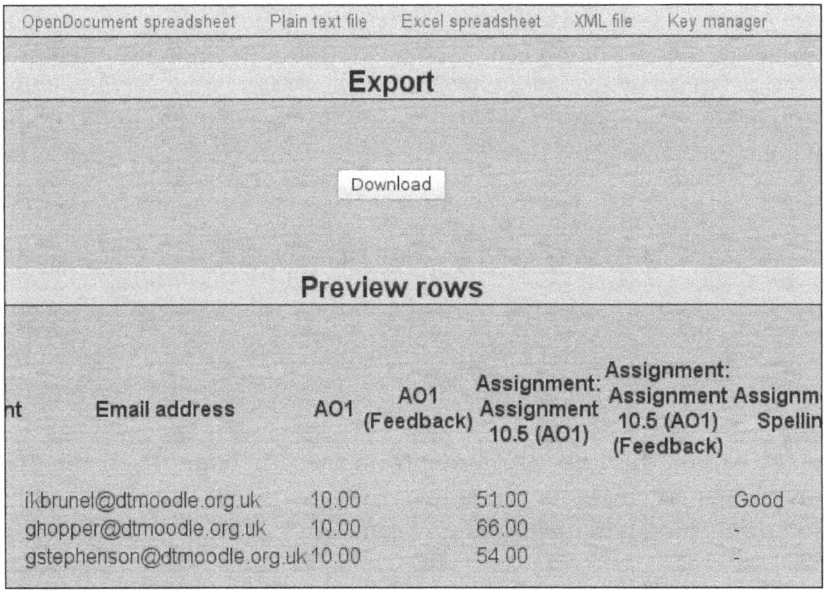

As you can see in the previous screenshot, the grades are exported to the screen to show you the details and can then be downloaded by selecting the **Download** button. One additional feature, which is only available to site administrators for security reasons, is the ability to export a web link to allow external access to the grades. An admin user will see an additional publishing option, as shown in the following screenshot:

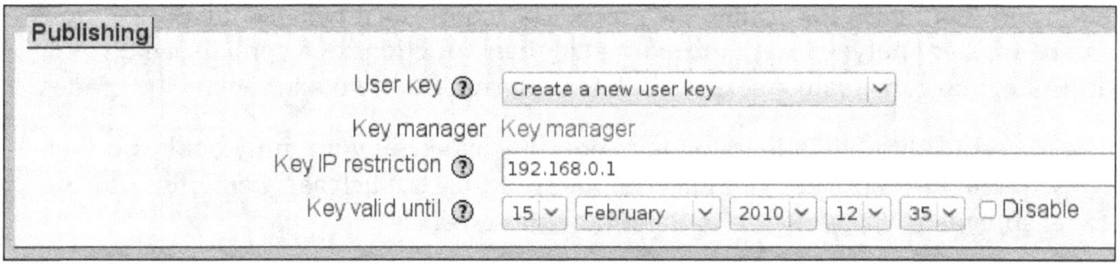

This will generate a web link and can be restricted to a specific computer address (IP) as well as a date and will also generate a secure key to prevent the data being picked up by third parties who should not be accessing it. The exported link is displayed in the following screenshot:

As mentioned earlier, this link can be sent from an exam board to an external moderator, who can then see for themselves the grades that have been applied without requiring a login to the Moodle system.

Modifying display options

The display options available for the gradebook are listed as **Settings** and **My Preferences** in the edit interface. These can be modified at the site level for all users and can be further modified at the course level. These are very much a personal choice and depend on what you would like to see in the gradebook and how your institute implements grading policies. All of the choices are clearly labeled and described. In most cases the default values would be enough for general use. The main options to consider for the report, beyond the general layout, would be whether or not to enable something like ranks. In some cases, it might be useful to have the rank of each student shown to either you or the students themselves, though this may not be advisable for motivational reasons. You might also like to change the number of students viewable and whether or not to lock the columns to make it easier when moving across a large amount of assignments. These options are available by clicking on the **Change report defaults** link, as shown in the following screenshot:

You can select some of the options and modify the display of your work area. Some of the options are shown in the following screenshot:

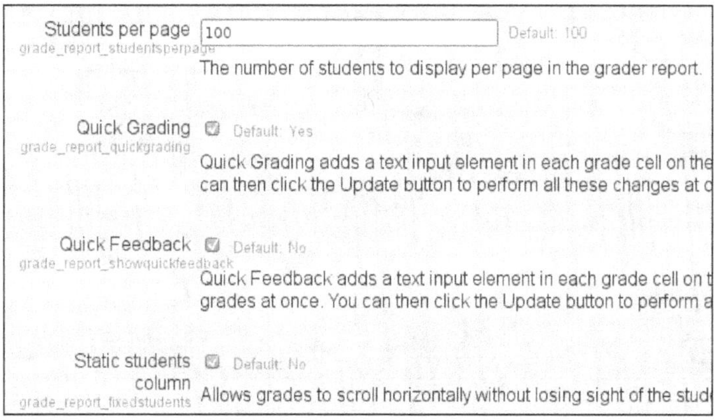

Option	Description and example
Students per page	How many students will be shown in the grader window? For small group sizes, where a detailed view is required, it could be set to 25. With large groups, where an overview is required, the default of 100 might be appropriate.
Quick grading	Ticking this option displays a small textbox next to all visible students. If all students have attended a workshop at a local college on plastering techniques, and this is an outcome, you can use this to give everyone a grade such as what they have achieved. You can quickly copy and paste it into all the boxes and then save your choice.
Quick feedback	As above, you can automatically assign a grade to all students, if it is the same. For example, you may give a generic feedback on a workshop of, "good basic skills in cooking hygiene".
Static students column	This option locks the student's name column so that you can scroll across a large set of grades and not lose their name. Very useful in large and complex classes.

Viewing your student grades

Once the various options, default or otherwise, have been selected, you can view the gradebook and begin to add feedback to student submissions to make sure they are maximizing their potential. When you click on the gradebook link from the administration panel on your course, or when you click on the view tab if you are already in the gradebook, it will display your class and all their grades. It should look similar to the following screenshot:

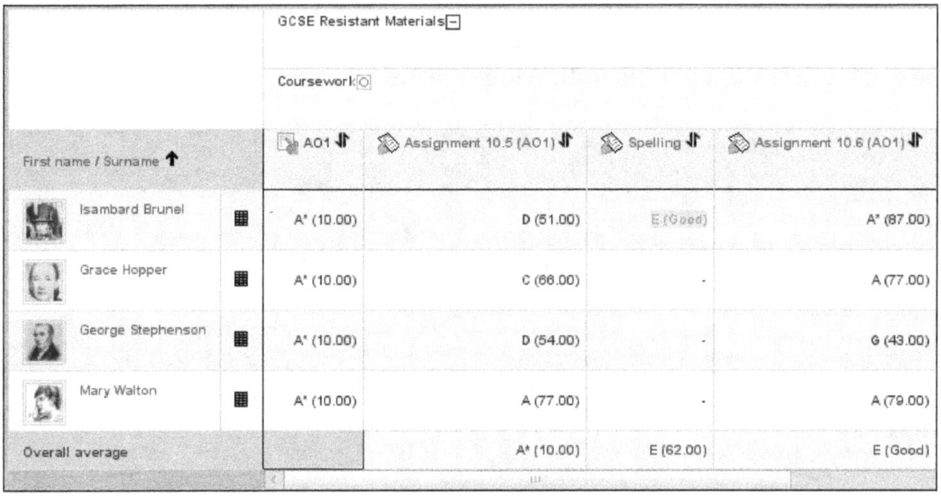

The previous screenshot is the default view, which is called the **Grader report**. This view shows an overview of all the students in your group and the grades that they have achieved, assuming that they have been marked manually or auto marked, such as quizzes. The view can be modified slightly by clicking on the collapsible or expandable **+/-** icons next to each column header name. For example, if you want to look in detail at just the examination material, you could collapse the coursework columns.

Displaying outcomes report

If you have enabled and used the outcomes on your course, there will be an additional panel to show you an overview of what courses contain the outcomes you have set and how many times a grade has been applied. You can look in more detail under the assignments themselves, but this gives a useful snapshot of how well outcomes are being realized. The following screenshot shows the overview for this course in development:

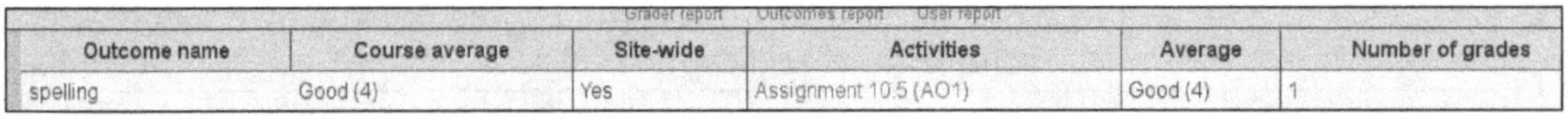

In the previous screenshot, we can get an indication that the general level of spelling is good. If it was some other outcome such as citizenship or IT competence, we could be confident that we had designed our course effectively and that the students were gaining the requisite competencies above and beyond their basic grades. In many Design Technology courses, it would be useful to get a quick idea that all the students were competent when using dangerous equipment, for example.

Assessing group performance

The user report allows us to select the entire group or individuals in the group to get a feel of how well they are meeting their targets. With groups enabled on the course, it also allows each teacher to access a drop-down list that will show them only the group of students in the course they are responsible for. In the following screenshot, there is a drop-down list in the top-right corner for us to make our selection. In this screenshot, we have chosen one of the students to get an overview of their work till date:

Select all or one user: Mary Walton

Grade	Range	Percentage	Rank	Feedback
A* (10.00)	- (0.00)–A* (10.00)	100.00 %	1/4	
A (77.00)	- (0.00)–A* (100.00)	77.00 %	1/4	Good work again Mary with some clear examples. The work you did with the small group was clearly thought out.
-	- (Disappointing)–A* (Excellent!)	-	-	
A (79.00)	- (0.00)–A* (100.00)	79.00 %	2/4	Good. Well researched and informative.
A* (40.00)	- (0.00)–A* (40.00)	100.00 %	1/4	
A (75.00)	- (0.00)–A* (100.00)	75.00 %	2/4	Good solid work.

In the previous screenshot, I can get an idea of what their grades are and even where they rank in terms of their classmates. If I was their personal tutor, I could then use this as the basis for writing a detailed report or for more one-to-one discussions about how they could improve their work.

Summary

The gradebook is very detailed, as it is designed for all aspects of grading that may be required in institutions across the spectrum. Having said that, it is also basic enough in its default state to give any educator a clear and detailed overview of the work their students are undertaking. It can be customized in terms of output and display to match your institution and departmental needs and can provide a solid base for quality interaction with students as part of a pastoral program. There is a wealth of detail on the gradebook on the Moodle site, and this chapter can only cover some of the more basic details. More comprehensive details and examples can be accessed at: `http://docs.moodle.org/en/Gradebook`.

Index

A

B

C

D

E

F

G

H

I

K

L

M

N

O

P

Q

R

S

T

U

V

W

X

Thank you for buying
Moodle 1.9 for Design and Technology

About Packt Publishing

Packt, pronounced 'packed', published its first book "*Mastering phpMyAdmin for Effective MySQL Management*" in April 2004 and subsequently continued to specialize in publishing highly focused books on specific technologies and solutions.

Our books and publications share the experiences of your fellow IT professionals in adapting and customizing today's systems, applications, and frameworks. Our solution based books give you the knowledge and power to customize the software and technologies you're using to get the job done. Packt books are more specific and less general than the IT books you have seen in the past. Our unique business model allows us to bring you more focused information, giving you more of what you need to know, and less of what you don't.

Packt is a modern, yet unique publishing company, which focuses on producing quality, cutting-edge books for communities of developers, administrators, and newbies alike. For more information, please visit our website: `www.packtpub.com`.

About Packt Open Source

In 2010, Packt launched two new brands, Packt Open Source and Packt Enterprise, in order to continue its focus on specialization. This book is part of the Packt Open Source brand, home to books published on software built around Open Source licences, and offering information to anybody from advanced developers to budding web designers. The Open Source brand also runs Packt's Open Source Royalty Scheme, by which Packt gives a royalty to each Open Source project about whose software a book is sold.

Writing for Packt

We welcome all inquiries from people who are interested in authoring. Book proposals should be sent to author@packtpub.com. If your book idea is still at an early stage and you would like to discuss it first before writing a formal book proposal, contact us; one of our commissioning editors will get in touch with you.

We're not just looking for published authors; if you have strong technical skills but no writing experience, our experienced editors can help you develop a writing career, or simply get some additional reward for your expertise.

[PACKT] open source
community experience distilled
PUBLISHING

Moodle 1.9 Teaching Techniques

ISBN: 978-1-849510-06-6 Paperback: 216 pages

Creative ways to build powerful and effective online courses

1. Motivate students from all backgrounds, generations, and learning styles
2. When and how to apply the different learning solutions with workarounds, providing alternative solutions
3. Easy-to-follow, step-by-step instructions with screenshots and examples for Moodle's powerful features
4. Especially suitable for university and professional teachers

---

Moodle 1.9 E-Learning Course Development

ISBN: 978-1-847193-53-7 Paperback: 384 pages

A complete guide to successful learning using Moodle

1. Updated for Moodle version 1.9
2. Straightforward coverage of installing and using the Moodle system
3. Working with Moodle features in all learning environments
4. A unique course-based approach focuses your attention on designing well-structured, interactive, and successful courses

Please check **www.PacktPub.com** for information on our titles

www.ingramcontent.com/pod-product-compliance
Lightning Source LLC
LaVergne TN
LVHW080035210926
848481LV00011B/3195
* 9 7 8 1 8 4 9 5 1 1 0 0 1 *